DESIGNING EDUCATION FOR THE FUTURE, NO. 1

Prospective Changes In Society By 1980

Edited by EDGAR L. MORPHET, *Director, and* CHARLES O. RYAN, *Associate Director, Designing Education for the Future: An Eight-State Project, Denver, Colorado*

Citation Press • New York • 1967

Library of Congress Catalog Card Number: 67-22887

1st printing, May 1967
Printed in the U.S.A.

PREFACE

At the close of the American Revolutionary War, the statement "Eternal vigilance is the price of liberty" became popular. After World War One, H. G. Wells expressed the same basic idea, with a modern application, when he said, "Human history becomes more and more a race between education and catastrophe."

During my many years in school teaching and administration, and more recently in educational publishing, these two statements, always vivid in my memory, never ceased giving me a deep sense of urgency in proceeding with the great task of vastly improving education and universalizing it in this country.

Seldom, if ever, has anyone given more meaning to the term "education" in so few words as did Mr. Wells. He was talking about the fast-moving accumulation of unprecedented power born of a technology never known to man in all history and capable of annihilating the slowly developed culture of the ages.

Against such a background of admonition and prophecy, it is indeed heartening to learn of the initiative taken by eight State Departments of Education in developing an Eight-State Project entitled "Designing Education for the Future" and supported generously by the U. S. Office of Education — a deliberate effort to keep education ahead in the race.

The initiators of the four-year project, launched in 1965, secured 16 carefully prepared papers by 24 authorities in various technical fields indicating what they believe will be the nature of many important facets of our society in 1980. These papers are published in *Prospective Changes in Society by 1980,* volume one in the "Designing Education for the Future" series.

The papers of the first volume were studied by 21 eminent educators who in turn prepared their respective statements of *Implications for Education of Prospective Changes in Society* for the second volume.

The third volume, entitled *Planning and Effecting Needed Changes in Education,* presents papers by other experts who have examined strategies and procedures for implementing changes in individual schools, school systems, and state educational agencies.

It should be stated that during the progress of the entire Project there were many conferences in which the writers thoroughly discussed the predictions and the implications.

JOHN W. STUDEBAKER
Chairman of the Editorial Boards
Scholastic Magazines, Inc.

DESIGNING EDUCATION FOR THE FUTURE:
An Eight-State Project

Policy Board and Project Staff

Sponsoring States	Chief State School Officers (Policy Board)	State Coordinators
ARIZONA	Sarah Folsom	Robert L. Pickering
COLORADO	Byron W. Hansford, *Chairman*	Russell B. Vlaanderen
IDAHO	D. F. Engelking	Robert S. Gibb
MONTANA	Harriet Miller	Earl B. Peterson
NEVADA	Byron F. Stetler	Lamar LeFevre
NEW MEXICO	Leonard J. De Layo	Thomas B. Bailey, Jr.
UTAH	Terrell H. Bell	Bernarr S. Furse
WYOMING	Cecil M. Shaw	Paul G. Graves

Edgar L. Morphet, *Project Director*

Charles O. Ryan, *Associate Director*

Financed by funds provided under the
Elementary and Secondary Education Act of 1965
(Public Law 89-10, Title V, Sec. 505)
and
the Sponsoring States

Project Office:

1362 Lincoln Street
Denver, Colorado 80203

FOREWORD

DESIGNING EDUCATION FOR THE FUTURE, an eight-state project, is one of the most exciting and significant projects of our time. It has the potential of having great impact on education and its inevitable change. The thrust of this project is of necessity in the nature of a study of desirable changes and the appropriate ways of providing some direction and impetus for these changes.

As has been stated many times we live in a period of ever-accelerating change. Our public schools and other educational institutions must prepare citizens to function effectively within this changing society and must provide an atmosphere which offers an internship for life in the future. In meeting this challenge, education is required to provide leadership of a broad nature to adjust and change in light of new demands.

State departments of education exist to serve the schools, and the schools exist to serve the society of which they are a part. Therefore, in attempting to determine the appropriate role for a state department of education in the future, we must first try to determine what society may be like in the future, and then what our schools and educational institutions should be like. This is the purpose of the present study.

This project is sponsored by the Chief State School Officers of the eight participating states. They, their State Boards and State Department of Education staff members recognize that their roles and responsibilities must change to meet the needs of a changing society that will require greatly improved programs of education in all states.

It is essential that the sponsoring state education agencies be fully prepared to provide the leadership required in their respective states to assure the kind and quality of education that will be essential for the future. This project should contribute significantly to that end, as well as to the broader purposes noted above, by providing valuable information and guidelines for effecting appropriate changes.

I am quite proud to be a part of this study, and I commend all who are associated with this project for their willingness to accept the challenges of the present and the future.

BYRON W. HANSFORD
Chairman, Policy Board

CONTENTS

xi

CHAPTER 1

The Project And The First Conference*

The American society will continue to experience an increasing rate of change. Many of these changes will have important implications for, and will necessitate changes in education. There is urgent need to attempt to anticipate the changes that are likely to occur in society during the next ten to fifteen years, to understand their implications for education, and to plan for adjustments that will be necessary to meet emerging needs.

Some of the prospective changes may be beneficial to society from a long range point of view; others may be harmful. Man, to some extent, can control the nature and direction of changes. With increased knowledge and understanding he should be in a constantly improving position to plan and prepare for those changes that are beneficial and to avoid some that could be disadvantageous or even disastrous. Thus, today's greatest hope and most urgent need is for a constantly improving and more realistic program of education for every member of society.

In this country, the citizens of each state have the basic responsibility for developing an adequate plan and program for the education of all residents. If any state does not meet its responsibilities realistically, both the state and the nation will be handicapped. During this period of rapid change it is particularly important that the people in every state attempt to appraise developments and to prepare long-range plans for meeting, as fully as possible, their responsibilities for education.

Arizona, Colorado, Idaho, Montana, Nevada, New Mexico, Utah and Wyoming, eight Western States that have many common interests and problems, have entered into an agreement to cooperate in an important project entitled DESIGNING EDUCATION FOR THE FUTURE: *An Eight-State Project*. This project is concerned ultimately with improving and strengthening the respective state agencies responsible for education. While each state is making its own appraisals and developing its own plans, these states are joining to study common problems relating to impending changes and their implications.

This project, necessarily, is concerned initially with all aspects of education for which the state agencies are responsible or have concerns, because all aspects are interrelated in one way or another. It should have important implications not only for state educational organization and responsibilities and for all agencies concerned with planning, but also for local organization and functioning, state-local school system relations, state relations to higher education, and for the issue of federal-state relations which is becoming more complicated and increasingly crucial.

*Edgar L. Morphet, Project Director, and Charles O. Ryan, Associate Director.

1

ORIGIN OF THE PROJECT

The basic concepts and ideas for this project grew out of considerations such as those discussed above. The Chief State School Officers (state superintendents and commissioners of education) of the eight participating states, members of their respective staffs, and others interested in these developments, have agreed that improvements in education are essential and should be carefully planned in the light of all available evidence. The chief state school officers have also agreed that the best approach to a study and solution of pending and prospective problems in education is through a cooperative project in which all eight states will participate. Two important concepts have been recognized by all concerned: (1) much important information and many challenging ideas can be provided through a small central staff and cooperative effort; and (2) the basic studies to be made and plans for effecting improvements in each state will need to be developed by competent leaders from within the state with counsel and assistance from other sources, as appropriate.

Fortunately the Elementary and Secondary Education Act of 1965 was enacted into law about the time the chief state school officers of the eight states, with the leadership of Colorado, were seriously considering proposals for this project. Title V, Section 505 of this act authorized funds to be used by the United States Commissioner of Education "to make grants to state educational agencies to pay part of the cost of experimental projects for developing state leadership or for the establishment of special services which, in the judgment of the Commissioner, hold promise of making a substantial contribution to the solution of problems common to the state educational agencies of all or several states."

A draft of the proposal for the project was submitted to the Commissioner wtihin a few months after the new law was enacted. On the basis of helpful suggestions from the Office of Education staff, the original proposal was revised and resubmitted. The project was approved effective December 9, 1965 to extend through June 30, 1969. The amount of federal funds authorized for the first year was $229,000; the amount for the second year was tentatively designated as $217,000. Each state was expected to provide supporting services or funds and is doing so. Colorado has been designated as the administering state for the federal funds provided. The central staff office is located in Denver.

THE GENERAL PLAN

The major purpose of the project is clearly indicated in the proposal: To assist each of the participating states to anticipate the changes that are likely to take place in this country, in the eight-state area and within the state during the next ten to fifteen years, and to plan and implement changes and improvements that should be made in the educational organization and program during that period. While some of the policies to be observed were incorporated in the proposal, the detailed steps and procedures needed to accomplish this purpose were appropriately left to the discretion of the policy board, the staff and the individual states.

The chief state school officers of the eight states were designated in the proposal as the policy board for the project. This board selected the central staff comprised of the project director and associate director, approved the budget and adopted the policies to be observed in conducting the project. Each state has selected a state coordinator who is responsible to the chief state school officer (or his designated representative) for planning and directing the studies and activities relating to the project that are conducted in the state.

The project staff, for planning purposes, is comprised of the director, the associate director, and the eight state coordinators. This staff has met periodically to develop recommendations on policies and budgetary matters for consideration by the policy board, to review proposals relating to the area conferences, to agree on policies and procedures recommended for consideration in each state, and to discuss other matters of mutual interest.

The project involves two distinct but closely related types of activities: (1) The area conferences and other aspects of the project planned by the staff and conducted primarily for the benefit of the participating states and their citizens; and (2) the development and implementation of plans for studies and other appropriate steps for the improvement of education within the state, for which each state is basically responsible. Each of these is discussed briefly below.

The Area Aspects of the Project

The central staff, with the cooperation and assistance of the state coordinators, is responsible for providing leadership and direction in planning and implementing the area aspects of the project. In addition to assisting the states with the development and implementation of their plans and providing the necessary administrative services, the major responsibility of this staff is to plan and conduct at least three major area conferences and arrange for the publication of the reports.

The first conference for which the papers included in this publication were prepared, was concerned primarily with *Prospective Changes in Society by 1980*. Such a conference was considered essential to provide a defensible basis for considering changes that should be made in various aspects of education. The fact is generally recognized that all major and many minor changes in society have some implications for education. However, in the past many of the needed changes in education have been made all too slowly to meet some of the urgent needs.

The second area conference, to be held in Salt Lake City, Utah, October 24-26 of this year, will be concerned with *Implications for Education of Prospective Changes in Society*. Fifteen basic papers, each of which will deal with some major aspect of education, are being prepared for this conference. Two additional papers will be devoted to the *major* implications for education of prospective changes in society. The substantial number of lay and educational leaders from each state who participate in these discussions or read the reports should thereafter be in a favorable position to begin meaningful discussions of the implications for changes in their respective states.

The third area conference, tentatively planned for the spring of 1967, will be devoted to *Planning and Change Processes*. It is anticipated that the people in each of the states will be concerned by that time with the development of detailed plans for effecting changes and improvements in their respective states and that this conference will provide stimulation and some guidance for them.

The State Aspects of the Project

The proposal provided for each state to appoint a competent person to serve full time as coordinator for the state aspects of the project. Each state coordinator is expected to provide the leadership needed to assure that all aspects are effectively planned and conducted in his state.

The process of evaluating existing provisions and planning needed changes in education presents many difficulties in any state. If recommendations are to be soundly conceived and implemented, many competent citizens should be involved. For this and other reasons, every state has either selected or is in the process of selecting an advisory committee for the project, comprised of some fifteen or more lay and educational leaders. This committee will advise with the coordinator on planning studies, analyzing data, and developing recommendations for the state. Funds are included in the budget to pay the expenses of meetings of the committee in the state and to enable at least four members to attend each of the area conferences.

Each state also has obtained the services of a competent out-of-state consultant who will work, as needed, with the coordinator and advisory committee in developing and implementing plans and preparing recommendations. Several of the states plan to appoint, at an appropriate time, special committees to study and prepare recommendations on certain aspects of the program for consideration by the consultant, coordinator and advisory committee.

The following projects are presently under way in each of the states:

(1) Obtaining from appropriate sources pertinent information on trends, developments and projections that will be needed as a basis for evaluation and planning.

(2) Planning special studies that may be needed to provide information not presently available, and obtaining the cooperation of agencies, organizations, higher institutions and individuals in position to make such studies.

(3) Making a study of and preparing a report on important changes that have been made in various aspects of education over a period of years, on when, how, and why each was made, and on some of the implications.

(4) Obtaining and summarizing reactions from educational and lay opinion leaders as to (a) the best features of the present educational program and organization for education, (b) the most serious weaknesses or problems and (c) the major changes that should be made.

(5) Developing plans to assure wide-spread study and discussion in the state of the papers prepared for and the issues considered at the area conferences, with special attention to the possible implications for changes in the educational organization and program in the state.

THE PAPERS FOR THE FIRST CONFERENCE

This publication includes the fifteen papers prepared for the first area conference held in Denver, Colorado, June 29-30 and July 1, 1966. Each of the first fourteen papers is concerned with prospective changes in some important aspect of American society (Chapters 2-15). The final chapter is devoted to a consideration of prospective major problems in society in 1980.

Despite the fact that this conference had to be planned and the papers completed within a period of three months, the persons invited to collaborate were so deeply impressed with the challenge and potential of the project that it was possible to obtain the services of authorities who are considered among the leaders in the nation in their respective areas. The papers prepared for the conference should be most stimulating and challenging to everyone who reads them.

The authors have attempted to base their projections of changes on the best evidence available. However this does not mean that all the anticipated changes will or should occur. As one of the authors pointed out: "Projection is not carried out in a vacuum. By our very attempts to project, we alter the future and render our projections inadequate." Another noted that projections, like plans, should not be considered infallible guides. They should be reviewed periodically as conditions change or new evidence becomes available, and should be revised whenever it is apparent that they are no longer defensible or useful.

While the primary attention of the authors was centered on prospective changes in society, some of them have suggested certain implications for education. It is hoped that readers and discussion groups will be interested in exploring this matter further in preparation for the second conference.

Everyone involved in developing plans for this first conference recognized that fifteen papers could not reasonably be expected to include all prospective changes in society. Even if several more papers could have been arranged, there would undoubtedly have been omissions. However, time and budgetary limitations prevented a more ambitious undertaking. The major purpose was to attempt to direct attention to some of the most significant prospective changes rather than to attempt to list all changes regardless of their importance. Even fifteen papers could not have been presented and discussed at a three-day conference, so a choice had to be made. The papers presented and discussed at the conference comprise Chapters 2, 4 to 10 inclusive, 12 and 16. Chapters 3, 11, 13, 14 and 15 include papers prepared for purposes of the conference but not presented or discussed.

CHAPTER 2

Natural Resource Trends
And Their Implications

JOSEPH L. FISHER*

The time is long past when people in this country can afford to plan their lives and activities against a time perspective extending only a few months or a few years ahead. In the world of increasing specialization and expanding technical and economic complexity, it will be prudent for young people in laying out their educational programs, to have in mind as clearly as possible the general lines of work they wish to follow far into the future of their lives. This selection, in turn, will depend partly on what American society will probably be like a decade, or two or three into the future; what kinds of jobs it will require, where the larger number of people will be living, how much leisure time people will have and what they should be doing with it, plus a large number of other highly relevent questions.

One ingredient of the future of basic and obvious importance is to be found in the natural resources trends and patterns. What resources and resource products will be required in 1980, and where will they be located or produced? How will the needs, desires, and effective demands of 1980's population for resources be satisfied most efficiently? The questions relate not only to the sheer quantity of food and fiber products, fresh water, fuels and electric power, metals and structural materials, and all the rest; of equal or even greater importance will be the qualitative aspects of the resource base of land, water, and air and the way people actually use, or abuse, the resource base.

These issues have to be of central concern for a society that wants to be better in 1980 than it is now or has been in the past. We shall want the material level of living to go on improving, hopefully in more selective ways than would be indicated simply by the trend in the gross national product. Attention will have to be given to the distribution of that product among regions, among income classes, among racial and national origin groups, and so forth. Certainly attention will have to be given to the regional distribution of the nation's prosperity in the Rocky Mountain states and elsewhere; we cannot afford to be content always with a good trend in national averages. And yet no region in the last third of the

---

*President, Resources for the Future, Inc., Washington, D.C. (a non-profit research and educational foundation concerned with the development of natural resources); served as economist and executive officer of the Council of Economic Advisers, Executive Office of the President (1947-53); has written, lectured, and consulted widely on economic problems of resource development and regional growth, and is an author of two recent books: *Resources in America's Future* (Hopkins, 1963 and *World Prospects for Natural Resources* (Hopkins, 1964.)

7

Twentieth Century can even think of standing on its own feet; each is a part of the whole, inextricably bound up in the trends and fortunes of all of the other regions, and beyond them of the other countries of the world. The time for regional chauvinism has long since past, if indeed it ever should have had a heyday.

It should go almost without saying that nothing is more important to regional welfare and to the material and cultural future of regions than the scope and quality of the educational programs they are able to establish and carry forward. I shall not belabor this point further in a general way, but later I shall try to say something about the important linkages between natural resources and education for the Rocky Mountain region.

The scheme of my paper is simple: first I want to set before you briefly but comprehensively some of the more significant trends in the resource sectors of the U.S. economy to the year 1980, which is the target year for consideration in this conference. Then I want to discuss briefly some of the implications of these trends for the United States, for the world, and particularly for the Rocky Mountain states. Finally I shall note a number of problems and opportunities for educators and education in general, and especially for the Rocky Mountain region.

REVIEW OF RESOURCE TRENDS

During recent years Resources for the Future has given a considerable amount of attention to the systematic delineation of economic and natural resource trends, past and future, for the United States.[1] It would be fair to say that we have tried to cast up a framework of the future within which problems, investment possibilities, policies, and public issues can be considered. We have been concerned that the alternative decisions and lines of action be consistent with a realistic measure of the potentialities of the future, and that they be consistent one with another in the separate resource fields. Such a framework is in no sense a plan or a blueprint of what has to be in the future; instead it is a set of guidelines or indicators of what is likely to happen under specified realistic assumptions regarding the underlying determinants of the economic and resource situation in the future. It is particularly important to look ahead in the resources field, as in the education field, because policies, programs, and activities have to be decided upon far in advance of the time when they will reach their maximum period of contribution. Thus, formal education of a person draws toward its close in the late teens or early twenties, but his economic and cultural contribution extends onward for the following four or five decades. A river development program of dams, reservoirs, and other facilities is decided upon at a moment of time, but its beneficial and perhaps harmful consequences continue on for many decades. Even in the financial sense we amortize such investments over a span of five or six decades. If one is going to open up a new mine,

---

[1] For example, see Hans H. Landsberg, Leonard L. Fischman and Joseph L. Fisher, *Resources in America's Future* (Baltimore: The Johns Hopkins Press for Resources For the Future, Inc., 1963); Sam H. Schurr and Bruce C. Netschert, *Energy In the American Economy;* Marion Clawson, R. Burnell Held, and Charles H. Stoddard, *Land for the Future.*

establish new ore processing facilities, create an irrigation project with all the related community and service infrastructure, he has to make such decisions in terms of the best, most systematic and comprehensive picture of the relevant future that it is possible to construct.

What is likely to be the size and shape of the U.S. economy in 1980? In Table 1, some of the basic aggregates are noted with 1980 projections made at a low, medium, and high level, based on past trends. The labor force for 1980 is predictable within a fairly narrow range, since all of the people who will be in the labor force at that time have already been born. One does not know exactly how many since this will depend on how many older people and women may be in the labor force, and on other factors: output per worker, what is commonly called labor productivity, is an uncertain thing; the estimates in the table are consistent with past trends, perhaps a little on the optimistic side, but not much. A small change in labor productivity, say half of one percent, amounts to a 25 percent absolute effect on gross national product. A two-thirds increase in GNP in the next fifteen years seems altogether reasonable; indeed if the rather higher rate of increase in the last several years continues, the 1980 GNP will be near the high estimate shown in the table rather than the medium. Implied in the medium GNP estimate is an annual rate of increase of slightly less than 4 percent.

Recently personnel of the National Planning Association have delineated what they call "aspiration goals" for the American economy for 1970 and 1975.[2] Attainment of these goals will involve an annual GNP

TABLE 1

Size of the U.S. Economy
1950, 1965, and Projected for 1980

	1950 (actual)	1965 (est.)	Levels of Demand	1980 (projected)
			L	226
Population (millions)	152	195	M	245
			H	279
			L	98
Labor Force (millions)	65	78	M	102
			H	109
			L	9.8
Output per worker	5.6	7.9	M	10.4
(thousands of 1960 dollars)			H	11.5
			L	965
Gross National Product	363	617	M	1,060
(billions of 1960 dollars)			H	1,250

L=Low, M=Medium, H=High

Source for 1950 and 1980: Landsberg, Fischman, and Fisher, *Resources in America's Future*, cited in footnote 1.

[2] Leonard A. Lecht, *Goals, Priorities, and Dollars* (New York: The Free Press, 1966)

increase of around 5.5 percent. "Aspiration goals" refer to the attainment, or at least good progress toward the achievement, of goals in the various sectors of the economy which are established by the best professional thinking in the several sectors.

The spread between low and high for each of the items in Table 1 simply means that in 1980 that particular item could realistically fall anywhere within the range, but the most likely outcome, on a judgment basis, is at the medium level. The labor force will increase in a fairly predictable way, hours of work per week are assumed to fall slightly, and output per worker is projected to increase at about 2 percent a year for the medium estimate. This, of course, will require continued capital investment, both for replacement and for new development, with the capital-output ratio continuing to move downward slightly. Productivity increases are obviously the resultant effect of improvements in technology, education and training, management, and other factors. Education and the improvements in technology that result mainly from education have been identified as the principal contributors to increasing productivity.[3] Also underlying these projections is an unemployment rate of about 4 percent of the labor force. If this could be reduced to 3 percent, not far from where it has been in recent months, and held at this level, there could well be 1 million more people at work in 1980 due entirely to this fact, and this would be the equivalent of something more than 10 billion dollars in output for that year.

In an economy that might grow as portrayed in Table 1, there would be associated increasing requirements for most of the natural resources and resource products. In fact natural resources and raw materials are the basic building blocks of economic growth; without an increasing flow of food and fiber, fuels, structural materials, and all the rest into the economic machine, the projected economic growth simply would not be attainable. This does not mean that natural resource inputs are more important than labor force or capital inputs; it simply means that they are basic and necessary. Table 2 shows requirements for selected natural resources in 1980 which would be more or less consistent with the aggregative projections of Table 1. These are shown here as examples only to give an indication of the resources ballpark in which we shall be playing in 1980. They provide useful reference points or benchmarks for testing policies, programs, and specific investments which will come up for consideration year by year as we approach 1980. In each instance the specific requirements for agricultural products, metals, fuels, and the rest are consistent with the aggregative projections, and are related to historical trends of specific resources or products themselves. The whole system of projections is comprehensive in the sense that individual items could actually work out that way and not carry us into a realm of impossibilities having in mind the limitations of the whole economy.

Of course the uncertainties are quite great when it comes to projecting demand for the great variety of resource products. One does not

---

[3] Edward F. Denison, *The Sources of Economic Growth in the United States and the Alternatives Before Us* (Supplementary Paper #13 published by Committee for Economic Development, 1962).

know what may appear during the years between now and 1980 by way of new products, new sources of old products, technological shifts which make possible substitutions of plentiful for scarce materials, new possibilities for imports and exports, by-products and various materials recyclings in industry which may be worked out, and so on. The economics

TABLE 2

Requirements for Selected Natural Resources,
1950, 1960, and projected for 1980

	1950	1960	1980
Cropland, including pasture (million acres)	478	447	443
Recreation land excluding reservoir areas and city parks (million acres)	42	44	76
Urban land, including city parks (million acres)	17	21	32
Timber (billion cubic feet)	12	12	19
Fresh water withdrawal depletions (billion gallons per day):			
East	10.7*	13.7	24.3
West	50.3*	59.7	68.7
Pacific Northwest	9.4*	11.1	13.5
Oil (billion barrels)	2.3	3.2	5.3
Natural gas, excluding NGL (trillion cubic feet)	6.8	12.9	23.5
Coal (million short tons)	523	436	630
Iron ore (million short tons)	117	131	209
Aluminum, primary (million short tons)	1.0	2.1	5.7
Copper, primary (million short tons)	1.7	1.7	2.6

*1954
Source: *Resources in America's Future.*

of relative cost shifts as these are translated into relative prices will govern in ways that are difficult to predict with any exactness. For example, new sources of oil and natural gas may be located in this country or abroad from conventional underground pools, or new materials may become economic such as oil shale or tar sands, or shifts may occur in the technology of fuel use which may make possible a substitution of electric power for oil or gas, and so on almost without end. Even in agriculture a bewildering array of substitutions is conceivable: we already know how fertilizer and machinery inputs can substitute for acres of crop land, but we do not know whether trends of the past in this respect will continue unabated into the future. Structural materials may be substituted one for another across a broad array of basic resource products from metals to timber to plastics which are produced in the chemical industries but derive basically from petroleum. But plastics may also arise from coal, and some of them from timber and other fiber sources.

In Table 2, several points are worth highlighting. The greatest increases in land use in 1980 are estimated to be for recreation land and for urban land. This is true even in absolute number of acres, as well as in percentage increase. We projected cropland more or less unchanged from 1960 to 1980, and this oddly enough is about the same as it was thirty or forty years ago. It could turn out to be an underestimate, depending largely on the amount of U.S. cropland devoted to wheat and other exports which may be required by India and other less developed countries. But this in turn depends critically upon the capacity of those countries to generate the foreign exchange with which to buy our food exports and upon our policies with regard to food for peace. Likewise, acres devoted to grazing and forests may not increase through 1980.

The estimates shown for fresh water withdrawal depletions (that is water actually withdrawn from lakes and streams and used up rather than returned) indicates a much greater percentage increase in the East than in the West, particularly in the so-called arid west. This is partly a reflection of the very high cost of developing additional supplies in the West, and hence is as much a supply as a demand projection. (Indeed this is one of the great difficulties in resource projections; demand and supply become intertwined so that it is difficult to know exactly which one is being projected.) The smaller increase in fresh water requirements in the West does not necessarily indicate a cessation of economic growth. It has been estimated elsewhere that a decrease of 5 percent in the amount of water used in irrigation agriculture would provide enough water for a doubling of industrial use. Furthermore, the value of water in terms of contribution to state and regional incomes in the West when water is used for industrial purposes might be forty or fifty times what it would be in typical agricultural use, on the basis of a variety of reasonable assumptions.[4]

The requirement for oil, natural gas, and coal in 1980 may confidently be expected to increase, probably more for oil and natural gas than for coal. Energy consumption, we think, will continue to increase at a slower rate than national production, but still it will increase quite a bit as indicated in Table 2. Substitutions among the three sources will take place according to the relative costs and prices, which in turn will depend upon discoveries, new extraction technology, shifting location of markets, and other factors. Most likely nuclear power will come into the picture; indeed recent events and decisions indicate that the floodgate is about to open with regard to this new source of electric power. Apparently the Tennessee Valley Authority is about to install two nuclear plants, each exceeding slightly 1 million kilowatts of capacity, very near the heart of the low cost coal region. Comparative studies seem to have indicated that nuclear power will be a bit cheaper than coal, in the range of 2.4 mills per kilowatt hour for nuclear. These would be very large plants and would put TVA into the nuclear business in a major way just as it is now in the coal based, steam power picture along with hydropower. Nuclear plants are footloose; their location does not depend on the location of fuel because the cost of transporting fuel to the plant site is a very small portion of total cost. What is

---

[4] Nathaniel Wollman, *The Value of Water in Alternative Uses* (Albuquerque, New Mexico, The University of New Mexico Press, 1962)

required is a large stable market to handle a nuclear base load, and a large sum to invest in the reactor, shielding, and other capital items.

Undoubtedly there will be increases in the requirements for iron ore, aluminum, copper, and a long list of other metals and non-metallics. In the next fifteen years as in the past there will be competition in numerous uses among two or more of the metals, as well as competition between the metals and timber based materials. Just how this will come out is difficult to predict. Therefore, if a low and a high estimate for aluminum had been shown, it would have covered a wide range with the high perhaps being five or six times the low. And depending upon how the aluminum use turns out, copper requirement will be high or low, and even the steel requirement will be affected. This kind of picture could be elaborated in considerably more detail, as is done in our study *Resources in America's Future.*

IMPLICATIONS FOR THE UNITED STATES AND THE WORLD

The first thing that has to be said is that the U. S. economy, large and diversified as it is, does not exist in isolation; it is part of a much larger world economy with which it is inter-connected at many points. Trade in raw materials has always been the basic element in world trade, and undoubtedly will continue to be so for many years ahead. The United States imports roughly one-fifth of its oil and more than that of its iron ore. For copper, lead, zinc, not to mention somewhat less important metals like tin, manganese, and a long list of others imports range from 50 percent on up to 100 percent. On the other side the United States exports large amounts of wheat, cotton, even rice, coal, sulphur, phosphates, and many others. If our exports of basic agricultural crops should suddenly be drastically curtailed, U. S. A. agriculture as a whole would go into a tailspin. Therefore, the trends in demand and supply from the other parts of the world are of vital importance to this country and to all its regions. A good beginning point is to compile a list of raw material exports and imports which have been important and will probably be important in the future, and then to consider world trends in demand for this list of items and the various world sources of supply. This can lead into analyses of great significance to the United States as a whole and to those regions especially concerned with individual items.

A second broad implication of our picture of resources in 1980 is the key role of technology as this is promoted through education and research and as it is translated ultimately to industrial production. If my picture of 1980 is an optimistic one so far as raw materials are concerned, then it is only because I have assumed continued technological advance across a broad front of agriculture, industry, and economic activity generally. This is what one means by a 2 or a 2½ percent annual rate of increase in productivity. Those resource industries or regions which fall behind in technological advance do really fall behind in a profound sense. Of utmost importance is the maintenance of all those things which make for technological advance including a careful selection of points for emphasis. Much has been written in recent years about the importance of not overlooking basic research as compared to applied research and development. Along with others I have stressed over and over again the additional importance of not overlooking research in management, economics and social science generally, and policy itself as an aid to insuring continued economic growth.

Another implication, related to the technological one just mentioned, will be the importance of programs of conservation and wise use of natural resources. Conservation, of course, is not an absolute goal all by itself but must be worked out realistically in terms of benefits and costs, alternative kinds of action, and a variety of ecological and cultural constraints. I do not need to emphasize the importance of land and water conservation in the West; perhaps I do need to emphasize that land and water in the West must be conserved and used wisely for those purposes which will return the maximum of benefits over cost, and I would conceive benefits and costs in broad social terms rather than narrow financial or economic terms.

Conservation now and for the future will be at least as much involved in preserving the quality of the natural environment as it will be in maintaining a capacity to produce quantities of goods. As technology and management assure raw materials for the future, our attention will switch to the qualitative aspects of abating water and air pollution, preventing pesticide damage, and improving the design and use of both the rural and urban landscape. Already this concern has found expression in state and federal laws and programs which have reached considerable magnitude, but are destined to grow rapidly in the coming years.

Finally, the resouce projections to 1980 and beyond seem to point to the need for much more policy and institutional experimentation, innovation, and testing than we have known in the past. Under the new Water Resources Planning Act the various river systems of the country are going to be subjected to much more comprehensive and interrelated kinds of planning and development than we have known before, with the exception of a few places. This legislation, as written and as being interpreted, wisely allows for diversity in institutional approaches in the various river basins. Particularly water quality programs are going to have to be conceived and put into operation on a river basin or regional scale. This leads to a host of challenging problems of planning, financing, establishment and enforcement of standards, the use of incentives to encourage private users to give attention to quality, and so on.

In the field of land use the need for institutional improvements may also be noted. In a way the most critical land use problems are to be found in the metropolitan areas, particularly on the fringes as the cities and suburbs extend out into the rural countryside. Here the shifts in use are dramatic, the conflicts heated, and our capacity to deal with situations limited. Attention will have to be directed toward the development of new metropolitan forms and organizations to deal with problems such as water supply, the handling of sewage, air pollution, transportation, and many others on a metropolitan scale. Monolithic government for metropolitan areas, with powers and responsibilities concentrated in one institution, does not seem to be in the cards and would be inconsistent with long established traditions for preserving diversity and a maximum of local autonomy. We must turn to the devising of new institutional arrangements such as metropolitan wide suburban land development authorities, transportation planning and development boards, and the like.

Implications for the Rocky Mountain States

Let me now center attention briefly on the eight-state Rocky Mountain area or region in which this conference is being held, with its principal center located in Denver but with important other centers elsewhere in the region. I shall not try to cover all possible implications of the 1980 resource picture, but shall discuss briefly a few important ones. I shall be dipping into our book *Resources in America's Future* quite a bit for examples.

Considering first some of the trends in agriculture over the next fifteen years that would seem to have a particular bearing on the Rocky Mountain region, one notices first the likelihood that per capita wheat consumption in this country, which was marked by a drop from 220 to 165 pounds between 1940 and 1960, is likely to show a much slower rate of decline over the next decade or two. But on a relative scale this shift will be large compared to that for other food products. One counter-trend should be noted, however; and that is the possibility that this region as well as other parts of the country will be called upon to supply large increases in wheat for export to the less developed, densely populated countries of south Asia and elsewhere. As noted earlier, national policy will be the significant element here. Already one can see the gathering of forces, political as well as economic, to re-direct American agriculture toward increasing acreages and much larger amounts of exports. In fact, one can see on the horizon a combination of forces including the traditional agricultural bloc, the western water development interests, shippers, enthusiasts for the food-for-peace or food-for-development idea, and perhaps others—all in a major new alignment which will press for increased agricultural development, additional water and irrigation projects, and large subsidized food export programs. But, short of a considerable move in this direction, the outlook has to be for not too much increase in wheat production in this country during the coming period of years. This, however, it turns out, will be of major importance to the eastern tier of the Rocky Mountain states which extend out into the Great Plains, as well as to other parts of the region in which are to be found valleys and pockets of land devoted to wheat.

Next one has to mention a continuation of the increasing per capita consumption of meat which has been so spectacular during the past 25 years. The recent years indicate no abatement in this tendency; indeed the high estimates for 1980 contained in our basic book will probably be exceeded well before that year. We are becoming the great beef eating country of the world in which steak is the most sought-after item in the menu, sometimes seemingly without too much regard to its much higher price compared to other items. Per capita consumption of beef already exceeds one hundred pounds a year, nearly double what it was in 1940, and the end of this is not in sight. All of this indicates shifts in acreage to feed grains, high protein concentrates, and pasture. Of course other parts of the country, notably the Southeast will be responding to this situation and outlook, and the Rocky Mountain region will have to find its place in competition.

The outlook for mutton and other meat, and for wool and hides, does not seem to offer anything like the possibilities for the West that can be seen for beef. Indeed in most of these others the West, and the nation as a whole, will be hard put to maintain recent absolute levels of production.

Turning now to forest products, our resource appraisal study indicated the possibility of supply difficulty toward the end of this century, but with no very great strain by the year 1980. Events of the past couple of years since the book was published lead us now to the view that the supply situation will be easier than we had thought, so that the mountain region would find competition rather keen with the Pacific Northwest and the Southeast in particular. The outlook is mixed: apparently there will be an abundance of hardwood supplies for any conceivable uses, but the pinch will continue with regard to high grade soft-wood saw timber. Those parts of the mountain West which have good stocks of saw-timber-size conifers should find quite good markets during the next period of years.

But according to many, the principal value of many forested lands in the future will not be for timber products but as a location for outdoor recreation. The rapid growth in what I like to call the outdoor recreation industry over recent years is by now quite widely recognized. Statistical and economic studies of outdoor recreation done principally by my colleague, Dr. Marion Clawson, have highlighted this trend. Depending upon what forms of recreation and areas one looks at, the annual rate of growth as measured by user-days has been and probably will continue to increase at between five and 10 percent per year. This puts outdoor recreation among the real growth industries of the country. Behind this growth are a number of factors: increasing family incomes, increasing population of course, more leisure time and vacations, increased mobility through air travel and wide ownership of automobiles, plus the psychological urge to escape from office and factory work into open spaces during vacation periods. All of these factors taken together seem to guarantee that outdoor recreation will absorb more time, planning attention, investment, and all the rest in the years ahead.

Dr. Clawson has found that the demand for what he calls resource-based outdoor recreation—that is, in the more remote mountains and wooded areas such as many of the national forests and national parks—has been increasing at especially rapid rates, although what he calls user-based and intermediate areas have also increased very rapidly. The annual rate of increase in user-days in national forests and national parks has been 10 to 12 percent for several decades past. Fortunately for the Rocky Mountain states there exists in this great region a tremendous extent of land of superb scenic and recreation value, much of it already in public ownership and therefore available for recreation use of anyone who wishes to come. Beyond this, of course, are the numerous possibilities for private recreational development on ranches, in cities and towns scattered through the region, on privately owned land around lakes and reservoirs, and so on. It is undoubtedly true that most of the national forests in the Rocky Mountain region can yield much higher benefits in recreation use than would be received from selling timber stumpage. A few years ago I estimated that, assuming a man-day of recreation in the national forests in the mountain West to be valued at $1.00, most of those forests already would return considerably more in recreation use than they do from sale of stumpage. One can dispute the $1.00 estimate and say that it should be $10.00 or 10 cents, and one can say that the value of scenery and a day in the mountains are not subject to monetary estimates. I offer the $1.00 only as an assumption to give some idea of the comparative values that may be involved in the two ways of using forests.

Fortunately recreation and timber uses of forests are frequently compatible. Recreationists usually want to go to the particularly scenic points, to the campgrounds, to the streams and lakes. If the forests are preserved in these zones, most of the recreation users would be well satisfied. In other cases recreation areas can be moved about so as to permit a cutting program to take place. Other areas, of course, are of such superb scenic value that they should be kept permanently in relatively undisturbed condition except as it may be necessary to interfere with the natural environment to provide access for people.

Recreation nowadays is frequently held out as a panacea for many kinds of areas that are experiencing economic difficulties. A word of caution is in order. In most parts of the country recreation is highly seasonal, frequently with no more than a two- or three-month active season. The economics of such a short term operation are very difficult to work out profitably, and investments are hard to justify. Frequently hopes and ambitions of individuals run far ahead of what can be justified. This is not to discourage such development; rather it is to urge that the economic side be calculated as carefully as possible before commitments of time and funds are made.

Adequate supplies of water for a variety of uses will continue to be a Western problem of intense interest. Supply adequacy, it should be pointed out, is a relative matter—relative to the importance of the uses to which the water is put, the cost of providing it, the prices paid for it, the economies, the substitutions that can be made, and other factors. I have already mentioned the lavish use of precious water in western irrigation. The possibilities for further conservation are striking; these include spreading thin films on reservoirs to reduce evaporation, lining irrigation canals, weeding out useless water-consuming trees and plants, and recycling and reclamation of industrial and municipal water. Desalinization of ocean and inland brackish water should be mentioned; also long distance, inter-basin transfer of water. Proposals along this latter line are exciting, if perhaps somewhat grandiose, and now embrace schemes as extensive as the whole western half of the continent. Of particular interest will be legal and institutional changes to facilitate a relative shift in western water use toward higher value municipal, industrial, and even recreational uses. The fostering of a more efficient market for water rights might be helpful and acceptable. (Some studies sponsored by Resources For the Future and undertaken in this region are probing in this direction.) The fact that most families in the humid East pay water bills as high as families in the arid West is a matter worth pondering. Those who hold that water development in the West should be subsidized by the nation as a whole in the interest of Western economic and social advancement, logically should favor a shift in water use from agriculture to industry where an acre foot of water could support much more in jobs and incomes. But, however these matters turn out, assuring water supplies will remain vital to the West.

Looking now at the energy resources, the prospects for the Rocky Mountain states as they might fit into national trends and patterns over the next fifteen years are full of uncertainty and excitement. Reserves of coal in the region and in adjoining states in the northern plains are fabulously large; they will remain distant from truly large manufacturing and population centers for the duration of the period under study here. But there they are, waiting in the wings for the time they may be called upon. To the extent that western coal can be used at the mine head, as in the production of electric power in the big plant in northwestern New Mexico, or for metallurgical or perhaps chemical industry purposes, Rocky Mountain coal may have a flowering of development earlier. Should coal gasification or liquefication come within the ambit of what is economic, then again western coal might rather suddenly begin to make a much larger contribution to the total energy supply of the country, not to mention the West.

The Rocky Mountain states also have rather large known reserves, and much larger potential reserves, of oil and natural gas, particularly in the southeastern part of the region. These are already being developed and are hooked in to national pipeline distribution systems. Their future will depend upon the unfolding of advantages here as compared to other locations of supplies.

Of more dramatic interest are the immense oil shale deposits in Colorado, Utah, and Wyoming. These have been known for many years; indeed troublesome and disputed claims for these lands were registered some decades ago. But actual development has been limited thus far to a few small, more or less pilot operations. Geological and economic studies seem to indicate firmly that large practical possibilities for mining the shale and extracting oil products from it are available by means of which products could be produced at only marginally higher costs than from conventional liquid underground sources. A 10 percent cost differential may be a good estimate. It is very difficult to say when the national economy will be ready to make substantial use of the Rocky Mountain oil shale. Most people seem to think it is merely a matter of time, although it must be conceded that people have been saying this for some years. In any case it is not too early for states and others interested in the region to bear down on a variety of studies and preliminary planning activities to get ready for the day when oil shale comes into its own.

A number of problems are worth further consideration. First is the disposition of the disputed oil claims, which apparently the Department of the Interior is now pressing to take care of. Second is to intensify research and development activities across the spectrum from mining through processing and distribution to see if further cost reductions can be achieved. The recent work being sponsored by a number of oil companies working through the Colorado School of Mines Research Foundation is promising, as is some other work being undertaken in the area. There has been much speculation about *in situ* retorting which, if it proves to be workable and economic, would have the immense advantage of not digging into the landscape and leaving huge unsightly piles of overburden behind. In addition, this method might greatly reduce the difficulties of water pollution in the very limited flow of streams in the area. In addition to research and development activities on shale itself, continued attention and study should be given to such matters as water supply and pollution, air pollution, landscape and wildlife effects, and community development.

Of importance for the next few years will be further consideration of the kinds of policies, particularly regarding leases, that the government may work out so as to attract private investment on a profitable scale without in any sense sacrificing legitimate public interests. The Oil Shale Board appointed by the Secretary of the Interior of which I served as chairman, reported on this subject a year and a half ago. While it did find agreement on many matters, it did not succeed in reaching consensus regarding this vital question of leasing terms. The group was arrayed along a line stretching from those who wanted the terms to be sufficiently easy that private industry would be attracted to making investments rather soon, to those who felt that any kind of leasing should await further information and research results regarding the extent of the resource, ways of exploiting it, and the like. My own view is that the government should consider announcing that several years hence it would offer a few properties of economic size for lease under terms which would be specified clearly so as to insure protection of the public interest in conservation, scenic amenity, and reasonable return on its property. I hope that something along this line can be worked out. This would make possible a few experimental leases for private development within a foreseeable period of time from which lessons could be learned regarding further leases for development of the resource. Meantime both private companies and government agencies should press forward vigorously with research and development activities.

Regarding the metallic minerals, it is difficult to know where to begin since each one of them is different in its economic characteristics and its place in the future, and yet there is a similarity about most of them. National demand for copper, lead, zinc, antimony, manganese, and many others will continue to rise, as will worldwide demand. The amount of the increase that will be drawn from the Mountain states will depend upon a number of factors: richness of deposits there, the amount and quality of capital brought to bear on their exploitation, the trends and substitutions among the metals and especially substitutions of non-metallics and plastics, the demand and supply trends in other parts of the world, the kinds of policies pursued by this government to regulate imports and provide incentives for domestic mining, plus many others. The more western mining activities depend upon import restrictions and government subsidies, the more shaky is the economic foundation for mineral activities in the Rocky Mountain region. It seems unlikely that metal mining will ever again in this region have the relative importance that it had in the late 19th and even the early 20th century. Metal mining employment already has been surpassed by several other categories of employment, but the region still depends significantly on shipments of metals and their products to other parts of the country for its "foreign exchange." Further discoveries may be expected in this region although it would be risky to depend on new discoveries. Perhaps it would be fair to view the metals as of continuing importance to the mountain economy, but of diminishing slowly in the relative sense.

Looking over the whole range of natural resources and resource products the future of the mountain West will continue to be closely linked with the national and world picture of demand and supply. The resource industries will continue to be more important in the mountain West than in the country as a whole because of their relatively greater employment and production. Their relative importance will probably continue to diminish, perhaps even slightly more rapidly than in the country as a whole which already has gone quite far in this direction. Water development will remain of vital concern and will be necessary to support much of any additional agricultural development, oil shale development, and manufacturing and urban development generally. Agriculture has been diminishing in all regions of the country; its future in the mountain West may be determined largely by the prospects for wheat and cattle. The picture for the latter has to be more optimistic than for the former. Outdoor recreation continues to be a major potential in view of national economic trends and styles of living, but investments in its development should be made with great care. Favorable policies by the national and state governments will be as helpful to the outdoor recreation industry as to the other resource industries. Fuels possibly represent the most exciting prospect for the future, partly because of the abundance and variety of fuels in the region but especially because of the great potentiality of oil shale. Metal mining and processing will continue to occupy a more important place in the economy of the mountain West than elsewhere in the country, but relatively speaking this emphasis may diminish in the future, with perhaps some metals going up but more going down in relation to the general growth of the region.

RESOURCE TRENDS AND EDUCATION

The trends in natural resources for the country as a whole and for the mountain West in particular, as depicted in the preceding sections, seem to point up several challenges for education. The conservation, development, and wise use of resources of water, land, air, and minerals may not require very many more people directly employed but they will require a highly trained professional group much larger in size than presently exists, numerous technicians in the middle levels both in existing fields and in some rather new lines altogether, more attention to basic principles at all levels in the school system, and a rich variety of educational activities and experiences for interested adult citizens. Our capacity to utilize our resource base in support of a larger population and a higher level of living will depend squarely upon educational advances in these fields; beyond this, our capacity to plan and manage our natural environment more tastefully and considerately, as well as more efficiently, will also depend on education.

At the professional level one can see an increasing need for a variety of scientists and engineers, plus additional persons with professional training in planning, management, and administration. These will be the persons to whom the country and the region will have to look in the future if the potentials for 1980 indicated earlier are to be reached, both in quantity of resource products and in improving the quality of the environment. I would expect to see employment opportunities increase rapidly for geologists, hydrologists, soil scientists, meteorologists, engineers of many kinds, economists, highly trained business and farm managers, among many others. Modern technology is being applied vigorously in virtually all of the resource activities from agriculture and ranching to mining and processing of raw materials. One of the reasons why employment in the resource industries has declined so much in recent years is that the professional competence of the key top personnel has risen so rapidly.

Through the middle levels of research and development, and resource planning and management one can foresee need for additional personnel more carefully trained for these pursuits. Conservation field technicians, park and forest wardens, research technicians, foremen and other key employees in mines and recreational enterprises and on farms and ranches, will be needed along with many others. Training programs in these fields, both in educational institutions and as extension activities, as well as on the job, offer important lines of activity for educators to think about. Only at the unskilled or semi-skilled levels is it likely that employment opportunities will decline.

In the elementary and secondary schools one can see the desirability of improved offerings to give all young people a greater appreciation of the role that resources play in economic and social development. Basic principles in ecology, conservation, biology, economics and many other fields have to be dealt with in the early years through appropriate learning experiences. The importance of direct field observation and experimentation should not be overlooked or postponed until the university or job years. Recognition of the fact that most people already live in cities, and that the proportion of urban dwellers will continue to increase, even in the more sparsely populated West, means that many learning experiences will have to be devised to appeal to urban youngsters. An understanding of water and air pollution will be more useful for the future perhaps than will visits to farms and ranches.

At the level of adult and citizen education there will be opportunity for numerous programs designed to promote general understanding of public issues in the resources field and the alternatives for policies and programs that should be considered. The need for an informed and well motivated citizenry extends beyond resources to many other subjects but, here in the West, resources have the center of the stage. To a major extent the well-being of Western society in 1980 will depend on intelligent and informed voters and how they cast their ballots between now and then.

I would not argue so much for separate courses or programs of re-source education at whatever level, although in many instances these are desirable and can be highly effective, as I would for trying to infuse natural resource considerations into all phases of school curriculums and other educational programs. At the university level, for example, natural re-source matters can be dealt with in almost all courses from zoology to political science to art and literature. Natural resources in the university curriculum may be likened to health or perhaps government; there can be special schools and programs for these subjects, but in addition and per-haps more important, they should enter appropriately into virtually all subjects taught. Here is a challenge for the curriculum makers, the text-book writers, the enthusiasts of interdisciplinary seminars, those who pre-pare laboratory manuals, and others. All of these remarks seem to me to have special relevance here in the mountain West where so obviously the natural resources and the natural environment bear directly and visibly on the lives and activities of all people who live in the area.

CHAPTER 3

Population Trends – Prologue To Educational Programs

PHILIP M. HAUSER* AND MARTIN TAITEL**

Education is a key activity. It is a strategic factor in the life of the individual, of the community, of the nation and of the world. With education of quality in adequate quantities, progress and development are not only possible, but well-nigh inevitable; without it, stagnation would loom ahead.

The task of designing and operating educational activities is, therefore, a heavy one. This Conference is an obvious and overt recognition of this. Directed toward providing basic ingredients—facts and expectations about the "purchasers" of education—for the decision-making process, it represents a sound initial step. The relevant knowledge assembled and digested will, of course, not guarantee good decisions, but it will increase the chances of success.

Prime among the relevant facts and expectations are those for the total number of persons, for the geographic distribution of persons and for the attributes of persons. Only a small part of the information about people relevant to the major decisions on education can be presented in this paper. In the main, we will cover the broad overall picture for the United States; to a lesser extent, for the Mountain Division with which this Conference is primarily concerned. It should be recognized, however, that most or at least a very large proportion of decisions are made for local situations which vary widely from the national, regional or state picture.

Also, it should be noted that we have drawn primarily upon the publications of the U.S. Bureau of the Census. Unfortunately, the bench-mark population data are over five years old, being from the Census of 1960. For some decades now, many of us have recommended that quinquennial population censuses be undertaken. Were such a program in effect, we could today be presenting at least preliminary results of an actual census rather than utilize statistics based upon limited sample data and even weaker foundations. and, we may note the contrast between our position today

*Professor of Sociology, and Director, Population Research and Training Center and Chicago Community Inventory, University of Chicago, since 1947; U.S. Bureau of the Census, 1938-50; U.S. Representative of Population Commission, United Nations, 1947-51; Assistant to Secretary of Commerce and Director, Office of Program Planning, U.S. Department of Commerce, 1945-57; Statistical Advisor to Government of Union of Burma, 1951-52; Statistical Advisor to Thailand, 1955-56. Publications: *The Study of Urbanization* (ed. with Leo F. Schnore), 1965; *Population Dilemma* (ed.), 1963; *Urbanization in Latin America* (ed.), 1961; *Urbanization in Asia and the Far East* (ed.), 1958; *Population and World Politics* (ed.), 1958, and many others.

**Consultant to Population Research and Training Center, University of Chicago, and other groups and organizations.　　University of Chicago. Author of numerous publications on projections and social statistics.

and our position just about five years ago, when we were preparing a similar body of material.[1] Indications of the shortcomings of our data collection programs appear in the large number of communities which request the Bureau of the Census to undertake special censuses in the years between censuses.

The sample data upon which we must place primary reliance at this time are designed primarily to provide estimates and projections for some important items for the United States as a whole. For this purpose, they are adequate. They are not, however, extensive enough to provide estimates of the desired reliability for smaller areas or smaller groups of persons. We caution the reader, therefore, to keep this in mind in applying the present material in such cases as the State of Nevada and the college age groups for individual states.

THE LONG VIEW FOR THE UNITED STATES

The United States has been one of the outstanding examples of rapid population growth. The long-term trend had been consistent growth *but at a declining rate*. The population doubled five times between 1790 and 1950—three times between 1790 and 1865 at intervals of 25 years, once in the 35-year period from 1865 to 1900, and once in the 50-year period from 1900 to 1950. Until about 1910, immigration and declining mortality rates were major factors on the side of rapid expansion. The Deep Depression's impact, together with immigration restrictions, brought both the birth rate and the growth rate to new lows during the 1930's. And, in fact, widely accepted population projections during the thirties, and some even in the forties, offered 165 million as the peak population for the United States to be reached around the turn of the century.[2] This is in contrast with 133 million in 1940, 63 million in 1890, 32 million in 1860 and 17 million in 1840.

But the marked environmental changes during the forties and fifties gave rise to an upsurge of marriage and fertility rates anticipated neither with regard to magnitude nor to duration. In consequence, the projections of the thirties were soon contradicted. The population of the United States passed the 165 million mark in 1955, is over 196 million today, and is being projected to exceed 300 million by the turn of the century.[3]

The population growth rate increased from 0.7 percent per annum in the thirties to 1.4 in the forties and then to 1.7 in the fifties. The war and post-war rates, however, were still well below the 3 and 2 percent per annum rates of the 19th and early 20th centuries. But in terms of the absolute number of persons, increases are very large. Thus, from 1950 to date, the increase has been about 45 million persons—or about the same number as the combined populations of Canada and Egypt.

[1] Hauser, Philip M. and Martin Taitel, "Population Trends—Prologue to Library Development," *Library Trends*, Vol. 10, No. 1 (July 1961), pp. 10-67.

[2] Whelpton, P. K., *Forecasts of the Population of the United States, 1945 to 1975*. U.S. Government Printing Office, Washington, D.C.: 1947, p. 41.

[3] U.S. Bureau of the Census, *Current Population Reports*, Series P-25, No. 286 (July 1964), after allowance for lower birth rates than assumed therein.

In looking forward to 1980, the important factor is fertility. Yet it is not possible to assess the effects of changing circumstances at this time. Experience is lacking with regard to reproductive behavior in an era of easy and effective birth-control, relative affluence and nuclear power as a factor in world politics. In addition, there is a growing appreciation on a world-wide scale of the inevitable consequences of sustained population growth—too many people for too little earth. How and at what population levels the people of the world will coordinate population and limited resources are, for the time being at least, not subject to precise determination.

Further, and most important to note, the consequences of large and rapid changes in birth rates will continue to be a feature of our population structure. Thus, the decline of the birth rate in the thirties led to a relatively *small* younger segment of the labor force in the fifties and sixties; the rapid rise in the birth rate in the decade or so following World War II will, during the relatively near-term future, bring relatively large college-age and child-bearing age groups. One consequence of the latter is that, even though the fertility level (i.e., average number of births per female) may decline, the number of births will increase and remain at a relatively high level between 1970 and 1980.

In the most recent projections by the Bureau of the Census, the total population of the United States for 1980 is shown as 241 million.* This projection is based upon the assumption of a moderate decline from the fertility level of 1962-65, which in turn appears to be significantly lower than the peak post war level. The projection also assumes that mortality rates will decline moderately and that net immigration will average about 400,000 per year. The mortality assumption is consistent with recorded changes over the past decade; the net immigration assumption is based upon an estimate of 371,000 average for 1961-1964 and an expected small increase as a result of the Immigration Act of 1965. Finally, the projections assume that there will be no disastrous war, widespread epidemic or similar catastrophic event.

A population of 241 million in 1980 would represent an increase after 1965 of over 47 million persons or 24.4 percent. Though such growth would be below the 28.1 percent for the 1950-1965 period, it would mean a greater increase in number, year by year, than occurred during the earlier period.

The Bureau of the Census projections for population for 1980 range from a low of 225 million to a high of 249 million. The whole of this difference reflects the range of reasonable possibilities for birth rates over the next decade and a half.

REGIONS AND STATES

The Bureau of the Census estimate of the number of inhabitants of the United States as of July 1, 1965 is 193.8 million. This represents a population of 42.5 million or 28.1 percent more than the April 1950

---

*The thirty-four tables prepared as an appendix to this paper are available through the project office. They could not be included in this publication because of space limitations.

Census figure of 151.3 million for the 50 States and the District of Columbia. These figures refer to the resident population, which excludes members of the Armed Forces and their dependents living abroad, crews of American vessels at sea or in foreign ports, and American citizens living in foreign countries.

California—a Western neighbor of the Mountain States—has replaced New York as the largest with an estimated population of 18.6 million in 1965. At the other extreme is Alaska, with a population just above one-quarter million. Thus, California has about 73 times as many inhabitants as Alaska.

Over 41 percent of our population lives in our six largest states— California, New York, Pennsylvania, Illinois, Texas and Ohio—each with over 10 million persons. Only 11 percent of our population resides in the 22 states and the District of Columbia, each of which has fewer than 2 million inhabitants. All of the Mountain States—the largest of which is Colorado with a population of just less than 2 million—are in this latter group.

Variation Among Regions and States

Population gains have not been evenly distributed throughout the country. Of the 42.5 million gain from 1950 to 1965, more than 43 percent was accounted for by 5 states, each of which gained more than 2 million inhabitants over the 15-year period. California alone gained over 5 million; New York and Florida, over 3 million each; Texas, 2.8 million; and Ohio, 2.3 million. At the other extreme were West Virginia and the District of Columbia, where population actually declined, and three States —Vermont, North Dakota, and South Dakota—each with a gain of less than 50,000. The eight Mountain States together gained a total of about 2.7 million inhabitants—less than each of four of the rapidly growing states mentioned above.

The West has been the fastest growing region since 1950. This is a continuation of the long-term trend maintained for more than a century. Further, the trend has—with few exceptions—held both for the Mountain Division and for the Pacific Division. From 1950 to 1965, the increase was 62 percent for the Pacific States and 53 percent for the Mountain States; in contrast, the rate for the U.S. as a whole was 28 percent.

Since 1950, variation of growth rates among the states has been substantial. Annual growth rates among the states in the fifties ranged from a decline of 0.7 percent per annum to an increase of 6.0 percent per annum; for the 5-year period, 1960-1965, the corresponding range was from a rate of decline of 0.6 percent per annum to a rate of increase of 9.1 percent per annum. Further, only West Virginia continued to lose population and Nevada had the greatest rate of increase from 1960 to 1965.

The marked unevenness of population change during the fifties is dramatically shown by the proportions for the various states of the counties which lost population. These data reflect the extent to which migration occurred within the nation. According to the 1960 Census, there were

3,110 counties (excluding 24 districts in Alaska for which 1950 data are not available). Despite the very large population increase of 18.5 percent for the entire nation, 1,536, or almost 50 percent, of these counties, actually lost population during the fifties as revealed by the Census tabulations. Some counties in every state, except Connecticut and Delaware (both with substantial population increases), lost population. Even in Florida, Nevada and Arizona, states with the largest rates of population increase, almost 20 percent of the counties registered population declines. In California, where population increased by over 5.1 million persons, 6 out of 58 counties lost population during the decade.

More important, for purposes of looking ahead at this time, is this: The diversity of population growth rates has been narrowing during the past few years. In the absence of a mid-decade census, precision is not possible on this important point. But the general drift is clear. First, for 1960-65, 40 states are included in a 0.5 to 2.4 percent range of annual growth rates; the comparable range for 1950-60 is 0.2 to 3.4 percent. Second, net migration between regions has declined since 1962; between 1962 and 1963, net migration totalled about 565,000 while between 1964 and 1965 the total was about 208,000.[4] The narrowing of the differences in rates of growth among the various parts of the nation is, it should be noted, not the result of a decline in the mobility of the population. Annual surveys taken since 1948 show the proportion of population moving within the country during a given year has been stable, ranging from 18.6 to 21.0 percent. Between 1964 and 1965 it was 20.1 percent.[5] It may be that the decline in net migration between states and regions reflects an evening out of basic economic, social and political conditions over the country. This observation, however, must be regarded as a tentative statement requiring investigation.

A complex of factors lies behind the differences in growth of geographical regions, of individual states, and of smaller areas. The surface manifestations are shown in statistics as components of change—migration, births, deaths. Behind them lie the more basic economic, social and political factors.

Underlying births and deaths—the natural increase factors—are such basic factors as racial and ethnic composition, education, income level, and age composition. These differ widely among the states and among localities within states. For example, Alaska, relatively youthful in both biologic and economic terms, had a relatively high crude birth rate of 28.1 per thousand and a relatively low crude death rate of 5.7 per thousand in 1964. In contrast, in much more mature Maine, the corresponding figures were 21.8 and 11.3, respectively.[6] The same is true for the Mountain States in contrast with the Middle Atlantic Division (New York, New Jersey and

---

[4] U.S. Bureau of the Census, *Current Population Reports,* Series P-20, No. 150 (April 14, 1966), Table A.

[5] *Ibid.,* Table 1.

[6] U.S. Public Health Service as reported in U.S. Bureau of the Census, *Statistical Abstract of the United States: 1965.* (86th ed.) Washington, D.C.: 1965, Tables 48 and 64.

Pennsylvania). Again, studies have consistently shown that fertility rates have varied with education and income.[7]

The mobility of our population, is probably greater than at any time since humans ceased being nomads. Thus, California and Florida, combining desirable climates with economic advantages, have drawn people to them in large numbers. By contrast, West Virginia, Arkansas and Mississippi, with problems of economics, law, and politics, have lost people, on balance, to other states. The eight Mountain States as a group, as well as the Pacific States, have been growing rapidly as a result of migration based upon particular advantages and conditions. But this has not been true for all of the Mountain States; Montana, Idaho and Wyoming, lacking some of the advantages of the other mountain states, have been growing but at much slower rates than Arizona, Colorado and Nevada.

Projections for Divisions and for the Mountain States

Projections for geographic divisions are based on the general underlying assumption that past trends in growth factors and growth patterns will continue. With regard to birth rates, the decline from the post-war peak has been taken into account, as has the tendency toward a narrowing of differences among areas. Similarly, following the decline which has already occurred during the past few years, the projections are based upon further declines in net migration between regions and states.

Differences in growth rates among the geographic divisions between 1965 and 1980 are projected as substantial. The projected rates for the Mountain and Pacific Divisions are the highest at around 39 percent; at the other extreme is the West North Central Division for which the rate is about 14 percent. However, this projected spread among the geographic divisions is much less than the estimated spread during the 1950-1965 period, when the rates of population increase ranged from less than 12 percent in the East South Central Division to almost 62 percent for the Pacific Division. The narrower spread projected follows the recent and expected trends of declining net migration and declining differences between regions and states in natural increase.

About 15 million or 31 percent of the total projected population increase between 1965 and 1980 will be accounted for by the Middle Atlantic and East South Central Divisions. Though their share of the total population will decline from 38.5 to 37 percent, they will continue as the most populous. These divisions are highly industrialized and urbanized, and further developments in those directions are anticipated. More of the projected increase—almost 18 million or 37.5 percent—is accounted for by the two next most populous Divisions, the South Atlantic and Pacific; their projected proportion of the total U.S. population is almost 30 percent, compared with an estimated 27 percent in 1965. These Divisions include not only areas with special climatic advantages, but also some which have demonstrated large industrial potentials. Should they continue to register

---

[7] Grabill, Wilson H., Clyde V. Kiser and Pascal K. Whelpton, *The Fertility of American Women*, John Wiley & Sons, Inc., New York: 1958, Chaps. 5 to 7.

markedly higher rates than the present more populous divisions, they would become the most populous parts of the nation.

Very mature New England, the agricultural West North Central Division, and the East South Central Division of the Deep South account for only 7 million or less than 15 percent of the projected total increase; according to the projections, they will account for only 19 percent of the population in 1980 in contrast with over 20 percent in 1965 and 23 percent in 1950. The West South Central Division, a mixture of the expansive Southwest and the Deep South is projected to continue to have almost 10 percent of the total population.

The Mountain Division, even with a projected expansion of over 3 million inhabitants or almost 40 percent, is computed to remain the smallest of the divisions with about 10.9 million inhabitants in 1980. Except between 1920 and 1930, the Mountain Division has been growing more rapidly than the U.S. as a whole since 1900. Continuation of this trend is anticipated, though the excess over the U.S. rate is projected to decline.

Because of the special interest of the Conference, projections for the eight individual States of the Mountain Division, together with the historical data from 1900 have been prepared and included in an appendix.* The projections for Nevada differ markedly from those of the Bureau of the Census upon which they are based. The Bureau of the Census had commented upon the difficulties in this instance, and, fortunately, our adjustment procedure as set forth in the tables provided a corrective.

Projections for Geographic Divisions and, even more so, for individual States, particularly if they are small, are subject to greater error than are the projections for the United States. The range of assumptions necessary to cover future possibilities is wide in comparison with those for the nation as a whole. A most important single item is that net internal migration does not have to be projected for the nation as a whole, and net immigration is subject to rather rigid limits for a long period ahead. Thus, the national birth rate becomes the most important consideration in projecting total U.S. population, in view of the marked stability to be expected for mortality rates. But for regions or states, not only is net migration an important and potentially erratic element, but local changes in birth and death rates (for example, say, in the East South Central States) may alter substantially the course of population growth in a state or region. Caution in using the figures is obviously necessary.

METROPOLITAN POPULATION: HISTORICAL OVERVIEW

Throughout its history, the population of the United States has become increasingly concentrated in urban places; and during the course of this century in metropolitan areas. In 1790, when the first census was taken, there were only 24 urban places in this country. They contained only 5 percent of the nation's population. Only two of them had more than 25,000 persons. By 1950, there were over 4,700 places in urban territory. They included almost 97 million persons or about 64 percent of the total popula-

---

*Available through the project office.

tion. The comparable figures for 1960 are 125 million persons, almost 70 percent of the total population, in about 6,000 urban places.[8]

Even more dramatic than urban growth has been the metropolitan explosion during this century. In 1900, areas which would have been classified as metropolitan under later Federal definitions numbered about 60 and contained fewer than 24 million persons, less than one-third of the nation's population. In 1950, about 56 percent of the population, almost 85 million persons, lived in 173 Standard Metropolitan Areas, while by 1960, 63 percent of the population, or almost 113 million persons, lived in 212 Standard Metropolitan Statistical Areas. Estimates for 1965 indicate at least 222 SMSA's with a total population of about 126 million. Further, expansion to a metropolitan population of about 170 million persons is projected for 1980.

The population has become increasingly concentrated in urban and metropolitan areas as a result of basic forces which determine the distribution of population: technological, economic, social and political. Most important, people have crowded into urban and metropolitan areas to form efficient producer and consumer units and in response to the lure of urbanism as a way of life.

For the 1960 Census, the Federal Government (through the Division of Statistical Standards of the Bureau of the Budget) introduced the term and definition now used for the areas called metropolitan; that is, "Standard Metropolitan Statistical Area" (abbreviated here to SMSA). This designation emphasizes that, for statistical and analytical purposes, areas are more or less arbitrarily delineated as metropolitan. For 1960, an SMSA was defined as one or more central cities of 50,000 or more persons, the balance of the county or counties containing such a city or cities, and such contiguous counties as, by certain criteria, are "essentially metropolitan in character and are socially and economically integrated with the central city."[9] Despite the arbitrary character of the definition, the SMSA data are closer representations of the actual realities of our grouping of economic activities and population than are statistics relating to cities alone.

There is an important definitional matter to be kept in mind in dealing with metropolitan population changes. This is the difference between (a) change in the number of persons in a specified class (e.g., living in a metropolis) and (b) change in the number living in a specified set of fixed areas (e.g., SMSA's). Differences between the two kinds of changes may be illustrated by contrasting the statements: (a) between 1950 and 1960, there was an increase of 28.4 million in the population classified as living in metropolitan areas satisfying specified population size and characteristics; and (b) at the same time, there was an increase of only 23.6 million in the population living in the fixed areas designated as SMSA's in 1960. In this case, the figures differ, mainly because 30 or more areas classified as SMSA's in 1960 would not have been so classified in 1950; hence, the 1950 population of these areas is excluded in the "same class" comparison and included in the "same area" comparison, while the 1960 popula-

---

[8] U.S. Bureau of the Census, *Census of Population: 1960*, Vol. I, Pt. 1, Tables 3 and 8.
[9] *Ibid.*, pp. xxxi-xxxii, for full details.

tion of those areas is included in both comparisons. In addition, of course, the boundaries of some SMSA's of 1950 had been enlarged by 1960.

Both kinds of comparisons provide insight into the nature and significance of population changes in the United States during recent decades.

Compilations of census data over the long-term have been made upon the basis of a "same class" definition of SMSA's. For the most part, other data provide only "equal area" comparisons. And, unfortunately, only very limited data are available for dates later than the census of 1960.

METROPOLITAN GROWTH: THE EXPLOSION OF THE FIFTIES

For the United States as a whole, SMSA population grew explosively during the fifties (26.7 percent for the 212 areas defined as SMSA's in 1960) by contrast with the growth outside SMSA's (7.2 percent). Of the total United States population increase of 28 million during the decade, about 23.5 million or 84 percent was accounted for by the 212 areas defined as SMSA's in 1960.

Regional Differences

Within this structure of changes, however, there were marked regional differences. In the Northeast, the division of population between metropolitan and nonmetropolitan changed only slightly during the fifties, rates of growth being about the same in and outside the areas of the 1960 SMSA's (13.0 and 13.6 percent, respectively). The pattern for the North Central States approximated that for the United States as a whole with increases of 23.5 percent in and 6.6 percent outside SMSA's. The most striking changes in the division of population between metropolitan residents and others during the fifties however, occurred in the South and the West.

In the South, the data for population change within the areas qualifying as SMSA's in 1960 do not adequately reflect the shift to metropolitan from nonmetropolitan residence. There were about 18 areas which crossed the SMSA definitional line between 1950 and 1960. When this is taken into account, there appears to have been a decline of around 800,000 persons in the nonmetropolitan population in the South; hence, metropolitan population growth exceeded the total population growth of about 7.8 million persons as a result of a net shift from nonmetropolitan to metropolitan population. This speaks of the very greatly increased importance to the South of industrial and service activities, as well as the importance of climatic advantages; it also bespeaks the sharp decline in the importance of agriculture and related activities in the South. Even so, despite the marked shift toward metropolitanization, the South remained the least metropolitanized region, with less than half its population in the SMSA's of 1960.

Essentially the same development occurred in the West as in the South during the fifties. About ten new areas qualified as SMSA's between

1950 and 1960. Taking this into account, it appears that the nonmetropolitan population in the West did not increase during the fifties, so that the population increase in the West was entirely of a metropolitan character.

Within the West, there were marked differences between the Pacific and the Mountain Divisions. Between 1950 and 1960, the proportion of the population of the Pacific Division in SMSA's (1960 areas) increased from 76.2 to 79.2 percent; in consequence, the Pacific Division had, by this measure, become as metropolized as the mature and highly industrialized Northeast Region. In contrast, the increase in the proportion of the Mountain Division's population in SMSA's was from 40.3 percent in 1950 to almost 49 percent in 1960. Thus, despite, the larger percentage increase in SMSA population in the Mountain Division than in the Pacific Division (63.9 as against 45.8 percent), the Mountain Division remained far less metropolized than the Pacific Division. And, it may be noted the change and level for the Mountain Division were about the same as for the South—the least metropolized region of the nation.

Of the 13 areas in the Mountain States which qualified as SMSA's in 1960, only 6 would have so qualified in 1950. And, the seven new "qualifiers" accounted for 26.3 percent of the population of the 1960 SMSA's of these states.

Highlights of the regional differences in population composition and change during the fifties, with reference to metropolitan population, may be indicated as follows:

Region and Division	For Areas of 1960 SMSA's		
	Percent of Total Population in SMSA's		Percent Change of Population in SMSA's
	1950	1960	
Total U.S.	59.0	62.9	26.4
Northeast	79.2	79.1	13.0
North Central	56.4	60.0	23.5
South	41.1	48.1	36.1
West—Total	67.1	71.8	48.5
Mountain Div.	40.3	48.9	63.9
Pacific Div.	76.2	79.2	45.8

Size Differences

There was relatively little difference between growth rates for the fifties among the various sizes of SMSA's as determined by 1960 population and characteristics. Except for the "500,000 to 1,000,000" inhabitant size class, with a rate of 36 percent, all fell within the narrow range of 23.2 to 25.8 percent.

Total population increases were concentrated in a few large SMSA's. The "big 5"—New York, Chicago, Los Angeles, Philadelphia and Detroit —contributed almost 6 million to the overall SMSA increase of 23.6 million; and the 19 SMSA's in the "1,000,000 to 3,000,000" size class almost another 6 million. At the other extreme, the 22 smallest SMSA's (population of less than 100,000 in 1960) contributed less than 350,000 inhabitants.

A large proportion of the SMSA population is, of course, concentrated in a relatively small number of areas. Thus, the 24 SMSA's with 1,000,000 or more inhabitants in 1960 contained about 55 percent of the total 1960 SMSA population. And, of course, a very small proportion of the SMSA population resided within a very large number of the smallest SMSA's—somewhat more than 14 percent in 111 SMSA's. Phenomena of this character have, of course, been well known to demographers and others for many years.

The distribution of metropolitan population among the size groups changed significantly during the fifties. Our five largest SMSA's in 1950, as well as in 1960, suffered a decline in relative importance within the SMSA family, even though their relative importance as a group within the United States increased somewhat during the fifties; they grew more rapidly than the rest of the United States combined, but not quite as rapidly as did the total metropolitan population. (The comparison has been made after adjustment for the definitional changes for the New York and Chicago SMSA's, so that the 1950 proportion for the "big 5" is 30.8 percent, rather than 34.7 percent.) The relative importance within the SMSA family of the large number of smaller SMSA's likewise declined during the fifties. Those with less than 500,000 persons accounted for 33.4 percent of the total SMSA population in 1950, but only 28.4 percent in 1960; and this was so despite an increase in the number of areas from 136 to 159. Thus, it was the larger, though not the largest, size groups which increased in relative importance during the fifties; for the second largest size class—the "1,000,000 to 3,000,000" class—the proportion of total metropolitan population increased from 19.4 to 26.4 percent. The increase in relative importance of SMSA's with 500,000 to 3,000,000 inhabitants was largely the result of a massive sliding up the size scale of areas but without any sliding up beyond the 3,000,000 level.

Under favorable economic, social and climatic conditions, growth rates of more than 50 percent in a decade may be expected to occur in the future as they have in the past. In the fifties, there were 30 SMSA's with such rates. Only one, Wichita, Kansas, fell outside the South and West; and 18 were in three states, California, Texas and Florida. Seven of the 13 Mountain State SMSA's were in this group. Finally, it should be noted, that 14 of the 30 would not have qualified as SMSA's in 1950, indicating that in the future, as in the past, opportunities for smaller communities to expand rapidly to metropolitan status may well be expected to occur.

Under unfavorable conditions—denudation of natural resources, and loss of comparative economic and social advantages—population stagnation and even decline may be expected. In the fifties, this apparently occurred in at least 20 SMSA's, eight with an actual loss of population and 12 with increases of less than 5 percent. Not one is in the West. The 10 in the South represent one extreme of widely varying conditions, of virtually an economic and social upheaval. Those in the Northeast and North Central regions appear to reflect a variety of underlying conditions—declining agriculture, exhaustion of natural resources, defeat in economic struggles.

Central Cities and Suburbs

Between 1900 and 1920, the ratio between central-city and suburban populations for metropolitan areas remained almost constant, about one-third in the suburbs and two-thirds in the central cities. Since 1920, that is, since there has been wide use of 20th-century transportation and communication technology, suburbia have outpaced the central cities. In 1950, well over two-fifths of the metropolitan population was in suburbia in 1960, nearly one-half. Suburbia increases of 19 million persons between 1950 and 1960 represent at least 70 percent of the total change in metropolitan population (on the "same class" basis).

The decade of the fifties was critical in the relation between central-city and suburban population growth. It may well be described as the decade of suburban boom and central-city bust. The population of the suburban areas (as of 1960) of the United States—i.e., the population outside central cities, but within the SMSA's—increased by 48.5 percent. By contrast, the population of the central-city areas (as of 1960) increased by only 10.8 percent. For many individual areas, of course, the difference was much greater.

The 1960 Census was the first of our Decennial Censuses to show population losses in a large number of cities. Eleven of the twelve largest cities in 1950 registered population declines.[10] During the decade, of the 257 central cities in the 212 SMSA's, 70 lost while 187 gained population.[11]

Such population losses do not necessarily imply economic decline or stagnation in a city or area. They may reflect an interchange of place of residence and place of work within an expanding metropolitan community. This interchange is indicated by the many cases where total SMSA population increased although, for one or more central cities, population declined, including four of the five largest areas: New York, Chicago, Philadelphia and Detroit.

The data already presented understate the population decline or stagnation in the inner cores of SMSA's. They do not show population increases accounted for by annexations.[12]. Overall, 4.9 million or over 86 percent of the central-city population increase was from annexations. But this is only part of the story. The significant increases of central-city population occurred in SMSA's of less than 1,000,000 persons (in 1960), i.e., the smaller and intermediate size cities, and these increases were accounted for in large measure by annexations. For SMSA's of more than 1,000,000 persons, the change in central city population was small and was exceeded by annexations. Thus, the inner cores of the metropolitan areas tended to grow very slowly or not at all because they were already filled. This is also reflected in the regional differences in central-city change. Major increases

---

[10] *Ibid.*, Table 29.

[11] *Ibid.*, Table 33.

[12] *Ibid.*, Tables Q and R and, for details, accompanying text.

occurred in the South and West and were, in large part, accounted for by annexations. In the North, annexations were an unimportant factor and totalled more than the central-city changes in population.

The patterns of population growth were accompanied by changes in patterns of land use and in the character of communities or neighborhoods within SMSA's. Students of the city have documented growth patterns which indicate that our metropolitan areas grew outward from one or more centers of origin.[13] Although characterized by both vertical and horizontal growth, the latter was the dominant form of development. The newer areas were always those farthest from centers of origin and embodied the new advances in technology. Our metropolitan areas tended to develop definite spatial patterns in terms of the age and the modernity of their residential structures.

Differences in physical facilities tended to produce a parallel socioeconomic stratification of the urban and metropolitan population. Persons of the lowest income, education, and occupational status, usually the newcomers to the urban environment, tended to occupy the less desirable residences toward the center of the city. Persons of higher income, education and social status tended to locate toward the peripheries of the metropolis. Agencies and institutions of all sorts tended to reflect, and are attuned to, the characteristics of the people contained in the areas in which they are located.

As our metropolitan plant aged, the early patterns of rapid growth have been paralleled by equally remarkable obsolescence and decay. Just as cities grew community by community, not structure by structure, so have the cities decayed, characterized by areas of substandard housing and by slums which have become a national disgrace. Federal, state and local programs for urban renewal have tended to consolidate efforts of slum clearance, rehabilitation and conservation. The start has been to rebuild the slum areas one community at a time. Populations of inner-zone areas are, under these programs being uprooted and dispersed to various sections of the metropolitan areas. Inner zones are being rebuilt or rehabilitated so as to attract higher as well as lower social and income groups. All this added to new developments in suburbia presages basic changes in the physical structure of our metropolitan areas, and in the manner in which they are used.

METROPOLITAN POPULATION: 1960-1964

Because of the crucial importance of the metropolitanization of the United States, the experience of the fifties, even though it has the aroma of "ancient history," has been presented in detail. For the more recent and more germane experience of the first half of the sixties, we must, unfortunately, rely upon sample surveys of limited size and upon indirect information, which can provide only estimates and fragments of limited

[13] Hauser, Philip M., *Population Perspectives*. Rutgers University Press, New Brunswick, N. J.: 1960, Chap. 4; Hoyt, Homer, *One Hundred Years of Land Values in Chicago*. University of Chicago Press, Chicago: 1933; Park, Robert E., and Ernest W. Burgess, *The City*. University of Chicago Press, Chicago: 1925, pp. 50 ff.

scope. Most important for this Conference, is that local, State and regional data are available in limited amounts only.

The general overall development of metropolitan population during the fifties and earlier continued during the first half of the sixties. According to Bureau of the Census estimates, the 212 SMSA's (1960 areas) again accounted for about 84 percent of the total United States population increase from 1960 to 1965, though the proportion was much less from 1960 to 1963 and much greater from 1963 to 1965. And, the proportion of United States population living in these 212 SMSA's (1960 areas) has, in consequence, increased further to 64.4 percent. The United States Bureau of the Budget, as of March 1965, had recognized 10 additional SMSA's so that, in terms of current areas, there are at least 222 SMSA's at the present time. These 222 SMSA's are estimated to contain 65 percent of our total resident population. This 65 percent includes, of course, the population of areas added to the 1960 areas of the earlier 212 SMSA's.

The pattern of little or no growth in central cities and rapid expansion in the suburbs has also continued. Of the estimated increase of 13 million in metropolitan population between 1960 and 1965, only 2.6 million was in central cities. For the first time, the population of central cities dropped below 50 percent of the total metropolitan population; in 1965, it is estimated to have been about 48 percent of the total, in 1960 it was 51.4 percent.

Similarly, there has apparently been a continuation of the changing relative importance of the various sizes of SMSA's within the SMSA family. Estimates of the populations of 55 large SMSA's (1964 area) indicate a further decline in the relative importance of SMSA's with less than 500,000 persons. In 1960, they contained about 28.3 percent of the SMSA population; but, according to the available estimates, 27.7 percent represents a maximum for 1964. (For these groups, net losses through "sliding up the size scale" cannot be determined from the data.) The details for the size classes for areas with 500,000 or more inhabitants are indicative, but unfortunately not definitive. They indicate declines in importance for the "3,000,000 or more" and for the "500,000 to 1,000,000" groups.

Growth rates by size of area and by region continued the earlier patterns. Of the three size groups for which data are available for the four-year 1960-64 period, the growth rate was least, 6.4 percent, for the "3,000,000 or more" and greatest, 8.9 percent, for the "500,000 to 1,000,000" size class. And, comparison with the Census estimates for all (212) SMSA's over the 1960-65 period indicates that the rates for the smaller size groups must have been lower than 8.9 percent, again conforming to the 1950-60 pattern.

The earlier pattern of regional differences in growth rates was also continued, i.e., rates increasing in the North-South-West order. This was true within each of the three size groups for which the data are available (a point not imediately verifiable for 1950 and 1960 since tabulations "by size by region" were not published by the Bureau of the Census).

SMSA's of intermediate size in the West—500,000 to 1,000,000 persons—
had the greatest growth rate: 19.0 percent. At the other extreme was the
"1,000,000 to 3,000,000" group in the North: 3.3 percent.

METROPOLITAN POPULATION: PROJECTIONS

The fundamental forces at work may be expected to continue to
operate over the next couple of decades with the expectation of further
growth of urban and metropolitan populations. They will account for
greater proportions of the total in 1970 than in 1965 and in 1980 than in
1970. This will be the case for the Mountain States as well as the United
States as a whole.

For the United States

Projections to 1980 for all metropolitan areas of the United States,
based upon a continuation of past trends, show an increase of about 45
million in the metropolitan population between 1965 and 1980 on the
"same class" basis. Such an increase would represent a number equal to
about 95 percent of the projected increase of 47.3 million in total population, and would result in more than 70 percent of the population being in
metropolitan areas in 1980.

Suburbs have been growing more rapidly than central cities because
of the impact of 20th-century technology and the relatively fixed boundaries of central cities. While technology was developing, the boundaries of
central cities remained relatively fixed despite annexations. On the average, the central city in the United States has been filled since the 1920's.
Since central cities became filled within their relatively fixed boundaries,
continued growth could take place only in suburbia, beyond the borders of
the city.

The forces accounting for the differential in the growth of suburbs
and central cities may be expected to continue operating during the next
decade or two. Of the projected increase of 45 million in the population
of metropolitan areas between 1965 and 1980, about 36 million is projected for absorption by suburbia. By 1980, of some 170 million people
in metropolitan areas, about 100 million are projected to be in suburbs,
about 70 million in central cities.

The spatial patterning of the physical residential plant of our metropolitan areas, with its correlative socio-economic stratification of the
population, is likely to be drastically modified. It is possible that, while
the obsolescent inner areas are replaced or renovated, decay will occur
in the suburban rings. With increased intervention and urban renewal programs, *it is likely that the physical and socio-economic character of a
community in the future will depend less upon the historical accident of its
origin and more upon the will of organized population groups as manifest
in their planning and development activities.*

It is also possible that, in the decades to come, an emergent pattern
of residence within the metropolitan area may become the modal one.
There is increasing evidence that, in accordance with the family cycle, the
family is tending toward a corresponding use of the metropolitan area. As

children come, their families tend to move to the outlying suburban area in order to place them in surroundings of green lawns and open spaces. As the last youngster departs for college or gets married to start his own family, the parents show a tendency to move back to a rebuilt or renovated inner zone of the metropolitan area.

Future growth of an individual metropolitan areas will, of course, depend upon both general, and special factors. Some guidance may, however, be gleaned from our past experience. Thus, if growth patterns remain the same, there will be, among the SMSA's, a small number of very large increases in numbers and a large number of very small increases.

For the Mountain States

Projections for the Mountain Division were prepared, as in the case of those for the total United States, upon the assumption of a continuation of past trends. However, they are not as reliable as those for the total United States. Further, the projections for the fixed 13 areas are more reliable than those on the "same class" basis; this is so, because the timing of conversions of a limited number of areas from a nonmetropolitan to a metropolitan classification is subject to considerable uncertainty.

According to the projections, the metropolitan population of the Mountain States is expected to increase by about 2.5 million between 1965 and 1980—from 4.1 to 6.6 million inhabitants. Such an increase would amount to 82 percent of the 3 million total increase in population projected for the Mountain Division. Less than half of this increase—45 percent—is expected to occur within the boundaries of the 13 SMSA's as of 1960. Some of the metropolitan expansion outside these areas has already been recognized, i.e., the designation, in 1963, of Ada County, Idaho, as a Standard Metropolitan Statistical Area.

The projected pace of metropolitanization in the Mountain States is greater than that projected for the United States as a whole. While the United States metropolitan population is projected to increase from 65 to 70 percent of the total, the increase for the Mountain Division is projected to rise from 53 in 1965 to 61 percent in 1980. In general terms, this conforms to an earlier period of development for the United States as a whole—say, the first 15 post-war years, 1945-1960. And, the development in the United States as a whole (particularly with respect to the smaller SMSA's) during those years may well serve as general guides and warnings to the Mountain States. In this paper, it is not possible to include projections for individual SMSA's or individual States. Some indications of the potentials for metropolitan growth may, however, be presented at this time. Obviously, past experience, both in the West and in the United States generally, indicate the 13 SMSA's as of 1960 may be expected to grow within their present boundaries. In addition, some of them may be expected to spread into contiguous territory. This has already been the case for the Salt Lake City SMSA which has expanded to include Davis County.

Finally, indications of possibilities for new SMSA's may be obtained from intensive study of cities which had 25,000 or more inhabitants in 1960, particularly if they have shown rapid growth hitherto. There are 5 of these in New Mexico; 2 each in Colorado, Idaho and Wyoming; one in Montana. There are none in Arizona, Nevada and Utah, but Yuma, Arizona, had just under 24,000 inhabitants in 1960 after more than doubling its population in the fifties. The full list[14] is as follows:

Urban Place	Population	
	1950	1960
Arizona:		
Yuma	9,145	23,974
Colorado:		
Fort Collins	14,937	25,027
Greeley	20,354	26,314
Idaho:		
Idaho Falls	19,218	33,161
Pocatello	26,131	28,534
Montana:		
Missoula	22,485	27,090
New Mexico:		
Carlsbad	17,975	25,541
Hobbs	13,875	26,275
Las Cruces	12,325	29,367
Roswell	25,738	39,593
Santa Fe	27,998	34,676
Wyoming:		
Casper	23,673	38,930
Cheyenne	31,935	43,505

Boise City, Idaho, has been omitted since it has already been designated an SMSA.

CITY AND COUNTRY POPULATION

While SMSA's are defined to obtain as close a representation of the actual realities of our larger population agglomerations as possible, urban territory is defined largely upon the basis of the existence of a charter granted by a state legislature for a relatively small area with 2,500 or more persons. (This applies even though the definition was modified in 1950 to include urban-fringes around cities of 50,000 or more and unincorporated places of 2,500 or more.) Most of the inhabitants of SMSA's are also in urban territory. But substantial numbers (25.7 million) reside in places of fewer than 50,000 inhabitants which are within urban territory but outside SMSA's. In addition, rural territory, with a total population of 13.3 million persons, lies within SMSA's. Hence, though the overlap is large, each basis of assembling data provides some information about population which the other does not.

Data available are of limited value for shedding light upon the size and structure of metropolitan areas or for purposes of counting people

14 U.S. Bureau of the Census, *Census of Population: 1960,* Vol. I, Pts. 4, 7, 14, 28, 30, 33, 46, 52, Tables 8.

by the extent to which they participate in "urbanism as a way of life." However, urban places accounted for all of the expansion of total population of the United States between 1950 and 1960, and, in addition, absorbed, on balance, some rural population. This was a continuation and an acceleration of the long-term trend of urbanization which brought the urban population to almost 70 percent of the total in 1960.

Urban

The number of cities climbing the size ladder during the fifties was far and above the number necessary to offset the downhill slides of some cities. Old places expanded into higher size classes, new places were formed, and there were some new arrivals from rural territory. The total number of places with 2,500 or more inhabitants increased from 4,300 in 1950 to 5,400 in 1960. Except for the largest size class, cities of 1,000,000 or more inhabitants, every size class showed an increase in the number of places. Cities of 50,000 or more inhabitants, each of metropolitan size, increased in number from 233 to 333. The net upward movement was facilitated by the long-used American procedure of expansion and annexation. The extent to which this growth occurred is illustrated by California, where 188 of some 212 incorporated places of 2,500 or more inhabitants in 1950 annexed territory during the decade.[15].

The relative importance of the various size groups within urban territory changed during the decade. It was the cities of intermediate size, populations between 10,000 and 100,000 inhabitants, which increased in relative importance. They contained less than 31 percent of the urban population in 1950, but more than 37 percent in 1960. Most of this growth was at the expense of our larger cities, particularly those with populations of 1,000,000 or more inhabitants. In large part, this change reflects the rapid growth of suburbs, i.e., of places really metropolitan in character by virtue of contiguity with large cities, while the larger cities, the central cities, were growing slowly, if at all. Finally, it may be noted, the smaller places, with populations of fewer than 10,000 persons, and "other urban" territory also declined slightly in importance during the decade.

In relation to the total population of the United States, it was the intermediate-size cities which increased in relative importance. They contained less than 20 percent of the total population in 1950, but almost 26 percent in 1960, and accounted for all the net increase in relative importance of urban territory. The larger cities declined slightly, and the smaller cities increased slightly in relative importance during the decade.

Rural and Farm

Until 1950, our rural population increased decade by decade, but, in general, *at a declining rate*. During the fifties, rural population actually declined; all of the overall population increase of 28 million and the 400,000 decline in rural territory was absorbed in urban territory.

---

[15] *Ibid.*, Vol. I, Pt. 6, Tables 3 and 9. The figure "212" is for all urban places and may include some unincorporated places.

Just as important as the absence of population growth in rural territory during the fifties was the shift of population from rural-farm to rural non-farm areas. Except for the depression thirties, the rural-farm population has been declining since 1910 when the first rural-farm Census count was made. In the forties, fifties and, thus far, in the sixties, the decline was sharp. Farm population decreased from about 30 million in 1940 to about 23 million in 1950, to about 16 million in 1960 and then to about 12 million in 1965.[16]

This decline has been stated in terms of the new definition of "farm population" introduced in 1960. The Department of Agriculture 1941 estimate for the year 1940 was used. Despite the change in definition, it is probably correct to say that the farm population of 32 million in 1910 decreased to 12 million in 1965. This conclusion is justified because the persons residing on "farms" without actually producing farm products, a group excluded from the 1960 definition, increased greatly between 1910 and 1960. Within rural territory there has been a major decline of persons living on farms who are directly dependent upon agricultural production for their livelihood. To some extent the decline in farm population may be the result of the development of "town" residence and "farm" work. In the main, however, statements on the decline in rural-farm population overlooks the increased mechanization and productivity of American agriculture. Acreage under cultivation throughout the entire period of decline of farm population has changed little, whereas productivity per acre has continued to increase greatly.

It may also be noted that during the fifties the distribution of rural population among "places" and "open territory" changed hardly at all. Furthermore, the number of places showed a net decline of little significance. Undoubtedly, some places moved from the rural to the urban classification during the fifties, while new places were born in rural territory.

Projections

By 1980, between 75 and 80 percent of our population may live in urban territory, which would place almost as many persons in urban territory in 1980 as there are in the entire United States today. This figure contrasts with about 64 percent in 1950 and almost 70 percent in 1960. Even so, it leaves room for a modest increase in rural population within the projected total increase.

Farm population may be expected to decline somewhat further in view of mechanization developments and productivity increases. By 1980, the farm population is likely to be fewer than 10 million persons.

GOVERNMENT STRUCTURE

In dealing with community services, the urban population approach, based on cities and legal entities, is more appropriate than the SMSA population approach. Such services tend to be organized, financed and ad-

---

[16] U.S. Dept. of Agriculture, Economic Research Service. *Farm Population, Estimates for 1910-62,* ERS-130 (October 1963)

ministered by individual government units rather than on an SMSA-wide basis. The mere number of governmental units is staggering—still over 90,000 in 1962 after a decline from over 100,000 in 1957. About one-third of these are school districts (which have declined in number) and another 18,000 are special districts (which have increased in number). Municipalities number about 18 thousand. Data from the 1962 *Census of Governments* [17] are as follows:

Governmental Unit	Number
Local governments, except school districts	56,508
Counties	3,043
Municipalities	18,000
Townships	17,142
Special districts	18,323
School districts	34,678
Other public school systems	2,341

The disparity between the legal entities (cities) and the population entities (SMSA's) poses problems for public agencies concerned with providing services to metropolitan populations. To serve well at low cost, an agency must make full use of the economics of large-scale operation. But this is not feasible with a large number of small purchasing units, (i.e., the relatively small governmental units). They act so as to limit agency size and the provision of integrated and unified services. This is true not only in rural, farm and small-town areas but also within our large metropolitan areas.

With the continuation of extensive urbanization and metropolitanization during the next few decades *will come increased recognition that our 20th-century technological, economic and demographic units have governmental structures of 18- and 19th-century origin and design.* Already there is a discernible trend toward changes in local government units to meet area-wide problems more adequately. Increasing numbers of elections have been held to consolidate city and county governments; in increasing numbers, special units have been created to deal with specific functions such as sanitation, drainage, water supply, and port facilities. It is certain that in the next decade or two, area-wide planning and functional governmental units will emerge at an accelerated pace. The sharp increase in the number of special districts and the sharp decline in the number of school districts between 1957 and 1962 shows, in bold relief, the lines of recent and future development.

RACIAL AND ETHNIC COMPOSITION

Throughout the history of the United States, its population has been relatively heterogeneous in its racial and ethnic composition. At the beginning, there were various European stocks and the native Indians. The infusion of African population during the 18th and early 19th centuries

---

[17] As reported in U.S. Bureau of the Census, *Statistical Abstract of the United States: 1965.* (86th ed.), Washington, D.C.: 1965, Table 565.

was followed by a wave of immigration of various European stocks during the 19th and early 20th centuries. Between 1820 and 1964, the Federal government managed to count about 43 million immigrants who came to the United States.[18] They came in large waves during the 19th and early 20th centuries. During the early part of the 20th century, sources of immigration to the United States shifted from Northern and Western to Southern and Eastern Europe—to Russians and Poles, including the Jewish groups, to Italians, Greeks, and other peoples from Eastern European nations, who left their homelands for the new opportunities beckoning in the rapidly developing United States. Direct Hispanic colonization or later migration from Spain and Portugal was limited in relation to the great currents from other areas of Europe; of the 43 million immigrants, only 193,000 came from Spain; only 295,000 from Portugal.[18] And all of Latin America and the West Indies together contributed 2.5 million of the total of 43 million immigrants. But, of the limited numbers permitted to enter the United States in recent decades, over 60 percent have been from Latin America and the West Indies, and about one-third of those were Mexicans.[18] Finally, migrants from Puerto Rico—not immigrants and not included as such—may be considered as ethnically and racially similar to immigrants from Mexico and Latin America.

The rapidity of our population growth and relative youth of this nation make the United States one of the more heterogeneous nations on the face of the earth, one which, in large measure, has yet to achieve unification or integration. As recently as 1950, for example, over a fifth of the population of the United States was either foreign-born or native-born of foreign or mixed parentage; and over a tenth were of nonwhite races. Even as late as 1960, only 70 percent of the population of the United States was native white of native parentage. As recently as 1900, little more than half of the population of the United States was native-white. Moreover, as recently as 1950, in four of our five largest cities, the native white population of native parentage constituted less than half of the total, ranging from 34 to 46 percent. Los Angeles was the only city among the five largest in the United States in which the native white population of native parentage was greater than half, and even there it was only 55 percent. The first generation in which virtually all the people of the United States share a common nativity is yet to come.

Large scale internal migration—the mechanism, in the main, by which population and opportunity are equated—within the United States has facilitated the acculturation both of immigrants and of diverse native-born groups. In the 19th and early 20th century, migratory flows were generally Westward, with the racial and ethnic characteristics of participants varying from time to time. To this general inter-regional Westward movement, have been added, since about 1940, major migratory flows into rapidly growing metropolitan areas and from farm to city.

[18] Immigration and Naturalization Service, U.S. Department of Justice, as reported in U.S. Bureau of the Census, *Statistical Abstract of the United States: 1965*, (86th ed.) Washington, D.C.: 1965, Table 117.

For the United States

The size of the foreign-born population depends, of course, upon the aging and mortality of the foreign-born already here and upon the volume of net immigration. In 1960, the foreign-born population was 5.4 percent of the total United States population; the foreign-born whites, 5.2 percent.[19] Despite heavy immigration, the foreign-born white population never exceeded 15 percent of the total—only in 1890 and in 1910 did it approach 15 percent. The subsequent decline was assured by the immigration limitation acts of the 1920's and later dates. Continuation of these policies in the decades ahead assures a further decline in the proportion of foreign-born. However, the number of foreign-born will remain about the same—about 10 million—under the assumption underlying the population projections presented in this paper, i.e., that net immigration will be about 400,000 per year.

As the foreign-born have declined both in relative importance and in number during recent decades, the nonwhite population, approximately 95 percent Negro, has not. From 10.2 percent of the total in 1930, the nonwhite population gradually increased to 11.4 percent in 1960. However, this small difference in the proportion of nonwhites reflects a large difference between the white and nonwhite growth rates. Thus, during the fifties, the nonwhite growth rate was 26.7 percent; the white, 17.5 percent. Continuation of such a difference in growth rates would lead to a nonwhite population in 1980 approaching 13 percent of the total population. And, with a continuation of recent and prospective patterns of concentration, large proportions would reside in the central cities of the larger SMSA's.

Along with the recent explosive growth of the nonwhite population, there have been massive and important changes in the location of that population. One facet of this growth has been the migratory flow of the Negroes from the South to the remainder of the country. This trend, started during World War I, has continued ever since, except for substantial diminution during the depression thirties. About 89 percent of the Negroes were in the South in 1910; by 1950, only about two-thirds were in the South; and by 1960, less than 60 percent. This decline may be expected to continue; and, as early as 1970, it is possible that as many Negroes may be in the North and West as in the South.

A second facet has been the increasing urbanization and metropolitanization of Negroes in the South as well as elsewhere. In 1910, before the flow of Negroes to the North and to urban places began, only 27 percent lived in urban places as defined by the Census (places of 2,500 inhabitants or more). By 1950, over 90 percent of the Negroes in the North and the West and about 48 percent of those in the South lived in cities.

By 1960—the latest date for which data are available, 58 percent of Negroes in the South lived in urban places; in the North and West, it was 95 percent. Further, almost 38 percent of the Negroes resided in the 24 largest SMSA's which include our 24 largest cities; and almost 65 percent resided in the 212 SMSA's as of 1960.

---

[19] U.S. Bureau of the Census, *Census of Population: 1960*, Vol. I, Pt. 1, Table 66.

A third facet has been the settling of the Negro in the central cities of SMSA's rather than the suburbs. For the 24 SMSA's containing the 24 largest cities, central-city Negro population numbered 83 percent of all Negroes in those SMSA's. As the Negroes moved into the inner-zones, the whites moved outward. Since the Negro population concentrated in relatively few areas within central cities, there was, in those areas, a large increase in population density.

There is evidence that in some respects the pathway followed by the immigrant groups in acquiring a place to live and economic and social status in the community is being followed by the Negro. The limited evidence that is available indicates that the Negro is climbing the social and economic ladder as measured by education, occupation and income. The evidence also indicates that he is moving outward from the inner zones of the city, which constituted his port of entry and, in fact, is beginning to knock at the door of the suburb. The most important respect in which Negro accommodation to his new environment differs from that of the immigrant is to be seen thus far in the continuation of the pattern of segregated residence. Although the time span involved is still a brief one, the evidence indicates increased rather than decreased segregation of the Negro within the cities.

The impact of the expansion, relocation and acculturation of the Negro population has been and will continue to be a major one. It cannot be predicated with accuracy, but will certainly be much greater than increases in numbers alone might indicate.

For the Mountain States

Rapid population growth, relatively large numbers of migrants, and rural and ethnic heterogeneity are familiar phenomena in the Mountain States. The white pioneers and settlers found Indians, Spanish-Colonials and their descendants, and residents of mixed parentage. Added to these groups over the decades have been Negroes and Asiatics, both immigrants and migrants. The outlook, as already noted, is for continued rapid population growth and for continued net in-migration, both immigrants and migrants. For the specifics on racial and ethnic characteristics and acculturation, the outlook is not so clear; in part, this arises because of the shortcomings of the statistics which do not adequately record either the historical developments or the current status; in part, this arises because of the diversity of the underlying conditions for the various groups.

Negroes. On a national basis, Negroes are the largest source of heterogeneity; at the same time, they are the largest group seeking acculturation by migration, education, political action. In the Mountain States, however, they numbered, in 1960, only 1.8 percent of the population or 123,000 persons; and this was as a result of more than tripling in number between 1940 and 1960. As elsewhere in the United States, they are concentrated in SMSA's and, within SMSA's, in central cities. In 1960, about 85,000 of the 95,000 Negroes in SMSA's were in the central cities; of the 95,000 in SMSA's, 57,000 were in the Denver and Phoenix SMSA's.

Relative to total population, the concentration was greatest in the Las Vegas SMSA; over 15 percent of the central city population was accounted for by about 10,000 Negroes.[20]

Whether the rapid growth of the Negro population, resulting from *relatively* high in-migration, has continued since 1960 is not known. *Total* nonwhite migration from the South to other regions appears to have been greater in 1963-65 than in 1960-63, but this is not definitive for the Mountain States. For looking ahead, perhaps the most reasonable expectation is for continued in-migration of Negroes; one reason for this is that they may be expected to participate in the general Westward migration of population, particularly as a disadvantaged racial and ethnic group both North and South.

Indians. In 1960, 188,000 of the 524,000 Indians in the United States resided in the Mountain States. Next to Caucasians, they constituted the largest single racial group. Furthermore, over 160,000 of the 188,000 Indians were in three states—Arizona (83,000), New Mexico (56,000) and Montana (21,000). Finally, in Census terminology, somewhat less than 70 percent of the Indians reside in rural non-farm territory.

Historically and currently, the Indian population is, in large part, a segregated population. In 1960, 86.4 percent—over 162,000 of the 188,000 Indians in the Mountain States resided in 13 Indian Areas, delineated as such by the Bureau of the Census in cooperation with the Bureau of Indian Affairs, U.S. Department of the Interior, and the Division of Health, U.S. Department of Health, Education and Welfare, for statistical purposes. "The areas generally contain an Indian population which is relatively homogeneous with respect to tribal and cultural affiliations." They are constructed in terms of whole counties and "do not necessarily represent federal reservations, although reservation land is included in varying proportions in many of them."[21]

Not only is the Indian population largely a segregated one, but it is also at the lower end of the economic and social ladder. Of the 13 Indian Areas, only one (Apache, New Mexico) reported a median individual income for men in 1959 in excess of $2,500; the others were under $1,500.[22] Of the 89,000 Indians 14 years old and over residing in the 13 Indian Areas in 1960, over 33,000 or 37.5 percent were functionally illiterate, i.e., had completed less than 5 years of schooling. In terms of median years of schooling for this age group, the maximum for any of the 13 Areas is 9.7 years (Apache, New Mexico, female)[23]; in contrast, the minimum for any Mountain State is 10.9 years and the average 11.5. For the Navajo, Navajo-Hopi and Navajo-Zuni Areas (Utah, Arizona and New Mexico, respectively), the maximum is 5.4 years (Navajo-Hopi, Arizona, male).[23]

In the past, the rate at which Indians have entered the mainstream of American life has been extremely slow. Present trends appear to indicate the rate is increasing. Should substantial numbers turn toward and join the

[20] *Ibid.*, Vol. II, *Nonwhite Population by Race*, Final Report PC(2)-1C.
[21] *Ibid.*, p. xii.
[22] *Ibid.*, Table 56.
[23] *Ibid.*, Table 51.

mainstream, it may be a challenge for the educational systems in the States and localities affected to provide education for persons originating in a tribal culture markedly different from that of the urban white population to which such systems have been oriented.

Mexicans and Whites of Other Hispanic Association. The number in this group exceeds, by far, the combined number of Negroes and Indians in the Mountain States. Reasonably comprehensive and precise statistical data, however, are not available for them. And, main reliance must be placed upon the special tabulations from the Censuses of 1950 and 1960 for which identification was based upon Spanish surnames.[24] These tabulations cover only 3 Mountain States—Arizona, Colorado, and New Mexico, and, in other respects, have severe limitations.

In 1960, the Spanish surname group in the three States numbered 621,000. This represented a 25 percent increase during the fifties—considerably less than the 45 percent increase for the total population of the three States, but more than the 18.5 percent for the United States as a whole. Since fertility of the Spanish surname group has been considerably greater than that of non-Spanish surname groups, the intermediate growth rate may simply reflect this. It is, however, also possible that some net in-migration has occurred, though less than for other groups in the three States.

The Mexican heritage appears to be a major, if not the dominant, one. In 1960, 8 percent of those with Spanish surnames were foreign-born—mostly Mexicans; an additional 16.7 percent were native with foreign or mixed parentage—again mostly Mexican. Thus, about 25 percent are definitely associated with a Mexican heritage. In addition, historic immigration and nativity data suggest that a substantial part of the native group of native parentage is also of Mexican origin,[25] though this may not apply to New Mexico. Regardless of the present extent of those of Mexican ancestry, current immigration patterns suggest continuation of a substantial Mexican-born group in the future.

The economic level of the Spanish surname group is well below the average. Median income in 1959 (of those with income) was just above $1,900 in each of the three States for which data are available. The corresponding State-wide figures range from $3,941 to $4,191. Even in urban places—where almost two-thirds of them reside—median income of those with Spanish surnames is less than $2,300.

Similarly, the educational level of those with Spanish surnames is much lower than the average. For them, median years of school completed for those 14 years old and over is just above 8 years—just about a grammar school education. The corresponding level for the three States is at or above 11 years—almost a high school education.

[24] *Ibid.,* Vol. II, *Persons of Spanish Surname,* Final Report PC(2)-1B.

[25] Taeuber, Irene B., "Migration and Transformation: Spanish Surname Populations and Puerto Ricans, "*Population Index,*" Vol. 32, No. 1 (January 1966), p. 7.

AGE STRUCTURE

Perhaps the most important single characteristic of a person is age. Activities of individuals change with the stage of the human life cycle, from infancy to retirement and eventual death. Each stage generates its own distinctive activities and demands.

In 1800, the "average" American was only 16 years old; in 1950, he was over 30. As late as the third quarter of the 19th century, over 40 percent of the population was under 15 years of age and only 4 percent, 60 years of age or more. Such an age structure is much like that of the underdeveloped areas of the world today. By 1950, however, the proportion of persons under 15 had declined to 27 percent, and those 60 and over had increased to 12 percent. Thus, by 1950, the United States had become "aged" on the basis of the United Nations classifications of nations by age.

Age changes of such magnitude and depth have significantly affected the character of American society. Perhaps the most striking feature of the data for the fifties and mid-sixties is found in the decreased median age of the population. From the moment of birth a person can only age. But a population may, over time, either age or grow younger. The explosive birth rates of the late forties and the fifties decreased the median age for the first time in the history of the United States, from 30.2 years in 1950 to 29.5 years in 1960, and then to 27.2 in 1965.

For the United States: 1950 to 1965

Even more significant than this decline in median age is the great variation in the percent of change during the decade and one-half ending in 1965 among the specific age groups. Thus, the number of children 10 and 11 years of age increased by over 70 percent. At the other extreme, the number of persons 25 to 34 years of age actually decreased; the number 25 to 29 years of age decreased in number by almost 9 percent during the decade and one-half.

These large differences between the growth rates of age groups were largely the result of fluctuations in birth rates. For example, the baby crop of the depression thirties, when birth rates were at all time lows, generated the 25 to 34 year olds of 1965; the baby crop of the prosperous twenties, when birth rates were much higher, generated the 20 to 29 year olds of 1950. The effect of the decline of birth rates was great enough to result in a decline in the number of 25 to 34 year-olds between 1950 and 1965, despite the larger child-bearing population and despite the lower mortality rates in the depression thirties. By contrast, the effect of the postwar rise in birth rates was sufficient to result in the "under 20" population expanding most rapidly during the 1950-65 period.

With regard to those persons 35 years of age and over, the declining birth rates of much earlier decades were, of course, important. But the counter-directional effects of the long-term mortality decline and the prior increase of the child-bearing population were sufficient to maintain growth at a rate close to the overall 28.1 percent increase from 1950 to 1965. In the case of the senior citizens, those 65 years of age and over, the increase in numbers was almost 35 percent during the decade and one-half. Thus, although the population of the United States grew younger during the period, as measured by median age, it also grew older as measured by the increase in the proportion of persons 65 years of age and over. This continuation of the "aging" trend over the decades brought the number of senior citizens to 9.4 percent of the total in 1965.

The decade of the fifties was, in a unique way, the decade of the elementary school child. The number of youngsters 5 to 13 years of age increased by 45 percent, as contrasted with less than 9 percent during the forties. To a lesser extent, it was also a decade for the high school group, which increased by 35 percent. For this group—those 14 to 17 years of age—the first-half of the sixties has been its half-decade. From 1960 to 1965, they increased in number by 24 percent in contrast to about 10.8 percent for the elementary school children. To this boom in numbers, perhaps, should be attributed a substantial share of the problems of our teenagers.

Curiously enough, it was also a boom decade and one-half for our senior citizen group so that both ends of our age structure increased more rapidly than the intermediate sector. Those 18 to 65 years of age, who include almost all of the working population of the country, increased by only 14 percent. As already noted some young adult groups actually declined in numbers.

For the United States: Projections to 1980

The projected rates of growth and expansions in numbers vary widely among the age groups. Between 1965 and 1980, the population 65 years of age and over will increase by some 5 million persons or by 27 percent. Since everyone who will be 65 years of age or over by 1980 has already been born, this projection can be accepted as quite accurate; uncertainty of birth rates is not a factor, and uncertainty of mortality and migration is of minor importance.

Increases for those 65 years of age and over will be at varying rates among various localities. Elderly persons have been migrating to places in the West and South with special climatic conditions, for example, to Florida, California and Arizona. This movement may be expected to continue during the sixties and seventies. It may also be noted that the senior citizens of 1980 will have attained higher levels of education and will have more leisure than their counterparts of earlier dates.

Like the senior citizens of 1980, those who will be from 35 to 64 years of age in 1980 are already here; thus, the projections for them are quite reliable. The rate of increase for the group 35 to 64 years of age, however, will be much smaller, only about 8 percent. This percentage represents an increase of only 5 million, less than that for our senior citizens. This broad group is composed almost entirely of active members of the labor force and persons well along in the course of marriage and parenthood.

A really explosive expansion in number will occur for the group 18 to 34 years of age. The increase will be 57 percent. In terms of numbers, it is an increase of almost 24 million persons, just over one-half of the projected 47 million overall increase in population. This group includes college students, new entrants to the labor force, newlyweds and young parents. Hence, the large projected increase for them is a warning signal of possibilities of a swamping of college and university facilities, a rise in unemployment while jobs also increase, and a large increase in the number of births.

The group which will be 14 to 17 years of age in 1980 are those born in 1962 to 1966. Practically all of them are here to be counted, and for the most part, they appear in the statistics now available. Hence, the projections for them are reliable, though not quite as reliable as those for age groups of 18 years or above. For them, an increase of almost 17 percent is projected (1965 to 1980), about 2.4 million teenagers. This is very small compared with the 67 percent or 5.7 million increase during the preceding 15-year period. Perhaps, as a result, an era of serious teenage problems will decline.

The major uncertainty for the group 5 to 13 years of age, the elementary school age group, is, of course, the birth rate during the years 1966 to 1975. The projections assume a moderate decline from the 1962-65 level for which fairly adequate data are available, and in that sense are conservative. Current birth rates are already well below the highs of the late fifties, but they may rise again, especially should international tension lessen and high levels of economic activity continue. On the other hand, the decline in birth rates could be greater than that assumed. In fact, however, important developments affecting the birth rate, but for which we have no guides in previous experience, have not yet been adequately assessed. On the conservative basis of projection used here, an increase of only 4 million or about 11 percent may be expected in the groups 5 to 13 years of age. Such an increase is in sharp contrast to the increase of 61 percent or 13.5 million children in the preceding 15-year period. Our schools and markets, we may feel certain, will feel no impact such as occurred during the latter period as a result of the postwar baby boom.

For the Mountain States

In broad sweep, the changing age structure—both recent and projected —parallels that for the total United States. There are, of course, differences in detail. In this connection, perhaps attention should be called to the fact that, for the Mountain States, no age group shows a reduction in number— either for 1960-65 or projected for 1965-80. This, of course, is a consequence of the larger growth rates, occasioned by substantial net in-migration, in the Mountain States in comparison with those for the total United States which are almost wholly the result of natural increase.

ENROLLMENT IN SCHOOLS

School enrollment depends on the number of persons in the various school-age groups and on their enrollment rates. As the American income level has increased, greater educational opportunities have been offered to and accepted by our younger citizens.

At least since 1910, school enrollment rates have increased. For the traditional elementary school age groups, they had come close to a practical maximum by 1950. Even as early as 1910, roughly 86 percent (and probably more) of the youngsters 7 to 13 years of age were enrolled in school;[26] by 1950, the enrollment rate was approaching 99 percent, and by 1960, almost every one of them was enrolled (over 99.5 percent). A small drop-off has occurred since then, but this appears to be a result of transient factors, perhaps only a lag in the provision of adequate facilities for our burgeoning population of 7 to 13 year olds. And, enrollment rates for our 6 year old children are not far behind. When enrollment in kindergarten is included, they are now over 98 percent, after a steady rise from roughly 52 percent (and probably more) in 1910. Even more than two-thirds of our 5-year olds are now enrolled, after a dramatic rise since 1940 when the rate of roughly 18 percent differed little from that of 1910. The bulk of these (perhaps 85 percent) are, of course, kindergarten children. Finally, it may be noted that the Bureau of the Census has recently[27] started to collect information on the school enrollment of 3 and 4 year-olds, this indicates that what used to be relatively rare may have started on the road to becoming common-place. For the 3 to 5 year-olds, the enrollment rise represents a change in our cultural pattern during the past half-century or so. Kindergarten is widely recognized as a standard beginning grade for public schools. There is a growing willingness to register precocious children who have not yet reached their 5th birthday. Nursery schools are becoming phenomena of the middle-income as well as upper-income groups, and are now being urged for low income and poverty groups.

For our children under 14, full exposure to schooling is in sight, that is in terms of enrollment. But this is not enough. There remain two acute and important problems, even for these groups. First, less than maximum enrollment is concentrated in small pockets of discrimination or poverty or both. Second, the quality of schooling is far below reasonable standards in a number of places and especially in city-slums and poverty stricken rural areas.

For the group 14 to 17 years of age, we are still far from achieving full exposure to a high school level of education. Despite a steady rise from roughly 43 percent in 1910, the school enrollment rate for those 16 and 17 years of age is still less than 88 percent. For those 14 and 15 years of age, the rate, after a steady rise from roughly 75 percent in 1910, is almost as high as the rate for the group 7 to 13 years of age. This gap between the younger and older high school ages indicates the minimum extent to which children are not completing a high school education—the magnitude of the drop-outs. It is a minimum since the enrollment rate for those 17 is less than for those 16 and for those 18 less than for those 17 years of age. As in the case of the younger children, less than maximum enrollment rates are concentrated in particular areas and among particular groups. For ex-

[26] U.S. Bureau of the Census, *Census of Papulation: 1960*, Vol. I, Pt. 1, Table 74.
[27] U.S. Bureau of the Census, *Current Population Reports*, Series P-20, No. 148 (February 8, 1966).

ample, in non-metropolitan areas, 85 percent of the white children 16 and 17 years of age are enrolled in school, but only 78 percent of the Negro children; similarly, in metropolitan areas the corresponding rates are 90 and 87 percent.[27]

For those 18 years old and above, enrollment rates are much lower, reflecting the fact that college and post-graduate education is obtained by relatively few. But for these age groups, there has been a sharp increase in enrollment rates since 1950, extending earlier advances. This reflects, not only greater participation in collegiate education particularly at the community college level, but also improved participation at the high school level. In connection with the latter, it may be noted that, of those 18 years of age who are enrolled in school, perhaps as many as 60 percent are in high school—the Census figure for 1960, the most recent year for which one is available.[28]

The most visible consequence of the changing age structure during the fifties was the tremendous pressure on kindergarten and elementary school facilities. The grade schools of the United States were inundated by the tidal wave of postwar babies who reached school-entrance age and filled the schools in the fifties and this continued into the sixties. Enrollment in kindergartens and elementary schools increased by 11 million children in the fifties and then another 3 million in the first half of the sixties, the total rise for the 15 year period running to 64 percent. This rise was somewhat less than the 61 percent increase for youngsters 5 to 13 years of age, the difference representing in part the increase in enrollment rates during the decade.

During the sixties and seventies, the pressure on the grade schools will sharply decrease. Between 1965 and 1980, enrollment may increase by over 4 million or by only 12 percent. This is approximately an average of 1 percent per annum, an easily managed rate. The major problems, therefore, will not be those of rapidly achieving net increases in total quantities of facilities and personnel. Rather, emphasis will be upon the relocation, improvement and replacement of physical facilities, upon the improvement of personnel and upon the innovation and development of materials and techniques.

Developments somewhat parallel to those in the elementary schools occurred in the high schools during the fifties and early sixties, but the increase was proportionately greater. Between 1950 and 1965, high school enrollment almost doubled, rising from 6.7 million to 13 million. And like the elementary schools this was considerably above the 67 percent increase of the high school age population. The difference represented, in large part, the rise of enrollment rates. Unlike the elementary schools, however, the high schools still have a few more years of rather rapid enrollment increases (about 13 percent between 1965 and 1970) before relief arrives in the form of smaller enrollment increases.

An explosive increase in enrollment of almost 60 percent occurred in our colleges and professional schools during the first half of the sixties.

---

[28] U.S. Bureau of the Census, *Census of Population: 1960*, Vol. I, Pt. 1, Table 167.

This followed on the heels of a less explosive increase of 61 percent in the fifties. Enrollment went from 2.2 million in 1950 to 5.7 million in 1965—an increase of 156 percent. Only in part does this represent an increase in the college age groups, the groups 18 to 21 years of age which increased by only 34 percent. In crude terms, the only ones available, about 80 percent of the explosive 1950-1965 increase in college and professional education has been the result of much greater rates of enrollment of the college age groups in institutions of higher education. A very large further increase of almost 3.5 million or 61 percent in enrollment is projected by 1980. However, current college enrollments have been swelled by the Selective Service policy of student deferments. Should this policy be modified, the enrollment expansion may be slowed though the longer-term trend will continue up at a rapid rate. Offsetting this, and also perhaps underestimated by the projections is the growing recognition of the need and the growing demand for community colleges.

In overall summary, school enrollment in 1980 is projected as about 64 million persons. This represents an increase of about 10 million persons, or about 18 percent, above the number enrolled in 1965. Both in number and in rate of increase, the change will be far less than from 1950 to 1965, when school enrollment increased 23.5 million persons or about 78 percent.

EDUCATIONAL ATTAINMENT

In 1940, the first year for which census data on years of schooling were collected, the "average" person 25 years of age and over in the United States had completed little more than an elementary school education, i.e., about 8.6 years of school. By 1950, median years of schooling had risen to 9.3; by 1960, to 10.6; and, by 1965, it is estimated, to a level approaching a high school education. This reflects the long term effects of rising enrollment rates beginning in the early part of the century. With a continuation of recent trends in educational improvement, a significant milestone will have been passed as the next decade is ushered in. Projections, and the conservative ones at that, indicate that, by 1970, the "average" American 25 years of age and over may have achieved a high school education; and, by 1980, median years of schooling will have risen further to 12.6 years. For those 25 to 29 years of age, an even higher level of attainment is projected. This, in turn, presages a continued rise in educational attainment to 1980 and beyond. Part of the rise in our educational level has been the reduction of the proportion of persons with little or no schooling. In 1940, about 13.6 percent of the population 25 years of age and over had fewer than 5 years of schooling, a level below that of functional illiteracy. In 1950, 11.1 percent were still in the group. By 1965, however, the proportion of functionally illiterate had declined to about 7.1 percent. Should the trend continue, the proportion will decline further to less than 4 percent in 1980.

With the effects of the rise in educational level added to the effects of increases in population, the numbers of high school and college graduates expanded rapidly. Since the expectations are for both factors to continue to rise, further increases in the numbers of such graduates are projected for the balance of the sixties and seventies.

In the adult population 25 years of age and over—all well beyond the age at which completion of our mass education high school programs is typically scheduled—the number of high school graduates increased by about 17 million persons, from 29.2 (conterminous U.S. only) to 46.6 (all U.S.) or by almost 60 percent during the decade and one-half from 1950 to 1965. In 1950, the high school graduates numbered 34 percent of all those in the "25 and over" age group; in 1965, the percentage was almost 45 percent. Sometime during the seventies, the high school graduates 25 years of age and over will pass a number equal to 50 percent of the corresponding total population. And, by 1980, the number may well approach 60 percent of the total. Between 1965 and 1980, a 28 million increase in the number of high school graduates (age 25 and over) is projected to bring the total to almost 75 million, an increase of about 60 percent, about the same as during the preceding 15 years.

For the college graduate group among the "25 years old and over" adults expansion of 73.3 percent, from 5.3 to 9.2 million, was at a greater rate than the high school group during the decade and one-half, 1950-1965. This difference in rate is projected to increase for the 1965 to 1980 period; the college graduate group is expected to increase by about 81 percent while the high school group will grow about 60 percent. By 1980, the number of college graduates in the adult "25 and over" population is projected to exceed 16 million. This figure would equal almost 13 percent of the total number of persons in the "25 and over" group, i.e., the number well-beyond the typical age of completion of a college education.

SUMMARY

The projections utilize conservative assumptions about the future. The critical one is the birth rate. If it should not decline during the sixties, and then remain at a lower level, the total population of the United States may well be over 250 million by 1980 and close to 350 million by the end of the century.

Differences in growth rates will change the distribution of population among the Geographic Divisions and regions. The South Atlantic Division will make a small relative gain. But, continuing a long-term trend, the West will make the major increase in relative importance. Within the Mountain Division, Arizona and Nevada are projected to register major increases in relative importance and New Mexico to retain its relative position. All or almost all of the increase in population between 1965 and 1980 will be in urban territory, most of it in metropolitan areas. This increase will leave between 75 and 80 percent of our population in urban territory and about 70 percent in metropolitan areas. Within metropolitan areas, close to 60 percent of the population will be in suburbs.

Expansion of population will not be uniform among SMSA's cities or counties. In fact, very wide variation may be expected within each type of smaller area.

The pace of metropolitanization is projected to be greater in the Mountain States than in the United States as a whole. Even so, the proportion of the population which is metropolitan will be less than—61 percent as against about 70 percent—for the total United States in 1980. And, past developments elsewhere in the United States may well serve as guides and warnings of the future in the Mountain States.

The need for modification of governmental structures of 18th- and 19th-century origin and design in the light of 20th-century conditions will receive increased recognition with the continuation of extensive urbanization and metropolitanization. The problems may be less acute in the Mountain States because of smaller population clusters and because of a relatively smaller total population.

Marked shifts in the composition of our population may be expected to continue. Perhaps the most significant is the changing age structure. In terms of average age, the population will be younger in 1980 than in 1965, but the underlying long-term increase in the proportion 65 years of age and over will continue. The most striking development during the last half of sixties and seventies will be increases ranging upwards of 55 percent in the groups from 20 to 35 years of age.

Assuming continuation of recent net immigration, by 1980, the foreign-born population will number only 4 percent of the total, and will have declined substantially in relative importance. By contrast, our nonwhite population, mostly Negro, growing more rapidly than the white population, will increase in importance and may well approach 13 percent of the total by 1980. Negroes will continue to migrate to the North and the West and will become more and more urbanized and metropolitanized.

With respect to racial and ethnic composition, the Mountain States differ significantly among themselves as well as from the total U.S. In common with other sections of the nation and with each other, they face problems of acculturation of racial and ethnic groups hitherto outside the mainstream of American life. In the Mountain States, these are now the Indians and Mexicans, together with others of Hispanic origin; and may later include the Negroes.

College and university enrollment in 1980 is projected to be more than 60 percent above the 1965 figure. Elsewhere, enrollment will expand at modest rates, far less than the explosive rates of the fifties and early sixties. For those Mountain States with rapid population growth rates, however, pressures upon educational facilities—particularly at the college level—may still be high.

Educational attainment levels will continue to rise so that, by 1980, the "average" adult 25 years of age and over will have received more than a high school education. By 1980, close to 60 percent of the persons 25 years of age and over will be high school graduates; about 13 percent of those 25 years of age and over, college graduates.

CHAPTER 4

The Medical Sciences

HERMAN E. HILLEBOE, M.D.* AND RAY E. TRUSSELL, M.D.**

What advances will there be in the medical sciences by 1980? How will they affect the organization and management of health services in the community? How can the emerging knowledge and new skills be harnessed to strengthen and improve school health services and education? These are the critical questions we are bold enough to tackle in our presentation today.

When asked in a recent article to peer into the last third of the 20th century, Elting Morison (20)[1] commented: "When the rate and variety of change seem to approach infinity, the task of relating what went before to what comes after seems immeasurable." This is particularly appropriate to describe the dilemma facing those who attempt to predict the future in the medical sciences. Yet we have no choice but to attempt to suggest possible answers so we can meet the challenges already appearing on the horizon. As civilization relentlessly advances, there is little hope of bringing our genetic endowments and physical environment into harmony without skillful planning. Forecasting is the first step in this essential long-range process.

SOME BASIC CONSIDERATIONS

Medical science and its application present a strange paradox today. As many of the major causes of ill health come more and more under control, the defective and disabled who might otherwise have perished are kept alive. In many parts of the world—even in developed countries—they have become an intolerable burden on society. To solve the riddle of this paradox requires fresh approaches to balancing needs and resources. The old way of doing things no longer suffices. The leaders of the health professions must come up with some better ways of solving accumulated problems and some fresh approaches to the new ones that technological development and urbanization have thrust upon us.

Before problems can be solved, they must be defined. Educators have taught health workers that conceptualization forms the basis for successful

*DeLamar Professor and Head of Division of Public Health Practice, Columbia Univesity School of Administrative Medicine since 1963; Commissioner of New York State Department of Health 1947-63; has held important Public Health Service positions, received honorary degrees from several Universities, and distinguished awards from a number of major organizations; is co-author (with Dr. Russell H. Morgan) of *Mass Radiology of the Chest* and senior author (with Dr. Granville W. Larrimore) of *Preventive Medicine* (1965).

**Director and DeLamar Professor, Columbia University School of Public Health and Administrative Medicine since 1955; Commissioner of Hospitals, New York City, 1961-63; Epidemiologist for Military Services during war and later in New York State Department of Health; author of numerous publications and frequent contributor to medical literature on various aspects of public health and preventive medicine.

[1] Each number in parenthesis refers to a correspondingly numbered reference at the end of the chapter.

implementation. Therefore, modern concepts of health are essential if clear definitions are to be formulated. What are these modern concepts that can provide the foundation for building a healthier world in which to live?

First and foremost is the vital role the health status of its people plays in the social and economic development of a nation. This implies a second concept—the inseparability of the medical and social needs of the individual and his family. Still another basic concept is the changing role of the health official, from police officer—enforcing quarantine of infectious diseases and abating nuisances—to community health leader. Furthermore, the organized community effort of health agencies to serve groups of individuals is being augmented by the application of preventive medicine by private practitioners to individuals.

This subtle change from a limited view of public health to a broad concept of community health presages the full flowering of human ecology, i.e., the relationship of the human being to his total environment—biological, physical, and social. The implications of this concept of comprehensive community health to our citizens' well-being reach far into the future.

Health then, is not simply a collection of facts and figures, but rather a generalized concept. The School Health Education Study group (11) looked upon health as a combination of three triads: 1) human well-being with its mental, physical, and social aspects; 2) human behavior with its cognitive, affective, and action domain; and 3) the focus of health on the individual, the family, and the community. The interrelation and interaction of these three triads give health the breadth of definition it rightfully deserves as a vital factor in society.

Furthermore, our concern for community health cannot be divorced from the problems of crime and delinquency, unemployment and poverty, inadequate housing and education. Duhl (6) looks upon urban man's loss of self-identity as the most prevalent disease of our time. The transplanted family from the country gets swallowed up in the metropolis and ends up as a number on a card, forced to wait endless hours in public clinics or welfare stations for necessary social and health services they have been accustomed to receiving on a more individualized and personal basis.

Psychiatrists, particularly in urban centers, identify a "social breakdown syndrome." This could well become the most common psychiatric diagnosis of the future. It affects whole families when illness strikes a home. Indeed, in most chronic ailments, the social aspects of illness far overshadow the disease itself. How can we hope for medical benefits without correction of the associated social evils of illness? Therefore, the aim of medicine—a social goal—is to keep individuals adjusted to their environment so they can be useful members of society or be readjusted when they have dropped out because of illness.

The social problems of the family are accentuated by the emotional and psychological overtones that accompany ill health and frequently spring from the cultural and ethnic roots of recently migrated people. According to J. D. Frank (7), the greatest threats to life and health are created by man himself; they can only be combatted successfully by changes in deeply in-grained attitudes and behavior.

The social costs of health programs enter into any appraisal of our efforts to eradicate human ailments or environmental hazards. Wolman (41) believes that the health profession must be realistic and confront it-self with less than total eradication measures. He urges us to select those means which promise most beneficial results at minimal social costs: "Life in a sterile environment—whether physical, chemical, biological or psycho-logical—is both improbable and undesirable."

Yet, as Coggeshall (2) has observed, advances in science and health care have stimulated individual health expectations. People are importuned by the radio, television, and other mass media to expect good health care. This attitude has increased the demand for health services, and prepaid medical care plans have helped to pay for this demand. The idea of "en-titlement" has come into the picture too. Morris' (22) opinion—that a disproportionate share of our growth needs to be directed to certain kinds of human needs that cannot be provided solely on a competitive market basis—is shared by many.

The Greek city planner, Doxiadis (5), believes that the expected urbanization in the decades ahead is contemporary man's greatest threat to survival. Beehive-like habitation deprives man of his basic liberties— to walk freely, to sit at leisure, to breathe fresh air, to drink pure water, to eat good food. The fight for privacy, dignity, and optimum health will be-come as determined as that for food, clothing, and shelter.

Weinerman (39) in describing anchor points in planning for tomor-row's health care, summarizes the new characteristics of man's ailments: 1) known elements of risk; 2) complex etiology; 3) non-preventability; 4) non-specificity; 5) multiple manifestations; 6) impaired social function, and 7) chronicity. The impairment of social functions demands treatment of the patient and his total situation rather than the disease alone. Our primary hope of solving community health problems is to help future health workers understand and apply the broad concepts of prevention— not just correction—to human ailments and environmental hazards (14). Prevention of occurrence, e.g., through immunizations, health education, and treatment of water supplies, is by far the most economic and efficient approach.

Prevention of progression, or minimizing ill effects, e.g., mass screening for early cancer, rehabilitation of stroke victims, early treatment of teen-age emotional disorders, is the second line of defense, once the ailment or hazard has appeared. Together, these two forms of prevention, often called respectively, primary and secondary, will enable the health leaders of to-morrow to keep ahead of both old and new problems arising out of human diseases, injuries, and defects.

ADVANCES IN THE MEDICAL SCIENCES, BY HEALTH PROBLEM AREAS

To encompass in one presentation all the advances in the medical sciences in the last ten years would necessitate writing many volumes. To predict the additional advances that may appear in the next fifteen years simply baffles the imagination. Therefore, it would perhaps be helpful to our discussion to think of health problem areas within the scope of the concept of "total community health" and to predict, for each area, some of the developments that may be anticipated.

In its full interpretation, the concept of community health consists of two interrelated segments—personal health and environmental health. This division offers a practical way of grouping health problems since the administrative approach in providing community health services differs for each segment. Such a grouping also is useful as a planning device (15).

Each of the health problem areas is affected by demographic variables in the population—by age and sex distributions, geographic differences, and varying socio-economic statuses of different communities of peoples. Population projections predict that there will be between 225-250 million people living in this country by 1980. The ratio of women to men is expected to be 100:70 and it is estimated that one-half of the people will be in the age-groups under 18 and over 65. About 80 percent of the population will be urban, with 40 percent of the urban total concentrated in metropolitan areas along the Eastern seaboard, the Great Lakes, and the West coast. Life expectation at birth should continue to inch forward. Life expectancy after 55 years of age, which has been relatively unchanged for the past two decades, will remain stable unless the cause and cure of major degenerative diseases (such as heart disease, cancer, stroke) are found.

Personal Health Problem Areas

The problem areas calling for personal health services can be conveniently grouped under six main headings. Some overlapping exists, but this is inevitable because of multiple causes and manifestations of human ailments. The relative importance of each of the categories varies with time and place and with a host of social and economic factors that will themselves be changing in the next decade and a half.

1. *Acute Medical and Surgical Illnesses* requiring hospital care (and ancillary institutional services). Further development of antibiotics can be anticipated for use in both medical and surgical conditions. This will have the effect of shortening hospital stay and extending the use of ambulatory services. Transplants of such vital organs as the liver and the kidneys —maybe even the heart—will become commonplace, once the immunological difficulties have been overcome. New techniques employing ultrasound, laser light beams, and freezing will enable the surgeon to probe the innermost reaches of the body, whenever removal of tissue is necessary for diagnosis or treatment. Such advances will prolong the lives and productivity of many men and women, but they may also overcrowd institutional facilities with completely disabled individuals whose death has been artificially delayed.

The use of auxiliary machines to carry on the work of the heart, kidneys, and lungs will unquestionably increase because of technological advances in engineering and medicine. At the same time, we will see increased collaboration among scientists from chemistry, physics, biology, and engineering and their medical colleagues to devise artificial spare parts to keep the human machine going.

2. *Chronic Illnesses* (especially among older adults) e.g., heart disease, cancer, and stroke (that together cause 70 percent of all deaths); arthritis; and diabetes. Heart diseases include coronary artery disease, high blood pressure, and hypertensive heart disease among adults. As yet, their etiology is unclear. But, Pickering (25) predicts that many of the degenerative diseases of the central nervous system (e.g., stroke) will be identified as biochemical lesions due to a genetic defect. Coronary disease will be identified as more than a dietary dysfunction; the genetic, social, and emotional factors are slowly coming to the fore. However, it is improbable that all the causes of this heart condition, and the knowledge necessary for more adequate control, will be uncovered in the next decade. The same is true of high blood pressure and hypertensive heart disease.

The Nobel Prize winner, Tatum (36), predicts that the basic causes of many forms of cancer will be established in the next few decades—that the suspected causes center on cell genetics and nucleic acid structure and function. He believes that virus infections, metabolic diseases, developmental defects, and malignant growths are actually interrelated and will be conquered by immunologic or specific chemical means.

In developed countries like the United States, chronic illnesses absorb an ever larger share of the health dollar. As greater numbers of persons live to older ages, more money and more medical care than ever before will be necessary to keep these oldsters reasonably comfortable. Consequently, all efforts to pinpoint causes and alleviate unnecessary suffering among the chronically ill, should be encouraged.

3. *Mental Disorders,* among adults include both illnesses and retardation. Alcoholism is included here because of its psychological component. The social aspects of alcoholism will be given increasing attention in a search for some of the precipitating factors in this illness with such grave social consequences.

The biochemical researchers of mental illness may bring us closer to the multiple causes of severe organic involvement. Schmitt (32) maintains that brain functions and their correlates in behavior represent major levels of complexity, with three disparate points of reference: 1) the molecular; 2) the neural (brain and nerves); 3) the behavioral: He surmises that until the discovery of a key to the system like the DNA-RNA-protein system of genetics, the advances will be slow. He further believes that the coordinated investigation of the three levels described is the central problem of the life sciences. These views are similar to those of Tatum (36) who has concluded that "the findings and concepts of molecular biology will play a leading role in the future of medicine."

We should see a shift in the care of the mentally ill from large state hospitals to community centers. Leading psychiatrists are coming to realize that many of the mental ills of older persons can be handled by general practitioners, both in and out of hospitals. This will help alleviate the shortage of psychiatrists and other scarce professional personnel. General physicians can be brought up-to-date by refresher courses given in community mental health centers.

As in the past, the urban areas will continue to contribute a major share of the mentally ill as a result of the poverty, unemployment, ignorance, and other handicapping conditions prevalent in these metroplexes.

The genetic aspects of mental retardation will be discussed under the heading of maternal and child health and family planning. However, in the next decade, we are apt to see a greater medical recognition of the need to make more exact diagnoses of mental retardation. Wherever possible, expanded efforts will be made to train the retarded to get along in the home rather than in the institution. This may help to mitigate the public's present attitude of hopelessness toward all the retarded.

4. *Maternal and Child Health and Family Planning.* In the next decade and a half, we can anticipate increased attention to the health problems of persons under 21 years of age. Richmond (29) believes that three major gaps exist which must be filled: 1) application of the pediatrician's knowledge to more children; 2) better distribution of services and professional personnel, and 3) new knowledge, especially in respiratory and allergic disorders, mental retardation, emotional disorders, and chronic illnesses. He thinks we should concentrate services in periodic care and immunizations. At the same time, infant mortality, accidents, dental disease, and handicaps must be further reduced.

The exciting developments in genetic counselling of parents (especially mothers), should reach a high level in the years ahead. Tatum (36) expresses the view that means will be found to introduce new genes or their products into defective cells of particular organs and that one may get at congenital defects by identifying genetic precursors. Meanwhile, Medawar (18), decries the fact that we are losing genetic endowments which, in the past, were essential for survival in coping with an arduous environment. Arguing that we are maintaining genetic endowments which are bad for survival, he feels that "marriage between two people who carry the same unfavorable recessive genes should be discouraged." Successful marriage counselling can reduce the babies born with mental retardation and other defects associated with metabolic disturbances, such as "PKU."

Another lead for future consideration is the discovery that malnutrition at a certain stage of the child's development may result in a degree of permanent impairment to his intellectual capacity. Payne (24) even goes so far as to say that "social and behavioral factors are equally, or more, important in the causation of disease and the determination of disease patterns in the population than biological factors."

Quite apart from its primary role in population control, family planning should soon come into its own key position in the protection of child and maternal health. The years ahead will see the development and extension of advice on family planning into every relevant aspect of community health services. Newer, simpler, and cheaper methods of contraception are in the offing. Research may even develop an immunizing agent that will prevent pregnancy from occurring.

5. *Infectious and Parasitic Diseases.* Acute communicable diseases still present problems in large cities and will continue to do so until social changes bring about comprehensive health services for all. In the next fifteen years, one may predict control of some of the causes of the common cold by chemical and biologic means. With the development of new drugs and antibiotics lethal to the tubercle bacilli, tuberculosis should soon be brought to an irreducible minimum, even in urban areas. But this will require community-wide programs of detection, diagnosis and treatment, rehabilitation, and life-long follow-up of known cases.

The parasitic diseases will continue to be prevalent, especially in cities and among migrants from the South, Puerto Rico, and tropical countries where such infestations are endemic.

6. *Accidental Injuries and Occupational Diseases.* This problem area, of course, has both personal and environmental aspects. It is the human factor and the need for personal health services that are of major concern here. In the next decade, we will see a better definition of the role of the host (man), the agent (vehicle or machine), and the environment (highway, home, place of work, recreation center) in the causation of accidents. We should also see a joint attack by industry, the government, and voluntary health groups aimed at the prevention of accident occurrence. At the same time, better emergency handling of accidental injuries, wherever they may happen, will be developed.

Recent federal legislative hearings point the way to stricter safety regulations in the design of automobiles, both to keep the driver from injury due to mechanical defects and to protect the passengers involved in car accidents. Klein and Haddon's (16) studies show that in buying a car today, an individual has a one in four chance of killing or injuring someone and probably a fifty-fifty chance of being hit by another's car.

Occupational hazards and illnesses will receive particular attention in smaller industries and businesses throughout the nation, whose health services have been neglected in the past. New methods of protecting workers against physical, chemical, and biological hazards will be developed at the insistence of both the unions and the health agencies.

Space flight and prolonged submarine duty add new dimensions to occupational health activities. Research findings from these new fields of medicine will find application in many aspects of community health.

Since accidents are the principal causes of death and disability in the younger age groups, increasing emphasis must be placed on planning to prevent their occurrence. Such planning will look for ways to utilize the full potential of school health services and school health education.

Environmental Health Problem Areas

In April 1966, the National Academy of Sciences made public a report (38) which described the pollution of the environment as "unprecedented and becoming desperate." Refuse production (4.5 pounds of solids per capita in 1965) is increasing with the population and growing at the rate of 4 percent a year. For example a single power plant burning coal or oil, can deliver several hundred tons of sulphur dioxide to the atmosphere daily. Unless drastic steps are taken, air pollution from such plants will be doubled by 1980.

Water pollution presents the same story. By 1980, sewers and waste pipes in the United States will discharge enough waste material, rich in organic food content for bacteria, to remove all the oxygen (making it unfit for aquatic life) from a volume of water equal to the dry-weather flow of the country's twenty-two river basins.

Having presented such devastating evidence, the Report poses a significant question: Within the financial resources available, how pure should the air and water be maintained to protect the health of the community and to meet recreational needs?

Another significant document on "Restoring the Quality of Our Environment" was published in November 1965 at the request of the President (28). The Report studies the main issue of pollution and considers the direction in which we should go. It further depicts the modern paradox of urban life and industrial expansion: "We are at the same time pollutors and sufferers from pollution." In its final recommendations, the President's Panel urged that "the public come to recognize individual rights to quality of living, as expressed by the absence of pollution, as it has come to recognize rights to education, to economic advance, and to public recreation."

It is evident from these excellent reports that new public policies and institutional arrangements will be needed in the near future before technological possibilities can be fully exploited. If the public can be motivated to demand action, the political authorities will provide the resources of money, manpower, and facilities.

The critical conditions we will face by 1980 will be accentuated long before that date in geographic and industrial areas where pollution is accumulating. These areas cannot wait fifteen years for a solution. It is essential that the federal government initiate regional research centers, provide financial grants-in-aid for planning and construction, and work cooperatively with states and urban centers in long-range planning. This action will necessitate changes in the organization of pollution-related activities at all levels of government.

Poverty, population, and pollution will continue to be pressing problems for many years ahead to leaders in the federal government, industry, and urban centers. The time is long overdue for the scientists and technologists to involve themselves in, or at least give advice on, the legal-political aspects of all forms of pollution of the air, water, and soil.

The problem areas of environmental health can be grouped under six main headings with some overlap (e.g., ionizing radiation in the air, water, and foods). The first two areas, water and air resources, have already been considered briefly in the introductory paragraphs of this section and will not be discussed further.

1. *Water Resources*—physical, chemical and biological contamination.

2. *Air Resources*—physical, chemical and biological contamination.

3. *Food and Pharmaceutical Resources*—purity and potency; physical, chemical, and biological contamination. We will see great advances in the packaging and storing of foods and in the development of low-cost protein sources, such as fish meal. The use of ionizing radiation as a means of preserving food and preventing spoilage will develop rapidly. Systems analysis of the needs of low-income groups should result in better distribution of the right foods to the right people at the right time (e.g., the distribution of acceptable surplus products from our abundant agricultural production).

Control of pharmaceuticals, e.g., drugs, biological products, hormones, therapeutic devices, should also make great strides forward in the next decade under the new leadership of the revitalized National Food and Drug Administration. Potency and safety will come under rigid controls with proof placed largely on the shoulders of manufacturers. Hopefully, health education may reduce quackery in the sale and use of drugs and allied products.

4. *Ionizing Radiation,* both man-made and from natural sources, will be placed under stricter federal and state controls than in the past. The principal sources of undue exposure—X-ray machines used in diagnostic medicine—will be minimized over the next ten years as a result of higher standards demanded of technicians, better surveillance, and more rigid enforcement of operating regulations. This is another example of prevention of occurrence—the absolute avoidance of unnecessary exposure not essential for accurate diagnosis. This concept calls for rigid application in reducing the number of examinations of school children for pulmonary tuberculosis and other chest diseases.

Automatic monitoring devices for air, water, food and soil will be developed on a nation-wide network to alert health agencies almost instantaneously of any increase in radiation. Such a network will be tied in with the Defense Department's monitoring of weapons testing throughout the world.

5. *Human Settlements and Residences.* Future concern will not be just for dwellings where people live, but also for adjacent spaces where they work and play. Housing and health authorities will team up with welfare agencies and voluntary associations to improve medical care programs in low-cost housing developments in urban centers. Medical care will be brought to the older citizens in their housing units, rather than having the oldsters neglect themselves because care is difficult to obtain. Noise control in urban areas will command additional attention because of the harmful psychological effects—already reaching alarming proportions.

6. *General Sanitation.* Solid wastes have already been mentioned under general remarks on pollution of air, water, and soil. In the next 10 to 15 years, the large cities will have to transport solid wastes away from urban areas and make permanent disposal to avoid pollution.

The use of pesticides and insecticides will be more clear-cut in terms of safety for human beings, other living things, and food sources. Research will be intensified to discover safer yet equally potent chemicals and biological materials—a challenge which will see agricultural scientists, chemists, biologists, and medical scientists team up for investigations and to provide service.

Medical and sanitary scientists alike agree that man cannot achieve optimum health in a contaminated environment. He will have to redirect the energies he expends in carelessly ruining his environment to keep the environment from ruining him. Urban designs of the future must therefore give a high priority to environmental hazards to health.

ADVANCES IN THE ORGANIZATION AND MANAGEMENT OF COMMUNITY HEALTH PROGRAMS

Closing the gaps between the knowledge and skills in the medical sciences and their application to all the members of the community will require the complete reorganization of community health programs. Old-fashioned methods of administration of health services can no longer be tolerated because the waste is too great, the price too high. Delay in delivery and distribution of care to those in need is inexcusable. Only the wide-spread application of modern public and business administration methods to the entire health field can lead to comprehensive community health services.

Advances in administrative organization and management have been applied successfully in industry and finance. The Defense Department and the Aeronautics and Space Administration have adopted planning, programming, and budgeting on a massive scale. The health industry, a $39 billion industry in 1965, should follow this pattern and more effectively solve its multitude of problems.

At the present time, the basic barrier to comprehensive services is the lack of national policy and planning for the entire field of community health. Responsibilities are now scattered among a dozen federal agencies. Moreover, fragmentation of programs exists in the Department of Health, Education, and Welfare itself. This lack of planning and the fragmentation into categorical approaches is naturally replicated in state health agencies and local agencies. Health administration in the United States today is truly a many-splintered thing.

Fortunately, the new heads in the Bureau of the Budget, and the Department of Health, Education, and Welfare, and the Public Health Service have recognized these deficiencies and are taking corrective action. But the voyage ahead will be long and rough. It will take pilots of unusual stamina and courage.

If leadership comes from the federal government, sound policy and planning patterns will be followed by the states and local health agencies—official, voluntary, and private. The government will need guidance in keeping the provision of direct services at a minimum and concentrating, instead, on the intelligent purchase of services from local community agencies. In this, the universities can play a dominant role. They should seek involvement in policy formulation and participate in planning from the initiatory to the evaluative stages. As the role of government in health becomes greater, the universities can also play the role of devil's advocate and help avoid rigidities in the operation of public facilities. Using their expert knowledge, university consultants can aid in preserving the best elements of the voluntary system and at the same time insist on high standards of care.

From recent meetings at the New York Academy of Medicine on the availability and accessibility of health services emerged some basic concepts needed to guide the provision of medical care in the years ahead. A sample of the opinions expressed may illustrate some directions. Mencher (19) for example, observed that trends within the practice of medicine have made it a large scale industry requiring the kind of financing and organization that only government can undertake effectively. Weinerman (39) bluntly stated that "there is no room for eligibility tests (for medical care) other than those of need," while Haviland (10) voiced the opinion that universal tax-supported medicine seems a certainty.

The federal health legislation in 1965 gave additional evidence of the scope and character of medical services people want, as expressed by their elected representatives to Congress and the White House. To meet the demands for such expanding services will require parallel advances in community health administration. Improvements needed will be discussed briefly under four headings: 1) finances; 2) manpower; 3) facilities; and 4) administrative organization and management.

Finances

Year by year, the federal government has been increasing its contribution to health programs—for service, research and training—and this practice will undoubtedly continue until resources catch up with needs and demands. The enactment into law of the Title XIX amendment to the Social Security Act of 1965 (34) indicates the trend of increasing federal participation in the care of the medically indigent (the old, the disabled, the blind, dependent children and other children under 21 years of age). The federal share varies from 50 to 83 percent; the state and local government divide the rest. Title XVIII of the amended Act provides for hospital and medical care for all people over 65, although of a somewhat limited scope—probably 60 percent of total costs. Title V of the amended Act extends benefits for maternal and child health and for the care of crippled children, especially the mentally retarded. A crystal ball is not necessary to predict how medical care will be predominantly financed in the future.

If complete chaos in providing medical care is to be avoided, the development of a single system of community health services is inevitable. Therefore, in the next decade and a half, we should see a pooling of resources for community health by official, voluntary, and private agencies throughout the nation. Moreover, we can hope for formal merging of some voluntary and private health agencies which share common problems, goals, and activities. In 1965, there were over 100,000 such health and welfare agencies in the country and they raised over $1.5 billion. Hence, their significance cannot be underestimated nor their potential contribution to services, education, and research minimized.

A very significant piece of legislation affecting financing for health programs was introduced in March 1966 by Senator Lister Hill, long influential in health legislation. Although this bill (S.3008) will be more fully discussed later in this presentation, let us say now that it replaces the Public Health Service's multitude of categorical grants-in-aid for health by just two types of grants—a comprehensive one and a project grant. In addition, the bill provides funds for planning and manpower needs.

It is apparent from prevailing legislative signs that we should soon have health insurance and extensive health care for the employed, self-employed, unemployed, and the dependents of all three classes. However, before comprehensive health care for all who need it is possible, great barriers of income and geography must be hurdled. In addition, better use of professional manpower is essential, even to the point of making radical changes such as substituting group practice for many of the present-day solo practitioners.

Manpower

New advances in the medical sciences cannot be applied on a large scale without greater numbers and new types of health manpower. In spite of the fact that over three million persons are employed in at least forty different occupations in the health field, we are desperately short of health manpower—professional, technical, and auxiliary. In fact, Surgeon General Stewart of the Public Health Service (35) estimates that one million new health workers will be needed in the next ten years.

Is this shortage a cause or a symptom of our difficulty? It would appear that it is primarily a symptom of the lack of modern organization and efficient management of available resources (31). A systems analysis of the health industry is the only logical first approach to a solution of the manpower problem. However, time is short, because a "lead time" of ten to fifteen years is necessary in recruiting and training professional personnel. For example, a minimum of eight years after high school is spent training a physician. After a year's internship, an additional three to seven years are still required for specialty training.

A few of the large number of concepts developed in recent years to guide us in meeting the manpower shortage will be mentioned. Although the validity of these concepts can be confirmed only after they have been evaluated, they nevertheless appear to be significant and warrant consideration.

First, lack of money prevents many young people from entering the ranks of the health sciences and the health industry. The only answer lies in federal and state scholarships for all who need help and can meet carefully determined qualifications.

Second, many professional personnel are performing tasks that could be done as well and more cheaply by technicians and auxiliary workers. In the next decade, we will see decayed teeth filled by dental assistants under the supervision of dentists. Mass X-ray films will be screened for abnormal shadows by technicians under the guidance of the radiologist. Laboratory tests will be carried out by automatic machines tended by laboratory workers under the direction of the pathologist. To conserve medical manpower, laboratories will be centralized and computerized to serve several hospitals and health centers. Non-medical administrators will be used to relieve physicians and other scientists of routine administrative tasks. However, the health professions will have to compete with business and industry for the bright young men and women on the threshold of careers in administration. Job satisfaction and advancement are equally as important as salaries.

Handicapped persons will fill more sedentary jobs, especially those with repetitive operations that would be boring to less motivated persons. The mentally retarded will be placed in jobs fitted to their limited mental capacities, but which make use of their physical stamina. For example, why could not more mentally retarded workers be employed as attendants at domiciliary institutions, particularly those for the mentally ill and physically disabled?

Haviland (10) advises us to be "alert to new ideas and fresh approaches to old needs." This advice is particularly relevant to recruiting and using health manpower. In May 1966, Secretary of Defense McNamara suggested two years of public service for every young man or woman on reaching maturity. This is worthwhile to consider. It would solve the draft problem, fill peace corps needs and aid in the maturation of our young people. It would teach them responsibility, offer a purpose in life, provide vocational opportunities and even incentives for going on to college and a professional career. If vocational guidance, training, and placement were built into the plan, such a public policy could be of considerable help in solving the health and other manpower shortages.

The intensified application of scientific advances will require the interdisciplinary efforts of a variety of specialists. The increasing specialization in the medical sciences is likely to continue, but at the same time, we must guard against lack of coordination among services. We need to avoid making health care of the individual too impersonal. This could happen if the focus of attention is put on a disease rather than on the individual or if mass production methods denigrate personal physician-patient relationships.

Facilities

In 1946, with the Public Health Service's Hospital Survey and Construction Act, the federal government took a giant step forward in providing funds for planning and building general hospitals, especially in rural areas. In the intervening twenty years, funds have been increased and provisions extended so that federal matching of state and local expenditures can now be applied to nursing homes, rehabilitation centers, diagnostic and treatment clinics, and community health centers.

In the next fifteen years, it is predictable that every conceivable type of facility—voluntary and governmental—for the care of both the healthy and the sick—will be under the umbrella of federal planning and construction funds. For the mentally retarded and ill, federal funds are also available for the operation of health centers. The most encouraging provision in these federal stimulatory grants is the requirement for statewide planning and priorities for type and location of hospitals on the basis of need. At the average construction costs in 1966 of $25,000-$35,000 per general hospital bed, no community can go it alone. The financial responsibility has to be shared by federal, state, and local sources, using both public and private funds.

Each community will have to plan jointly with neighboring communities in its region to provide the vast network of health facilities required by advances in the medical sciences. Medical teaching centers will form the core for satellites of hospitals, nursing homes, and rehabilitation and health centers in the surrounding areas. Such regional planning and distribution of health facilities is a rational approach to meet increasing demands for service, teaching, and research. In addition, continuation education for physicians and other professional personnel can be provided from the core medical centers staffed with full-time personnel for this activity. Professionals receiving such training can then return to the satellite centers from which they came and spread the knowledge they have received. Continuation education will be essential to maintain and improve the quality of medical care.

Furthermore, we shall see an extension of higher standards for medical facilities and an accrediting system that is scrupulously enforced by state and local health agencies, staffed with specialists to do the job. Existing accreditation under voluntary auspices, however, cannot reach those hospitals and nursing homes which do not wish to comply. The Social Security Administration has already promulgated standards for all nursing homes, laboratories, and home care services, for those groups that wish to provide services under the Medicare Act (Title XVIII, 1965 Social Security Amendments). This is a step in the right direction.

Better and less expensive care will be given by transferring patients rapidly from one facility to another. Of course, the facility used will depend on the condition of the patient—does he need a bed full-time or part-time, a place to rest, a wheel chair, transportation to an ambulatory clinic, or just a visit to his home by a social worker, nurse, or housekeeper? Hospital beds are too expensive to build and maintain, for a patient to stay in residence one hour longer than is necessary. At the present rate of increase, the average cost of hospital care will be close to $100 per day by 1972. Advances in medical sciences and the increasing cost of equipment, supplies, and specialized workers are driving hospital costs sky high. Thus, it is essential that hospital services be neither wasted nor abused.

Health care facilities of the future will be located for the convenience of consumers rather than the purveyors of health services. The problem is not solely one of accessibility and availability, but also of motivating those in need of preventive and therapeutic care to use the facilities. This may require opening many health centers in the evenings to permit daytime workers to bring in their families at convenient times. In some instances, this will mean seven-day a week functioning of hospitals and their outpatient departments to complement the around-the-clock services of emergency rooms.

Hospitals absorb the biggest share of the medical care dollar and the public has the right to demand that this huge sum of money be spent efficiently with a maximum of benefits. The use of modern administrative methods is well advanced in operation of many hospitals, particularly the larger ones. Still needed is the extension of these methods to all hospitals and other health care facilities in every community. Innovation can create optimum conditions to bring together the families who need comprehensive personal health services with the facilities where such services are provided.

Organization and Management

Planning health programs involves conceptualization and implementation (14). Implementation can be subdivided into two interdependent parts: a Plan of Action and Budgetary Allocation. Operational feasibility and systematic accomplishment are the major concerns of the Plan of Action. Distributive action is the focus of resource allocation. In other words, administration of a health program is the apex of a triad with organization and management at the other two points. Once the concepts are developed, experts in community health and in administration can use these concepts as a basis for developing strategies of action. It is in this context that we shall discuss advances in administrative organization and management which can be applied in the health field in view of expected changes in the medical sciences by 1980.

Geographical reorganization of health services is likely to be the key administrative change in the next fifteen years. The old political boundaries —federal, state, local—no longer make sense as a means of bringing new knowledge and skills to every community. As John Grant (9) said after years of experience in Puerto Rico, "Regionalization is the only way to bridge the existing gap between medical knowledge and its social use."

Federal and state health agencies will remain the main source of funds and of proposed legislation and new interstate and intrastate regions will become operating entities. Some metropolitan centers will be a composite of parts of both types of regions.

Personal health services will be given on a "market area" basis. Environmental health services will be provided on a cachement area basis, with variations for air and water pollution and solid wastes. Planning and programming will be regional; budget allocation of resources can then be made on the basis of common agreement among participating groups.

Manpower and facilities will be distributed on a regional basis because of the complexity of diagnostic methods and therapies to be applied. There will be a need to distribute specialists regionally in order to give service, do research, and help with continuing education for professional personnel, e.g., in the Heart Disease, Cancer, and Stroke Regional Programs (26).

The next fifteen years should also bring official and voluntary agencies together in closer collaboration. Too frequently these groups—often sharing the same goals—have been competitive and suspicious of one another's work. But the problems of community health are so great and so much needs to be done, that no room exists for duplication of effort or waste motion. Each has a particular job to do. Joint planning can lead to division of work and cohesion of services.

Unlike official agencies, the voluntary agencies are not subject to laws that restrict the direction or content of their programs. With the approval of their boards of directors, they can spend as much as they wish on health education, public persuasion, or plain propaganda. So, we can anticipate that the voluntary health agencies will increase their effectiveness and public support by increasing citizen participation in volunteer health services, by formal interagency agreements on programs, and by strict accountability of performance to the public which contributes the funds.

The official agencies also have some reorganization to accomplish at all governmental levels—federal, state and local. Fragmentation is rampant. Competition for the tax dollar is open and often political. Many departments flagrantly raid each other for professional personnel. To alleviate this situation, we should see an extension of Interdepartmental Health Councils at all levels of government where policy is determined, to begin the task of combining similar functions, serving as clearing houses for new programs, and assisting the executive and legislative branches in long-range planning.

Community health and mental health centers should be combined, at least geographically, for greater effectiveness in serving the same families. Health departments and the medical offices of welfare departments should also be under the same medical administration instead of wasting time competing with each other. It may well be that many more states will emulate the five states that already have combined health and welfare services into one agency.

In May 1966, the Mayor of New York placed the Departments of Health and Hospitals and the official agencies concerned with Mental Health, Medical Welfare and the Medical Examiner under a medical "czar" to supervise and coordinate all health activities. This is a sound approach to obtaining comprehensiveness and continuity in community health services. The former Commissioner of Hospitals in New York City (37) also made an effective approach to improving the quality of care by affiliating each municipal hospital with a great teaching hospital or medical center. These are the innovations that the leaders in every large city will need to follow in the future.

One significant development following in the wake of advances in the medical sciences—actually one that made many of the advances possible—is the widespread use of electronic data processing in all phases of community health. These computer systems will be used by regional health groups for planning, for research and for day-to-day operations in every type of health facility. This will include such diverse functions as keeping track of dirty linen for the hospital laundry to monitoring the amount of strontium-90 in the baby's daily supply of milk. Computers will be used to record laboratory reports, to help interpret electrocardiograms, and even to suggest differential diagnosis on the basis of recorded signs and symptoms. They will answer telephonic questions put to information and referral centers by persons seeking health and welfare services in the community.

It would not be feasible or economical for every small hospital or health center to have its own equipment for electronic data processing. Instead, each smaller facility can tie into a computer center in a nearby teaching hospital or medical center large enough to warrant such a unit. Since a rapid communication system is the foundation for the effective administration of a regional health program, a computer network in every region of the country, whether state or interstate, will be essential to the success of expanding federal health programs in the coming years.

International computer programs will also be at work to protect the health of people throughout the world. In June 1966, the World Health Organization established an International Drug Monitoring System to help avoid disasters like that of the thalidomide babies who were born without arms, legs or other parts of their bodies.

When commenting on new federal legislation, Wilbur Cohen, the Under Secretary of Health, Education, and Welfare (3), recently noted that over the past five years, (and particularly in 1965) we have witnessed an unprecedented series of legislative triumphs. A thirty-year battle for health insurance has been won (Title XVIII); a single category of medical assistance replaced four categories of public assistance (Title XIX); a regional system of programs for heart disease, cancer, and stroke victims has been inaugurated; legislation to staff community mental health centers was enacted; vocational services for the disabled and programs for handicapped children were expanded. Cohen feels that legislative enactments for education, civil rights, and the attack on basic causes of poverty are of similar importance. He predicts great accomplishments in the fields of education, health, and social services in the next ten years. Because Mr. Cohen was one of the principal architects of the Social Security Amendments of 1965 (34), his predictions carry weight and are particularly relevant to planning for the future health and welfare of the younger members of our communities.

Every one of these legislative innovations will have a lasting impact on the organization and management of community health services. Furthermore, they would not have been possible without the great advances in the medical sciences of the last two decades. Now, the task facing us is to blend these new developments into the matrix of community life and to organize our resources to meet the growing demands for comprehensive health services.

If enacted, one other Congressional bill will have a pervasive effect on every community health activity and will help strengthen the organization and management of all health programs. Senate Bill 3008, mentioned earlier, provides funds for planning by a state agency, for combining categorical health grants into one comprehensive grant for all health services and provides for project grants to cover problems not handled by the general grants, as well as financial aid for meeting the manpower shortage.

These are improvements that state health officers have been trying for years to accomplish.

This bill, if enacted into law, can change the existing piecemeal pattern of approaching health problems more than any other legislation since the passage of the Public Health Service Act in 1944. It will make possible a problem-centered approach to replace the political-jurisdictional bartering of the past. It can lead to the development, within a few years, of regional health areas, effective policy and planning councils, and close collaboration of official and voluntary agencies working in the regions. Its effects should permeate the local communities. Deliberate action planning of programs should replace crisis action, i.e., the crash approach which has proved to be so wasteful and frustrating.

It is, of course, a calculated risk to count on the passage of any bill in Congress. But S. 3008 is so sound, its sponsor so influential, and its backing by official and voluntary health agencies so whole-hearted, that the risk appears minimal. Therefore, every health agency concerned should begin to plan for changes under the reorganization of state and local health programs. If S. 3008 becomes law, it may well be the administrative mechanism that will rapidly bridge the gap between medical scientific knowledge and its application in every community.

IMPLICATIONS FOR SCHOOL HEALTH SERVICES

In 1900, infectious diseases such as pneumonia, diphtheria, measles, whooping cough, scarlet fever, and tuberculosis were the major causes of illness and death in infancy and childhood. In 1966, the contribution of these diseases to childhood deaths, except for pneumonia and influenza (whose risk is substantially reduced), is negligible. Advances in the medical sciences and social betterment have accounted for this remarkable improvement.

At present, the greatest number of childhood deaths derive from accidents, congenital anomalies, and cancer. Also included as growth progresses are deaths from chronic diseases like diabetes, epilepsy, and the residue of congenital malformations. Added to these, of course, as causes of morbidity, are the more common conditions of dental caries, visual and hearing defects. They cause few deaths, but are major sources of disability. Yet, despite these many disorders, the risk of death is lower in childhood than at any other age of life.

As Yankauer (42) has pointed out, the childhood origin of much mental retardation and anti-social and neurotic patterns of behavior is well recognized. The high incidence of these and other mental disorders in culturally and economically deprived groups is well documented.

Poverty disrupts the growth processes and health of children. It also affects the cohesion and dignity of the family unit. A simultaneous attack on the basic causes of poverty is a prerequisite for improving the health of children. Urbanization, poverty, and ill health have a debilitating effect on whole families, and the children in such families often suffer severe damage. The effects of a bad start can last a lifetime.

With the exception of malignancies of childhood and many congenital malformations, the knowledge is available to reduce the ill effects of many of these mental and physical disabilities. The greatest deficiency is the lack of application of what we know to the great mass of persons in the ages from childhood to maturity. Therefore, in the area of social effort, drastic changes in the delivery and distribution of health services are necessary. The community itself needs to accept responsibility and demand action before comprehensive health care of high quality can be made available.

To apply to the early age groups present knowledge and new knowledge from expected advances in the medical sciences, a fresh look at school health services is imperative. The content and direction of these services require a complete overhaul in most communities of the nation. Fortunately, recent federal legislation and proposals for community health organization from such groups as the National Commission on Community Health Services (23) give us some guidelines for the future. Let us consider some of the steps that can and should be taken.

First and foremost, the next fifteen years should witness a blending of school and community health services. The school is a part of the community and its health services should function as an integral part of comprehensive health services.

In the past, the real block to progress has been the financial plight of the medically indigent and their children. The 1965 Amendments to the Social Security Act have greatly reduced that obstacle. Title XIX of the Act provides comprehensive personal health services to all persons under 21 years from medically indigent families. Title V, Maternal and Child Health, provides special benefits for school and pre-school children, including dentistry. Title II, Crippled Children, expands services for handicapped children, including the mentally retarded. Moreover, other federal agencies are extending health and social services. For example, the Office of Economic Opportunity is giving special attention to underprivileged children, particularly the pre-school (Operation Headstart).

The synchronization of these new resources with those already existing in the state and local communities is going to take time and the most skillful reorganization. Efficient management of school health services as a part of community health programs will require a high order of management even after program plans are developed and agreed upon. Interchange of health records between schools and health agencies will be facilitated by computerized central systems of Records and Reports. It is conceivable that in the next decade identification systems will be developed which will assign a social security number to each child on the first day of school or preferably at birth.

School nurses and visiting nurses in both public and private agencies and schools will need to be combined into one functional group. They will serve entire families, including the school children, so as to make full use of limited professional personnel. At the same time, high standards of comprehensive health services for every school child will be developed by educational and health experts. These standards will be enforced by official health agencies as a part of their statewide accrediting process for all health services and facilities.

On another front, fluoridation of public water supplies will undoubtedly be extended in the next ten years. When this is coupled with preventive therapeutic dental services in all the schools, it should be possible to markedly reduce the dental caries problem for the first time in the history of school health.

IMPLICATIONS FOR SCHOOL HEALTH EDUCATION

It has become evident that acceptance and application of basic knowledge about health is essential if each individual is to take prompt advantage of the advances in medical science, protect himself against the hazards of medical quackery, and achieve an optimum level of health for himself, his family, and his community (33). Since the development of favorable health practices is so dependent on the knowledge people have about their health, it is vital that the concepts learned be correct, that is, based on the latest knowledge and developments in the medical sciences. The most efficient and appropriate age for such instruction is during an individual's formal schooling experience, when attitudes are being formed and some habits can be modified. Thus, high quality health education for the entire school-age group is a necessary part of both public and private school instruction. This group may soon include persons from three to twenty years of age.

The teaching of health should be based upon broad concepts that include an understanding and acceptance of the individual's responsibility for solving personal, family, and community health problems. When such conceptual goals achieve reality, a more knowledgeable adult population should result, for it is hoped that much of what children learn now they will later practice as adults.

In 1961, the School Health Education Study staff began a series of investigations among school administrators, teachers, and students using a structured sample of elementary schools in 38 states. The Study aimed to shed light on three broad questions: What is the nature of school instruction in the public schools in the United States? What do students know and think about health? How can the findings be used to improve health instruction in the schools?

The study results indicate major deficiencies in what children know about their health, how health concepts are taught, and in the nature of the instructional materials used. The number of misconceptions and general ignorance about health led the researchers to conclude that in a majority of our public schools, health instruction is either grossly inadequate or virtually non-existent.

It was clear that a national approach to the problem was needed, starting with a revision of school health curricula and including modifications in the training given health teachers. Equally important was the necessity to create a climate in the school system that would give appropriate priority and adequate funds to health instruction.

The School Health Education Study has concerned itself mainly with national curriculum development. During 1963 and 1964, a group of educators and health experts teamed up to create and test an entirely new health curriculum. Unanimous agreement was soon reached that a conceptual approach to school health education offered exciting possibilities for health teaching and learning. Consequently, a unified concept of health was constructed and three key process concepts for the health curriculum material were delineated: 1) growing and developing, 2) decision-making about one's own health, and 3) interaction with others on health matters. Ten conceptual statements were then subheaded under the key concepts and represented the major organizing elements of the curriculum. Further subheaded under the ten directional indicators were 31 substantive elements. Students' goals in terms of health knowledge in the cognitive, affective, and action domains were formulated for the ten concepts and 31 elements. The details of the experimental curriculum are available in the Study's publication: "Health Education: A Conceptual Approach" (11).

Teaching-learning guides and experimental lesson plans were devised, with revisions and rewriting done by consulting specialists in health, education and related fields. Finally, in February 1965, the materials were tried out in four school systems in the country, using two of the key concepts under "Decision-Making" and "Interaction." The results are now being evaluated and preliminary reports are quite satisfactory, both to the Study group and the experimental teachers. From now until 1969, the remaining eight concepts, accompanying teaching-learning guides, and resource packets will be developed and tested. They will soon be made commercially available for general use.

We have described this project in some detail because of the School Health Education Study's uniqueness and the potential value of its contribution to school health education. One of the authors (Dr. Hilleboe) was chairman of the Advisory Committee to the Study staff. For a health administrator, it was highly educational and a most satisfying experience.

Many problems of adolescent children and teenagers (particularly in urban areas) stem from unstable socio-economic and psychological factors. Yet these problems also reflect misinformation about boy-girl relationships, sex, family life, alcohol, cigarettes, drugs, and the individual's role in community living. Misinformation often leads to distorted attitudes (17); together, these frequently culminate in anti-social action. Health instruction in the schools does offer hope of preventing some adolescents from falling into the unhealthy traps of premature drinking and smoking, promiscuity and illegitimate births, venereal disease and the use of habit-forming substances. Education for good health, of course, cannot exist in a vacuum. Ethics and responsibility must also be considered, at the same time, in the school and in the home.

During the next fifteen years, school health education should assume its rightfully prominent role in affecting community health activities. Just as school health and community health services are inseparable, school health education and community health education programs should become complementary parts of the whole network of health communications. In the long run, the quality and extent of community health is determined partly by the knowledge and attitudes citizens possess but, even more, by the behavior they demonstrate. School health education and school health services can help to prepare the children of today to become responsible parents and community leaders of tomorrow.

CONCLUDING REMARKS

Many of the advances made in the medical sciences during the past ten years have been the direct result of vast sums of money appropriated for research by the federal government. Inherent in these appropriations has been a mandate from Congress to translate new knowledge and skills into benefits for all the people. Paralleling these advances in the medical sciences, a burgeoning of interest and activity in the area of social reform has occurred. Because health is so essential to economic and social development, reform in the provision of comprehensive health services seems a natural accompaniment to these social reforms.

If oncoming generations are to benefit fully from present and predictable advances in the medical sciences major decisions must be made about how health resources will be organized and managed in the future. Jealously guarded professional prerogatives and vested bureaucratic interests will have to take a backseat to modern administrative methods. At the same time, the combined efforts and planning of governmental and university leaders, augmented by voluntary health agencies and philanthropic foundations, will be required. In the final analysis, achievement of the goals we have suggested is possible only if the concerted efforts of some of our nation's best brains are put to the task.

Thus, those of you responsible for "Designing Education for the Future," whatever your special field of interests, face a formidable challenge. This Conference is a significant step in the direction of the cooperative endeavors the future health and welfare of the nation require, bringing together as it does, so many specialists to offer their concepts of the task ahead.

1 Bowles, Frank. The Dual Purpose of Revolution. Presented at the Annual Conference on Higher Education, March 14, 1966.

2 Coggeshall, L. T. Planning for Medical Progress Through Education. Association of American Medical Colleges (Chicago) 1965.

3 Cohen, W. J. Social Policy for the Nineteen Seventies. Department of Health, Education, and Welfare Indicators, U.S. Department of Health, Education, and Welfare, May 1966, p. 8.

4 Converging Social Trends—Emerging Social Problems. U.S. Welfare Administration Publ. No. 6, (Washington, D.C.) 1963.

5 Doxiadis, C. A. Ekistics of Public Health. International Journal of Public Health, 8:60, 1965.

6 Duhl, L. J. Urbanization, Poverty and Health. Bulletin of the New York Academy of Medicine, 42:369 (May), 1966.

7 Frank, J. D. The Doctor's Job Tomorrow. The Pharos (April), 1966, p. 45.

8 Governor's Committee on Hospital Costs, Report of the. Private Printing, December 1965.

9 Grant, John. Health Care for the Community: Selected Papers. American Journal of Hygiene Monograph Series No. 21, Johns Hopkins University Press, (Baltimore) 1963, p. 184.

10 Haviland, J. W. Steps in Meeting the Nation's Health Goals. Bulletin of the New York Academy of Medicine, 41:1255 (December), 1965.

[11] Health Education: A Conceptual Approach. School Health Education Study, (Washington, D.C.) 1964.

[12] Hilleboe, H. E. The Changing Role of Government in Health Affairs. Bulletin of the New York Academy of Medicine, 41:1343 (December), 1965.

[13] Hilleboe, H. E. and Larimore, G. W. Preventive Medicine (Second Edition). W. B. Saunders and Co., (Philadelphia) 1965.

[14] Hilleboe, H. E. and Schaefer, Morris. Health Planning Guide (For Human Ailments and Environmental Hazards). In press, May 1966.

[15] Hilleboe, H. E. and Schaefer, Morris. Planning for Community Health by Problem Areas. Prepared for WHO Meeting on Health Planning, September 1966.

[16] Klein, D. and Haddon, W. Prospects for Safer Autos, Consumer Reports, 30:176, 1965.

[17] Masters, W. H. and Johnson, V. E. Human Sexual Response. Little, Brown and Co., (Boston) 1966.

[18] Medawar, P. B. Do Advances in Medicine Lead to Genetic Deterioration? Mayo Clinic Proceedings, 40:23-33 (January), 1965.

[19] Mencher, S. Trends in Government's Health Roles. Bulletin of the New York Academy of Medicine, 41:1350 (December), 1965.

[20] Morison, E. E. It's Two-Thirds of a Century—We've Made it so Far. New York Times Magazine, April 26, 1966, p. 34.

[21] Morris, J. N. Some Current Trends in Public Health. Proceedings of the Royal Society: Series B: Biological Sciences, 159:65-80 (December), 1963.

[22] Morris, Robert. Steps in Removing Barriers to Health Care. Bulletin of the New York Academy of Medicine, 41:1248-1275 (December), 1965.

[23] National Commission on Community Health Services. Health is a Community Affair. (Bethesda) 1966.

[24] Payne, A. M. Innovation Out of Unity. Milbank Memorial Fund Sixtieth Anniversary, (Denver), April 1966.

[25] Pickering, Sir George. Degenerative Diseases: Past, Present, and Future. Unpublished paper presented at the College of Physicians and Surgeons, Columbia University, New York, May 26, 1966.

[26] President's Commission on Heart Disease, Cancer, and Stroke, Report of the. Vol. I and II, U.S. Government Printing Office, (Washington, D.C.) 1965.

[27] Reston, James. The Computer That Turned Philosopher. The New York Times, May 22, 1966.

[28] Restoring the Quality of Our Environment. Report of the Environmental Pollution Problem, President's Science Advisory Committee, The White House, November 1965.

[29] Richmond, J. B. Gaps in the Nation's Services for Children. Bulletin of the New York Academy of Medicine, 41:1237 (December), 1965.

[30] Rutstein, D. O. Toward the Medicine of the Future. Bulletin of the New York Academy of Medicine, 41:1389-1401 (December), 1965.

[31] Schaefer, Morris and Hilleboe, H. E. The Health Manpower Crisis: Cause or Symptom? To be published in the American Journal of Public Health, November 1966 (est.).

[32] Schmitt, F. O. Molecular Dynamics and Brain Function. Unpublished paper presented at the College of Physicians and Surgeons, Columbia University, New York, May 26, 1966.

[33] The School Health Education Study—A Summary Report. Private Printing by the School Health Education Study, (Washington, D.C.) 1964.

[34] Social Security Laws (Compilation of). House of Representatives Doc. No. 312, U.S. Government Printing Office, (Washington, D.C.) 1966.

[35] Stewart, W. A. Manpower for Better Health Services. Public Health Reports, 81:393 (May), 1966.

[36] Tatum, E. L. Molecular Biology, Nucleic Acids and the Future of Medicine. Unpublished paper given at the College of Physicians and Surgeons, Columbia University, New York, May 26, 1966.

[37] Trussell, Ray E. Quality of Medical Care as A Challenge to Public Health. American Journal of Public Health, 55:173, 1965.

[38] Waste Management and Control. National Academy of Sciences—National Research Publ. No. 1400, (Washington, D.C.) 1966.

[39] Weinerman, E. R. Anchor Points Underlying the Planning for Tomorrow's Health Care. Bulletin of the New York Academy of Medicine, 41:1213-1226 (December), 1965.

[40] Williams, C. D. What is Health Education? Lancet, 1,7448:1205 (May 28), 1966.

[41] Wolman, Abel. Hippocrates Revisited. Herman E. Hilleboe Prize Lecture, New York State Annual Health Conference, (New York) May 25, 1966.

[42] Yankauer, Alfred. Maternal and Child Health Problems. Annals of the American Academy of Political and Social Sciences, 355:112 (September), 1964.

CHAPTER 5

Prospective Economic Developments

GERHARD COLM*

With the Assistance of Mrs. Carol S. Carson

Future educational requirements have to be seen in the frame of prospective economic developments. If I would, however, undertake to sketch what American economic life will be like in 1980, you may very well say that, with all the political, social, and technological uncertainties of our age, it is futile to prophesy the economic future 10 to 15 years ahead. In making economic projections we are, however, not engaging in the parlor game of crystal gazing. In education, as in some other fields of public and private responsibilities, decisions have to be made today which will have their full impact only a decade or longer from now. Granted all uncertainties, as human beings—who like to be regarded as at least partly rational—we want to make decisions today which to the greatest possible extent will serve the needs of the future.

PROJECTIONS AS A TOOL FOR EDUCATIONAL PLANNING

Economic projections should not be regarded merely as predictions, but as a tool for present planning. The test of their usefulness is not whether statements made today happen to prove accurate ten years later, but whether they have helped us to make more prudent decisions. Therefore, projections are not one-shot undertakings, but must be considered rather as a continuing effort. We try to anticipate the future, but must continue to observe developments as they unfold and to correct our projections when new, previously unknown factors come in to play, or when previous judgments need to be corrected.

As a frame of reference for the projections which are presented in this paper, the following methodological explanations may be useful. We distinguish between two different but closely interrelated kinds of projections. The first are of a *quasi-normative* character. They are designed to reflect the economic potential in a nation and the aspirations people have as individuals and as members of various groups (including voluntary organizations, public, national and supernational organizations).

Second, projections can be designed to formulate the *most probable* course. We call these estimates "judgment" projections because they re-

*Chief Economist, National Planning Association, Washington, D.C. since 1952; awarded Bernard Harms Prize from Institute for World Economics; has held professorships in prominent universities in Germany and the United States, has been Advisor or Consultant to numerous Government organizations, and has served on numerous missions to other countries; Author (with Theodore Geiger) of *Economy of the American People* 1961; and of other books and numerous articles and monographs in economics and public finance.

81

flect not only the probable effects of market forces, but also a judgment of the extent to which the government is likely to pursue the goals of the target projections and to what extent the government is likely to succeed or fail in that effort.

Target projections are used mainly to analyze policies that may be needed to promote full utilization of the potential and to approximate the goals of individuals, groups, and the nation. Judgment projections are useful as benchmarks for planning specific government programs, such as in education or transportation, or for private business planning.

The projections used in this report are those of the "judgment" type. But to repeat, because they are designed to reflect probabilities, they include government policies which are likely to be forthcoming in pursuit of national goals.

This symposium is intended to help in the long-term planning of education for the states in the Rocky Mountain area. But because the mountain states are a region of the United States, their educational requirements can be analyzed only within the framework of national educational requirements. Similarly economic projections for the mountain states must use national projections as their frame, but in addition must reflect special developments which are likely to take place in this region.

Economic projections can be useful for educational planning in three major respects. First, educational planning must be based on estimates of financial requirements for education. These are determined by costs per student and future student enrollment. The latter are based, in turn, on demographic data which imply, among other factors, economic differentials by regions and consequent internal migration. Second, economic developments affect the tax yields and future changes in tax structures which determine the financial resources available to meet educational expenditures. Third, a broad picture of the social and economic outlook can help to envisage the kind of education that will be required to meet the needs of the future.

Dr. Ahmad-Samarrie, a member of the staff of the National Planning Association (Center for Economic Projections), has prepared a special set of projections for 1970 and 1980 in which prospective developments for the nation as a whole are contrasted with those for the mountain states (see Supplement).

DEMOGRAPHIC PROJECTIONS AND PROJECTIONS
OF EDUCATION REQUIREMENTS

Most basic are projections of future population. Population in the mountain states is expected to increase from 6.9 to 10.8 million, or by 55.9 percent, from 1960 to 1980. This compares with an increase of 35.9 percent for the United States as a whole. The projected increase in school-age population shows approximately the same differential development as for total population in the United States and in the eight mountain states (see Table 4 of the Supplement). Thus, the population projections suggest that the mountain states will have a heavier load in providing educational facilities than the United States as a whole.

Projections of enrollment for the various levels of education for the United States as a whole are shown in the table below. College enrollment in 1980 would be by young people born in the years 1958-62, a period in which the birth rate had begun to decline. The very large increase in college enrollment, therefore, reflects more the increase in the rate of enrollment than an extraordinary increase in population in these age groups.

Projected Increase in Enrollment, 1960-1980

(For the United States—In Thousands)

	1960	1980	percent increase, 1960-1980
Elementary school or kindergarten	32,441	39,791	22.7%
High school	10,249	15,679	53.0
College	3,570	10,866	304.4
Total	46,259	66,336	43.4

Note: Based on Series B population projections and a "relatively rapid" increase in future enrollment rates computed as the average annual percent reduction, between 1950-52 and 1962-64, in the proportion of each age not enrolled in school, with a ceiling enrollment rate of 99.8 percent at any age. Alternative population and enrollment rates were also given in the source. SOURCE: "Projections of School and College Enrollment in the United States to 1985", Bureau of the Census, *Current Population Reports,* Series P-25, No. 338, May 31, 1966.

Projected enrollment figures by states for the same period are not available. However, Selma Mushkin and Eugene P. McLoone have made estimates for the period from 1962 to 1970 which are indicative of the trend of development.[1] These estimates show an increase by 26.2 percent (30.5 percent including pre-primary) for enrollment in public elementary and secondary schools for the eight-state area, compared with a 15.2 percent (19.6 percent including pre-primary) increase for the United States as a whole.

Projected costs of education increase substantially more than the projected numerical enrollment. Even excluding any general inflationary trend, costs of education increase more than the increase in the number of students because expenditures per pupil are rising as a result of, among other things, greater expenditures for science and similar specialized equipment and inclusion in the projections of expenditures for special summer and after-school enrichment programs, and because of the rising percentage of enrollment in high schools in comparison with less expensive elementary schools. According to the estimates by Mushkin and McLoone, the expenditures for public local schools in the eight mountain states are projected to rise by 88.4 percent compared with the increase in the United States as a whole of 74.7 percent for the period 1962 to 1970. We have every reason to assume that the expenditures will rise more than in proportion to enrollment beyond 1970 to 1980 as well, although no such estimates are available.

[1] *Local School Expenditures: 1970 Projections* (Chicago, The Council of State Governments, 1965).

Also with respect to public higher education, projected expenditures rise faster than enrollment for the period 1962 to 1970[2], again not counting the effects of a possible general price rise. In contrast to the projections for elementary and secondary education, for higher education the projected increases in enrollment and expenditure in the eight mountain states will be somewhat less than the increases in the United States as a whole.

Increase in Selected Education Indicators, 1962-1970

	Increase 1962 to 1970
Enrollment in public elementary and secondary schools[a]	
Mountain state region	26.2 - 30.5%
United States	15.2 - 19.6%
Total expenditures for public local schools[b]	
Mountain state region	88.4%
United States	74.7%
Total property tax collections[c]	
Mountain state region	65.3%
United States	62.2%
(GNP increase assumed for projection)	55.4%
Enrollment for degree credit in public colleges and universities[d]	
Mountain state region	101.3%
United States	107.0%
Total expenditures, capital and current, of public colleges and universities[e]	
Mountain state region	176.0%
United States	199.2%

[a] Selma J. Mushkin and Eugene P. McLoone, *Local School Expenditures: 1970 Projections* (Chicago, The Council of State Governments, 1965), pp. 17 and 19. Higher percentager represents inclusion of preprimary enrollment, fall 1962 to fall 1970.

[b] Ibid., p. 58; school year 1961-62 to calendar year 1970; Census of Governments definition.

[c] Based on data from Selma J. Mushkin, *Property Taxes: The 1970 Outlook* (Chicago, The Council of State Governments, 1965). A rate of lag of 0.83 percent, meaning that for each 1 percent increase in market value the assessed values rise only 0.83 percent, that prevailed in 1956-61 was applied to projected increase in market value of the general property tax base (excluding public utilities and autos). The effective tax rate, assumed in 1970 to be generally the same as that existing in 1962, was used to calculate the general property tax. Projected collections from special property taxes and the tax on automobiles and public utilities were then added to arrive at total property tax collections.

[d] U.S. Department of Health, Education, & Welfare, *Opening (Fall) Enrollment in Higher Education, 1962: Institutional Data;* and Selma J. Mushkin and Eugene P. McLoone, *Public Spending for Higher Education, 1970* (Chicago, The Council of State Governments, 1965), p. 46, fall 1962 to fall 1970. The Mushkin-McLoone projections of total enrollment (public and private) from which these projections of public enrollment are derived (see footnote p. 5) differ somewhat from the data presented in the table on page 4.

[e] Selma J. Mushkin and Eugene P. McLoone, *Public Spending for Higher Education, 1970,* p. 52; fiscal year 1962 to calendar year 1970.

---

[2] Selma J. Mushkin and Eugene P. McLoone, *Public Spending for Higher Education, 1970* (Chicago, The Council of State Governments, 1965). Two important assumptions on which these projections are based on: (1) the pattern of migration of college students to out-of-state schools is assumed to continue that existing in 1963; and (2) enrollment in private colleges and universities is assumed to continue the trend of increase from 1955 to 1963, with public enrollment being the residual of total enrollment less private enrollment.

With respect to financial resources for education, I will limit my discussion to public elementary and secondary schools. Most public elementary and secondary school expenditures are financed by local tax resources, of which the property tax provides about 90 percent. Very often concern has been expressed that, in contrast with the rapidly rising requirements for school expenditures, property tax collections are likely to follow general economic developments only with considerable time lag. This view has been questioned by those who emphasize the rapid rise in property values. In a study (in the same series mentioned above) by the Council of State Governments, Dr. Mushkin has projected the prospective increase in property values for the period 1962 to 1970.[3] Using her figures we can estimate the property tax collections assuming a "lag" in assessment practices similar to that of the 1956-61 period. Under these assumptions the property tax collections in the mountain states are likely to increase by 65.3 percent; in the United States as a whole, by 62.2 percent. Thus, for the mountain states, where property tax receipts are projected to rise by 65 percent, expenditures are projected to rise by 88 percent, which is considerably greater. For the United States as a whole the projected expenditures also rise faster than projected property tax collections, although the differential—a 75 percent rise in expenditures and a 62 percent rise in receipts—is not as great as in the mountain states.

I am not in a position to evaluate the accuracy of Dr. Mushkin's estimates in detail, but we should probably note two qualifications. It might be that for a longer-run perspective, the need for improvement in quality of education, and thereby in expenditures, may be underestimated. It might also be that there will be a greater lag in reassessment of property values in the future than in the past because of reduced pressure on local authorities to keep their collections in line with educational expenditures. This possible reduced pressure might be traced to (1) the slower growth in the school-age population which is projected for the future, and (2) the possibilities of alternative sources of finance, such as expansion of federal aid. If either or both of these are the case, the result would be to widen the gap between expenditures and property tax collections even more than is shown in the projections.

THE NATIONAL TAX STRUCTURE AND THE
POSSIBILITIES FOR FINANCING EDUCATION

The observations on prospective tax revenue of the federal government on the one hand and of state-local governments on the other were based on the assumption of no substantial changes in the national tax structure as a whole. Specifically, it was assumed that the income tax would remain the backbone of the federal tax system, and the property

---

[3] *Property Taxes: The 1970 Outlook* (Chicago, The Council of State Governments, 1965). I am grateful to Dr. Mushkin for her assistance in adapting these projections to the framework of this paper.

tax (largely real estate) would continue to be the main source for financing local expenditures, with sales taxes (general sales and excises) a major contributor to state finance. In addition, grants-in-aid play an important role in state-local finance. Is it likely that the national tax structure and especially federal-state-local financial relationships will remain unchanged during the next 15-year period? It is interesting to note (see following table) that no drastic change in the major patterns of the national tax system has taken place during the previous 15-year period. Noticeable, however, is the growing importance of grants-in-aid for the financing of state and local functions. In 1963, 11.6 percent of state and local expenditures were financed by federal grants-in-aid as compared with 9.7 percent in 1950. This percentage is bound to increase further as a result of new legislation. Noteworthy is also the growing importance of payroll taxes for financing social insurance.

Source of Government Revenue As a Percentage of Expeditures, 1950 and 1964-65

	1 9 5 0				1 9 6 4 - 6 5			
	Federal	State	Local	Totalᶜ	Federal	State	Local	Totalᶜ
Income taxes (individual & corporate)	58.5	8.6	—	39.3	57.1	12.3	0.7	39.0
General sales taxes	—	11.3	—	—	—	14.7	2.3	3.9
Selective sales taxes	17.4ᵈ	19.9	2.9ᵉ	18.5ᵉ	12.1ᵈ	18.2	1.4	12.1ᵈ
Property taxes	—	2.0	41.2	10.4	—	1.8	39.7	11.1
Other taxes	2.5	10.6	2.4	4.4	2.8	10.3	1.4	4.5
Non-tax revenues	10.9	11.3	20.6	14.4	10.0	12.7	22.0	15.1
Insurance trust revenueᵃ	7.8	11.9	1.2	7.8	14.7	14.5	1.4	12.9
Intergovernmental revenue	—	15.9	25.9	—	—	22.6	27.2	—
Borrowingᵇ	2.9	7.9	5.3	5.1	3.3	-7.2	3.8	1.5

Note: Components may not add to 100% due to rounding.

ᵃ Mostly payroll taxes; ᵇ Expenditures less revenue; ᶜ Excludes duplicative transactions between levels of government; ᵈ Includes customs duties; ᵉ Separate data not available.

SOURCES: U.S. Department of Commerce, Bureau of the Census, *Historical Statistics on Government Finances and Employment* (vol. VI, No. 4, of the 1962 Census of Governments), 1964; and *Governmental Finances in 1964-65*, June 1966.

What observable tendencies may bring about modification during the coming decades? There is, first, the certainty that both federal expenditures and tax revenues will continue to rise and, second, the probability that in an economy of reasonable growth, tax yields (under existing tax rates) will tend to increase more than expenditures, especially if the current increase in defense expenditures should be only temporary and may be followed by arms reduction. This would then lead to the possibility of a repeated reduction in federal income tax rates. If at the same time the financial needs of state-local governments continue to rise, there will be renewed pressure not only for additional grant-in-aid programs, but also for increased revenue from the state and local governments' own sources.

Here two possible developments may be mentioned.

1. Several states and even some local governments use individual and corporate income taxes as a source of revenue. Most states are reluctant to impose such taxes—or at least at high rates—because they are a "locational" factor for wealthy individuals and corporations with a high degree of mobility in their choice of residence or location of operations. To encourage wider and more uniform use of the income tax at the state level, a federal tax credit—similar to the present estate tax credit—has been proposed. The joint use of computers by federal and state authorities could simplify the burden both for the income-tax payers and the income-tax administration. One could imagine that the taxpayer fills out only one return with relevant information and that the computer calculates the tax liability under the laws both of the federal government and of the state in which the taxpayer resides. While I believe that some shift may occur in the relative share the federal government and state governments obtain from income taxes, I do not expect a substantial change in the relative importance of this tax source in the totality of the national tax system.

2. A growing number of states have been using general sales taxes as a source of revenue. For a long time it has been suggested that general sales taxes be made more equitable and less harmful by the use of the "value added" tax principle. It is probably true that a value-added tax can obtain more revenue without creating harmful distortions than could be obtained from a conventional general sales or turnover tax. If the states should face a situation in which more money needs to be obtained from tax sources other than income taxes, they might do so by adopting the value-added tax device.

Recently this tax has been advocated also as a partial substitute for the corporation income tax. Under the GATT (General Agreement on Tariffs and Trade) rules a sales tax may be rebated for exports, but a corporate income tax may not. This is a competitive disadvantage for countries which have no national sales (or comparable indirect) tax but which depend instead on corporate income taxes. Recently the Committee for Economic Development has advocated substitution of the value-added tax for a major portion of the federal corporate income tax—not only in connection with export rebates. I do not expect that the federal government will adopt a general sales tax, in any form, as a major source of revenue, except under conditions of a serious war contingency. The value-added tax has, I believe, more promise as a refinement of state sales taxes.

In general, I expect also on the federal level more refinement than a drastic change in the tax structure. It may well be that some of the nominal top-bracket tax rates may be further reduced in exchange for plugging existing loopholes.

The experience with the long deliberation of the 1964-65 tax reduction in support of steady economic growth and with the uncertainty about possible tax increases to combat current inflationary trends may lead to adoption of greater flexibility in the federal income tax. I do not expect delegation of authority to the President to adopt tax changes, but there is in Congress itself a growing conviction that simplified legislative procedures for making temporary changes in tax liabilities should be adopted. This, too, would not require a substantial change in the national tax structure.

Alternatives for Financing Education

From our discussion about expenditure projections for education and possible development of federal and state-local financial resources, the following alternatives for future educational financing emerge.

1. There is, of course, the possibility that desirable expenditures for education will be held down because of inadequate financial resources. With the prospective increase in productivity and total production the nation certainly can "afford" to meet the dollar requirements for future education. However, this may necessitate some adjustments in federal-state-local financial relationships.

2. Local governments may increase their own financial resources, particularly by raising property tax rates and by reducing the time lag between property tax assessments and the development of real estate values. The property tax, however, is regressive; that is, property tax obligations claim a higher percentage of income of persons at the lower end of the income scale than they do for persons in the high-income classes. Continued increases in the property tax, especially if it is possible to reduce federal taxes again, increase the undesirable regressive elements in the total tax structure.

3. The states may increase their tax resources and provide additional funds for education. As we have seen, this could be done either by increasing the use of sales taxes or by a wider adoption of income taxes. I believe it is probable that the states—not only for education but also for other increasing state-local requirements—will make increased use of general sales taxes, particularly if their distorting economic effect is mitigated by the use of the value-added tax method. But, sales taxes are also regressive, irrespective of the form in which they are adopted, although some increases will probably be regarded as politically acceptable if the yield is put to use for the benefit of the majority of voters. Sales tax increase beyond a certain point, however, does not appear likely, particularly if at the same time the federal individual and corporate income taxes can be reduced. It is not very likely that the proportion of the individual and corporate income tax in the national tax system as a whole will be substantially increased. There is, though, a definite possibility that state income taxes will be raised when federal income tax rates are reduced. This would require, however, some device by which the use of the income tax at the state level would be made more uniform and the burden on government and taxpayers of having multiple income taxes

would be reduced. The most extreme form of such simplification would be the tax-sharing device which is used in other countries with federal structure but which in America is believed to interfere too much with political self-determination by the states.

4. The tax-sharing device is in effect very similar to the so-called Heller-Pechman plan for federal grants to the states without specific determination of the purpose for which the grants are to be used. While both the tax-sharing and these block grants could help financial conditions of states—and indirectly local governments—and preserve the progressive nature of the national tax system, it would not assure that the additional resources would be used for education in general or for specific educational programs.

5. This leaves as the last possibility continuation and expansion of the present policy by which federal aid is given to education or to certain aspects of education. This course has been followed in recent years with the passage of the Elementary and Secondary Education Act of 1965, the National Defense Education Act, the Higher Education Facilities Act of 1963, and others. If the use of federal grants is further increased it is likely that the almost chaotic multiplicity of existing grant programs[4] will lead to some consolidation without, however, necessarily adopting the system of block grants.

These various possibilities are not exclusive alternatives. Most likely will be some combination: namely, some increase in state-local tax revenue associated with some measure of return, plus an increase in federal grants associated with a simplification of provisions for grants.

IMPLICATIONS FOR EDUCATION

When considering educational planning for such a long period ahead, there is a much broader issue than comparison of prospective enrollments and costs with the projected financial resources. This broader issue deals with the kind of emphasis education should have for the period which we are considering.

Ours has been called the age of technology. It is really up to future historians to find out what is the most important characteristic of our present age. A wise man said, the unique character of the present age is that it happens to be the one in which we are living! Perhaps the most important fact of our age is that the old world order is in process of liquidation and that we are going through the birth pangs of a new international order. Or the "population explosion" and the ability and the determination to do something about it may be the most important characteristic. Whatever the most important characteristic of our present and foreseeable period, there is no question that we are going through a period of very spectacular technological changes. These technological changes affect all aspects of our political, social, and economic life. By focusing on this

---

[4] There are at present more than 250 federal grant programs. See "Catalog of Federal Aids to State and Local Governments [Second Supplement, January 10, 1966]", prepared for the Subcommittee on Intergovernmental Relations of the Committee on Government Operations, United States Senate, by the Legislative Reference Service of the Library of Congress, issued April 6, 1966.

aspect we do not deny the importance of other related characteristics of our age.

From the viewpoint of technology, three historical phases may be distinguished. The period of the longest part of human history might be characterized as one where production was carried out by human beings with the aid of certain artifacts or tools. The second phase, or the first industrial revolution, can be characterized as a period in which human beings directed and serviced machines used in production. The third phase, which is the age of automation or cybernetics, can be characterized as a period in which control machinery begins to direct production machinery. This is a period in which machines perform not only physical and routine clerical activities but also assist in certain managerial functions. Some people, including a few experts on electronic technology, believe that automation and cybernetics will soon push the human being out of the production process.[5] One expert on automation has said that 15 years from now 2 or 3 percent of the population could do all the work that has to be done to satisfy the material needs of our society. Considering the spectacular technological advances of, let us say, the last 25 years, these views about what the age of automation and cybernetics may have in store over the next 10 or 20 years may not appear Utopian. In this case, the consequences for future education would be most radical. It would drastically change the whole ethical, economic, and social basis of society as we have known it in the past. The basis of our social, ethical, and economic systems has been the fact that man must work in order to earn a living. If we are entering an age in which only few workers are needed in the production process, people must obtain purchasing power regardless of whether they do remunerative work or not, and in which for most people nonremunerative work must give a meaning to their lives. The emphasis would no longer be on the need to work but on the need to develop a society based on no-work. It is obvious that this would present entirely new tasks for education. In this context we can understand what David Riesman meant when he said that modern technology threatens us with total destruction or total meaninglessness. If this is so, it is the major task of international politics to prevent total destruction and the major task of philosophers and educators to prevent total meaninglessness.

Economists can be expected to evaluate the likelihood that this technological explosion with all its consequencs for education and other aspects of life will take place in the near future. The economist can best express his evaluation by estimating the effect of technological developments on productivity, that is the output in goods and services per man-hour. If manpower is virtually being pushed out of the production process, productivity, by this measurement, would shoot up.

While I believe that the economic and social consequences of current technological developments deserve the most serious attention, the views to which I have referred grossly exaggerate, in my opinion, the likely immediate economic and social effect of the technological revolution.

---

[5] Ralph Helstein, Gerard Piel, Robert Theobald, "Jobs, Machines, and People: A Conversation," Center for the Study of Democratic Institutions, 1964.

This exaggeration is of such a nature that in my opinion, the policy advice that follows from it would have very harmful political and social consequences. We have reason to assume that the *revolution* in science and technological ability contrasts with the *evolution* of productivity in production. In opposition to the views which I have reported, I believe that the modern technology will make it feasible to meet many more needs and provide many more services, rather than replacing virtually all labor. For the next 10 to 20 years, I believe so much needs to be done in the fight against poverty here and abroad, in rebuilding our cities and improving our transportation systems that even with use of all feasible technology we can make full and effective use of those who are able and willing to work.

In contrast to those who believe that productivity is rising dramatically, most economists believe in a more evolutionary long-term increase in productivity. There are several factors that lend support to this latter view.

• Not all technological possibilities that replace manpower with machines are commercially profitable. In space exploration we have become accustomed to scientific development and practical application going almost hand in hand at a breathtaking pace. But we must remember that this is a program where costs count very little. The case of commercial application of technology is drastically different.

• Many technological advances result in better service, such as faster bank statements or faster and more accurate airline reservations. Better service of this type is not fully reflected in the increase in productivity as it is measured in statistics.

• Some technological advances could replace a human worker, but are best used in combination with a human. A learning machine can tell a student when he has made a mistake, but such machines cannot replace the personal influence of the teacher. The coming of such machines may not lessen the need for teachers, but may improve instruction.

• Modern technology, while making labor-saving devices possible in some fields, also requires highly labor-intensive work in research laboratories and in servicing of these devices.

• Technological developments often have harmful side effects, such as pollution of air and rivers, which require costly countermeasures.

• Increased productivity leads to greater affluence, which in turn means that the greatest increases in demand are for labor, recreation, entertainment, and education services. Also, the standardization of products associated with mechanization and automation also engenders demand for the opposite, the highly individualized artistic work by handicraft methods. Thus the increase in productivity sets in motion its own countereffect.

• As technological unemployment becomes a problem of serious proportions, the labor unions increase their insistence on job security measures which increase the costs of adoption of labor-saving devices and thereby retard their adoption.

Actually over a period of the last fifty years the average annual rate of increase in productivity in the private sector was 2.6 percent. During the last five years it was 3.6 percent, but over this period the economy moved from the recession level of 1960-61 to the level of relatively high employment, which superimposes the extraordinary cyclical increases in productivity on the secular increase. For the next decade or so I assume an annual average increase of about 3 percent, which would be higher than the historical rate but lower than the dramatic increase which some of the technocrats anticipate for the immediate future. With this rate of increase in productivity, and with a labor force expanding at an average rate of 1.7 percent per year, we have two main building blocks for our projection of total production; using these assumptions, total production of goods and services will rise from about $676 billion a year in 1965 to $1¼ trillion by 1980 (in constant prices).

By taking this less sanguine point of view with respect to the replacement of labor by machines, I do not want to underestimate at all the significant impact of technology on labor requirements. There are two important considerations. 1) Some labor is being replaced by automatic equipment, and this would create technological unemployment unless there is an offsetting expanding production of new and improved goods and services and opening up of new markets (particularly the potential market represented by population groups suffering from poverty and deprivation). In contrast with the view I have criticized, a study of existing deficiencies leads to the conclusion that policy should focus on satisfying the great, yet unfilled needs, rather than on pulling people who wish to work out of the production process. 2) The technological changes are bringing about drastic changes in the skill requirements for labor. There is less need for unskilled labor to perform functions which machines can do much better, and there is less need for skills which require years of apprenticeship and training. Instead, we need a highly alert labor force equipped with basic human skills and adjustability to new tasks. There will also be a demand for more people with professional training in humanities and science.

Our analysis of the prospective increase in productivity and of the needs and aspirations of the people leads us to emphasize policies which support the realization of these needs and aspirations, and which promote the adjustment of the labor force to the requirements of the technological age.

As productivity increases, not explosively, but substantially, actual hours of work will be reduced, not drastically, but steadily. At the present time most of the rank and file laborers still prefer a higher wage income (partly through payment of overtime) to a drastic reduction in the hours of work. However, hours of work now average about 38½ per week, and by 1980 we anticipate something like a 36-hour work week. In addition, it may become common to have a sabbatical for labor; that is, a period in which a worker, after several years of work, may need retraining or additional training, travel, or to pursue some other activity of his choice.

Also, the advances in medicine on the one hand, and improvement in old-age and survivor insurance programs on the other, will permit a longer period of productive retirement. Thus we need a new direction in education which, in addition to preparing people for the job requirements of our technological age, also prepares them for a constructive use of their leisure time.

I believe it would be wrong to conclude that we should replace our philosophy of work by one of non-work (nonremunerative work, that is) but we should supplement education for the work that needs to be done with education for a gradual increase in the opportunities for nonremunerative but useful activities. It is not an either/or situation, but one which suggests the need to dovetail these two educational objectives that follow from our economic analysis. This means that education has a great and growing responsibility in helping to develop the abilities and skills required by our technological age. We have, however, also the great opportunity to use some part of the resources which result from this technological development not only for such narrowly defined utilitarian purposes but beyond that for a truly humanitarian education. Unless we succeed in this, the technological achievements may ultimately be of little value. They may, indeed, have a more negative, destructive than constructive effect.

SUPPLEMENT

Demographic And Economic Projections For 1970 and 1980, United States And Mountain State Area*

The attached tables summarize past and projected changes in key economic demographic variables in the eight-state Western region relative to those in the nation. The states are Arizona, New Mexico, Montana, Idaho, Wyoming, Utah, Colorado, and Nevada. The projections for the combined region are the results of separate estimates for individual states. The 1950-60 decade is the frame of reference for analysis of past changes. The projections cover the period through 1980; they are based on the regional work carried out by the National Planning Association and periodically published in the Regional Economic Projects Series.

Table 1 shows resident population by age and sex. Resident population refers to total population exclusive of armed forces abroad; it is the sum of civilian population and armed forces personnel stationed in every state. *Sources:* 1960 data are calculated from Bureau of the Census, *United States Census of Population,* 1960 (area reports), and *Current Population*

---
*Prepared by Ahmad Al-Samarrie, National Planning Association (Center for Economic Projection).

Estimates, Series P-25. The 1970 and 1980 values are projected by the NPA—see brief statement of projection methodology.

Table 2 shows labor force estimates by broad age groups. Labor force refers to the number of persons 14 years and over residing in each state who are able, willing, and seeking to work. It includes the civilian employed, the armed forces stationed in each state, and the unemployed persons in the state. *Sources:* same as for Table 1.

Table 3 shows civilian employment data by broad industry groupings. The data are in concept equivalent to the national civilian employment estimates reported in the *Monthly Report on the Labor Force.* That is, they represent a count of persons employed in the state (including wage and salary workers, the self-employed, and unpaid family workers, but excluding dual job holders). No such data are published in official sources and had to be estimated by NPA. The employment data by industry are classified on the basis of the latest (1957) Standard Industrial Classification, and also were estimated by the NPA from a variety of sources.

Table 4 is a summary table showing the economic performance of the multi-state region relative to that of the nation.

A Statement of Methodology

The National Planning Association publishes five- and ten-year economic and demographic projections by states and multi-state regions. The projections cover the following set of indicators: population and inter-state migration by sex and five-year age groups; labor force and labor force participation rates by age and sex; civilian employment by two-digit manufacturing and one-digit nonmanufacturing industries; personal income by broad functional groupings; and gross national product for broad industry divisions. The state projections are consistent with the corresponding national values, periodically published in the NPA's National Economic Projections Series.

The projections of state population, labor force, and employment are highly integrated (interrelated) in our system. This can be made clear by outlining the steps necessary for the estimation of labor force. These entail: (1) the projections of labor force participation rates for specific age and sex groups; (2) the projections of resident population by age and sex assuming initially the absence of net inter-state migration, i.e., "closed" population projections; (3) the projections of state civilian employment by explicit analysis of future employment changes in specific industry division; and (4) the estimation of net interstate migration by relating the projected changes in civilian employment to the composite changes in the working age population and the corresponding labor force participation rates, and making preliminary assumptions about the future rates of unemployment in different states.

The projections of labor force participation rates represent largely judgment extrapolation of the 1940-50 and 1950-60 trends in the state-to-national ratios of age—and sex—specific participation rates (from the decennial population censuses), and multiplying the results by the BLS projected national participation rates.

State closed population is projected by adding to the base year state population, future estimates of natural increase—the excess of births over deaths. Births during a period are estimated by multiplying the number of females between the ages of 15 and 44 years by the corresponding state female fertility rates. The estimates of deaths assume that the death rate for each age-sex-color group in every state is the same as for the nation.

The projections of state civilian employment are the composite results of separate employment projections for thirty industrial sectors, most of which are manufacturing industries. State employment, by industry, is projected—using, in part, national industry control totals and "differential" shift analysis—evaluating the past and prospective competitive abilities of states to capture an increasing share of the changing national industry employment.

Finally, the analysis of inter-state migration is the principal mechanism by which we link the demographic and employment projections and maintain consistency among them. This consistency is achieved through a process of successive approximations involving the three sets of projections described above, viz., closed population, labor force participation rates, and state employment.

Brief Analysis of Trends

1. Measured by any indicator, the eight-state Western region has achieved a high rate of economic growth during the postwar years. For example, between 1950 and 1960 population increased by roughly 35 percent, compared to about 18 percent for the nation as a whole. A significant large part of this increase was the result of net migration of people into the region in search of more favorable employment opportunities and amenities (pleasant climate). Looking at individual states within the region, Nevada heads the list with a population growth of about 80 percent during the 1950's, followed by Arizona (75 percent), New Mexico (39 percent), Colorado (32 percent), and Utah (30 percent). Montana, Idaho, and Wyoming lagged behind many states in the rate of population growth, reflecting the heavy out-migration of people from predominantly farm areas because of rapid mechanization and consolidation of farms.

2. The pace of net migration into the multi-state region is projected to slow down over the next two decades as other parts of the country (particularly the South) improve their relative economic performance. As a result, the gap in the rate of population growth between the multi-state region and the rest of the nation may narrow considerably; however, the region will still experience a rate of demographic growth well over the national average over the projected period.

3. The growth in population hides diverse movements in specific age groups:

(a)   Because of the postwar population explosion, there was a sharp rise in the number and proportion of the younger age groups in the population of the multi-state region during the last decade. In 1950, people under 15 years of age numbered about 1.6 million and represented about 31 percent of the population. By 1960 their number had grown to 2.4 million, or 35 percent of total population. The same general pattern holds true for the nation. It is, however, significant to note that the share of the younger age groups in total population is much higher in the multi-state Western region than it is in the nation. (This is because the fertility rate is higher in the region than in the rest of the country.) The projections to 1980 show a sizable absolute increase in the number of the younger age groups, although in relative terms the increase is insignificant.

(b)   There was a sharp decrease in the proportions of the 15-34 year age groups in the total population of both the nation and the multi-state region during the last decade. This reflects the coming of age of people born during the 1930's and early 1940's, periods characterized by relatively low fertility rates. The baby boom of the immediate postwar years will mean a sharp increase in the number and proportion of these age groups, chiefly those between 25 and 34 years, over the next decade and a half.

(c)   In contrast, there will be a sharp reduction in the percentage share of people between the ages of 35 and 55 years in total population of both the nation and the Western region over the 1960-80 period.

4.   Total civilian employment is projected to increase from 2.4 million in 1960 to roughly 4.1 million in 1980, i.e., an increase of about 73 percent during this period. This compares with a 40 percent employment growth for the nation as a whole.

The bulk of the projected increase in total employment will originate in the non-commodity industry groups, particularly services, governments and trade. These industries account for a much higher percent of the multi-state Western region than of the nation. Manufacturing, on the other hand, plays a relatively small part in the economy of the region, although it is experiencing a much faster employment growth than its counterpart in the rest of the country.

5.   The region's per capita personal income is currently below the national average; however, the gap between the two are expected to narrow down considerably so that by 1980 the region's per capita income may approach the national average of $3680 (expressed in 1964 prices).

TABLE 1

Population By Age Groups
Total (In Thousands) and Percent Distribution
United States and the Eight-state Region.
1960, 1970, and 1980

United States

Age Groups	1960 Total	Pct.	1970 Total	Pct.	1980 Total	Pct.
0-4	20,364.3	11.2	21,895.0	10.5	28,345.0	11.6
5-9	18,825.3	19.9	20,918.7	19.8	25,215.0	19.3
10-14	16,910.3		20,510.3		22,094.0	
15-19	13,349.2	7.4	18,887.5	9.1	20,790.0	8.5
20-24	10,847.2	12.0	16,894.0	14.7	20,331.0	16.1
25-29	10,819.2		13,689.5		19,082.0	
30-34	11,901.2	13.5	11,319.6	10.7	17,234.0	12.8
35-39	12,481.2		11,011.0		13,832.0	
40-44	11,640.2	12.6	11,876.5	11.6	13,333.0	9.1
45-49	10,912.2		12,212.2		10,814.0	
50-54	9,650.2	10.1	11,115.5	10.1	11,355.0	9.2
55-59	8,464.1		10,042.0		11,279.0	
60-64	7,162.1	4.0	8,453.4	4.1	9,777.0	4.0
65 and over	16,659.3	9.3	19,542.5	9.4	23,086.0	9.4
TOTAL	179,986.0	100.0	208,367.7	100.0	244,567.0	100.0
Pop. 5-19	49,084.8		60,316.5		68,099.0	
% of total Population	27.3		28.9		27.8	

Eight-State Area*

Age Groups	1960 Total	Pct.	1970 Total	Pct.	1980 Total	Pct.
0-4	884.7	12.8	1,027.6	11.7	1,380.9	12.7
5-9	813.6	22.0	978.2	21.7	1,133.8	20.2
10-14	704.7		921.9		1,067.1	
15-19	542.6	7.8	829.5	9.5	1,012.9	9.3
20-24	448.4	12.8	725.2	15.0	913.4	16.2
25-29	436.9		590.2		856.3	
30-34	453.3	13.2	510.1	11.3	781.1	13.0
35-39	464.5		477.6		635.9	
40-44	428.1	11.8	477.7	10.9	523.2	9.2
45-49	388.8		475.4		479.5	
50-54	328.6	8.7	425.3	9.1	467.3	8.4
55-59	274.1		369.6		446.5	
60-64	224.3	3.2	295.9	3.4	376.6	3.4
65 and over	534.4	7.7	646.4	7.4	824.3	7.6
TOTAL	6,927.0	100.0	8,750.6	100.0	10,898.8	100.0
Pop. 5-19	2,060.9		2,729.6		3,213.8	
% of total Population	29.8		31.2		29.5	

*Includes Arizona, New Mexico, Montana, Idaho, Wyoming, Utah, Colorado, and Nevada.

TABLE 2

Labor Force By Age Groups, United States and
Eight-state Region, 1960, 1970, and 1980

Total (In Thousands)

AGE GROUP	United States			Eight-State Region		
	1960	1970	1980	1960	1970	1980
14-24	13,525.0	19,576.0	23,740.0	565.3	876.3	1,173.3
25-34	14,881.0	16,667.0	24,797.0	571.8	720.2	1,020.2
35-44	16,547.0	16,346.0	18,395.0	609.9	681.9	846.4
45-64	24,135.0	28,809.0	30,530.0	818.3	1,074.6	1,233.6
65 and over	3,241.0	3,389.0	3,436.0	110.7	115.8	125.0
Total	72,329.0	84,787.0	100,898.0	2,676.0	3,468.8	4,398.5
	Percent Distribution Among Age Groups					
14-24	18.7	23.1	23.5	21.1	25.3	26.7
25-34	20.6	19.7	24.6	21.4	20.8	23.2
35-44	22.9	19.3	18.2	22.8	19.6	19.2
45-64	33.4	34.0	30.3	30.6	31.0	28.1
65 and over	4.5	4.0	3.4	4.1	3.3	2.8

TABLE 3

Civilian Employment By Industrial Sector,
United States and Eight-state Region
(Thousands)

Industries	United States			Eight-State Region		
	1960	1970	1980	1960	1970	1980
Agriculture	5,801.0	4,295.4	3,380.1	270.3	206.6	171.6
Mining	600.0	539.4	484.4	74.3	69.4	66.8
Construction	3,734.0	4,738.7	6,086.8	174.3	250.2	360.0
Manufacturing	17,067.8	19,529.0	21,208.9	272.8	388.0	449.5
T. C. P. U.*	4,267.4	4,140.6	4,149.2	175.8	172.6	184.2
Trade	13,069.9	15,116.7	17,813.7	494.0	643.3	895.5
F. I. R. E.**	2,934.0	3,919.4	5,061.9	94.9	135.0	185.0
Services	11,336.7	14,898.9	20,635.6	454.6	665.9	938.5
Civilian Govt.	7,868.0	11,539.0	15,038.8	386.6	629.0	890.0
Total	66,678.9	78,717.2	93,859.4	2,397.6	3,160.0	4,141.1
Percent Distribution						
Agriculture	8.7	5.5	3.6	11.3	6.5	4.1
Mining	0.9	0.7	0.5	3.1	2.3	1.6
Construction	5.6	6.0	6.5	7.3	7.9	8.7
Manufacturing	25.6	24.8	22.6	11.4	12.3	10.9
T. C. P. U.*	6.4	5.3	4.4	7.3	5.4	4.4
Trade	19.6	19.2	19.0	20.6	20.3	21.6
F. I. R. E.**	4.4	5.0	5.4	3.9	4.3	4.5
Services	17.0	18.9	22.0	19.0	21.1	22.7
Civilian Govt.	11.8	14.6	16.0	16.1	19.9	21.5
Total	100.0	100.0	100.0	100.0	100.0	100.0

*Transportation, Communication and Public Utilities.
**Finance, Insurance and Real Estate.

TABLE 4

Comparison Between The United States and
Eight-state Region In Key Indicators

	Total				Decennial Pct. Rate of Change		
	1950	1960	1970	1980	1950-60	1960-70	1970-80
Population (thousands)							
United States	151,241.0	179,986.0	208,367.7	244,567.0	19.0	15.8	17.4
Mountain states	5,120.0	6,927.0	8,750.6	10,898.8	35.3	26.3	23.4
Population, Ages 5-19 (thousands)							
United States	—	49,084.8	60,316.5	68,099.0	40.1	22.9	12.9
Mountain states	—	2,060.9	2,729.6	3,213.8	53.2	32.4	17.7
Employment (thousands)							
United States	59,746.9	66,678.9	78,717.2	93,859.4	11.6	18.1	19.1
Mountain states	1,855.4	2,397.6	3,160.0	4,141.1	29.2	31.8	31.0
Personal Income (millions in 1964 dollars)							
United States	$228,152.0	$416,425.0	$626,231.4	$900,000.0	44.5	50.4	43.7
Mountain states	9,075.0	14,908.0	25,213.7	39,178.0	64.3	69.1	55.4
Personal Income Per Capita (in 1960 dollars)							
United States	$ 1,906.0	$ 2,314.0	$ 3,005.0	$ 3,680.0	21.4	29.9	22.5
Mountain states	1,772.0	2,152.0	2,881.0	3,595.0	21.5	33.9	25.9

CHAPTER 6

The American Partnership:

The Next Half Generation

DANIEL J. ELAZAR*

Nineteen eighty is only fourteen years away. Nevertheless, the task of projecting into the future and describing with accuracy the shape of the American federal system and its component parts in that year is no easy one. We stand, in 1966, just past the midpoint of our generation, some twenty years after the unleashing of America's postwar frontier and approximately five years after the beginning of the great thrust of governmental activity designed to help us accommodate ourselves to the new world of metropolitanism opened up since 1945. To gain some notion of how difficult projection is at this moment in our history, we need only think of the problems someone living in 1938, five years after the launching of the New Deal, would have had to predict accurately the shape of American life in 1952. Nor is this simply a matter of the indeterminacy of world affairs, though looming behind everything we may say here today are the great and imponderable questions of global war and peace. Even the domestic convolutions that can occur in fourteen years, roughly half a generation, can, as we well know, be unbelievably great in an age of rapid change; witness the changes in the status of American Negroes since 1954. Furthermore, projection is not carried out in a vacuum. By our very attempts to project, we alter the future and render our projections inadequate. This is especially true in our country because the American system of government has proved to be both durable and resilient, able to confront many new situations and absorb many changes without serious alteration in its basic character in part because men have acted contrary to projections they have made.

Rather than try to predict the future with its many unknowns, it first behooves us to understand the basic character of the American federal system—that combination of elements which has remained constant through generations of change—and to delineate the way in which that system has confronted new problems and accommodated itself to them. If we are able to do those two things, perhaps we will be in a position to identify trends and specify alternatives that will enable us not to predict but to act.

*Associate Professor of Political Science, Temple University; consultant to numerous agencies and organizations; published books include: *The American Partnership* (a study of the evolution of federal-state cooperation in the United States in the nineteenth century), *American Federalism: A View from the States* (a study of the contemporary system of federal-state-local relations from the vantage point of the states), and (editor of) Morton Grodzins' *The American System: A New View of Government in the United States,* 1966 (an overview of the entire cooperative system)

THE FEDERAL SYSTEM AS A PARTNERSHIP

In recent years there has been much talk of a "new federalism." The substance of this talk has been that we are now embarked on a new age of intergovernmental relations in this country, one which gives the federal government a greater role in domestic affairs than ever before and a particularly strong role in setting national standards to which the states and their local subdivisions must conform. There is no doubt some truth in the labeling of recent developments as new departures, to the extent that they represent federal involvement in new ways in old programs and in old ways in new programs. But the recent discussions simply reflect a growing awareness of an old truth; that our federal system has always been characterized by the cooperative interrelationship of federal, state, and local governments. Indeed, there are hardly any activities, be they local law enforcement or foreign affairs, which do not involve all three levels of government is some meaningful way. This was as true of 1816 or 1866 as it is of 1966. This patterned sharing of governmental activity by all levels of government reflects the fact that all three levels serve the same people, generally share the goals, and are faced with the same demands. American governments have traditionally assumed responsibilities only in response to public demand but when the demand has arisen, it has invariably been addressed to all governments more or less simultaneously. The twentieth century, with its great increase in the overall velocity of government and its emphasis on the complexity of public activities, has only served to sharpen the degree of interrelationship necessary for our political system to function successfully. Consequently it serves little purpose to think of the federal, state, and local governments separately without considering the way in which they function as parts of a single system.

Intergovernmental cooperation, no matter how patterned or routinized, is not to be confused with governmental centralization. The various levels of government in this country, no matter how much they collaborate with each other, have consistently maintained their own separate integrities within the framework of a common partnership. Indeed, the cooperative system implies the existence of partners with legitimate "personalities" and aspirations. Thus the single system is also a system of systems.

By now, certain basic principles of intergovernmental collaboration have become part of the American governmental tradition. Among them are: national supremacy, broad national legislative and appropriation powers, noncentralized government, and maximum local control. National supremacy has long been accepted by the American people reflecting the fact that we are one nation. The states are not constituted by separate peoples as in Yugoslavia or by special linguistic groups as in India, but are historically differentiated subdivisions of a single national society. The Constitution itself, as written and as interpreted by the courts over the years, gives the national government strong legislative and appropriation powers. Since the 1930's, these powers have been virtually unlimited by common agreement if only because the complexity of the nation's social and economic order has made it impossible to distinguish between erstwhile truly national and exclusively local functions.

At the same time, the national government is not a *central* government. There is no single center of authority or power in the United States, rather there are many centers: located in the fifty states as well as in Washington by constitutional design, in myriad localities by constitutional tradition, and in non-governmental institutions as well. Thus government in this country is not *decentralized* by virtue of decisions made in Washington but is *noncentralized* by the very terms of the constitutional compact which gives the states (and, by extension, their local subdivisions) primary authority as a matter of right.

The existence of noncentralized government has meant that, despite the increase in both the nation and state roles in many programs, domestic activities from education to the war on poverty are subject at all times to maximum local control. The larger governments set standards, provide funds, offer technical assistance, and do many important things to stimulate local activity, but ultimate control over the programs remains, to a great extent, vested in the local community.

The basic principles of American federalism are guaranteed through a number of key mechanisms. Among them are: separate administrative structures at each level of government; a nondisciplined, noncentralized party system; routinized political "interference" in administration; regular intergovernmental consultation; and a system of grants-in-aid from higher to lower levels of government.

The nation, the states, and the localities are all entitled to maintain separate governmental structures even as they cooperate functionally. Indeed, their structual autonomy serves to make cooperation possible without consolidation becoming its inevitable byproduct. Consequently, every government and the political forces which support it value structural independence as a means of "sitting in on" the great American political game.

The party system, based for constitutional and practical political reasons on nearly autonomous political organizations in the fifty states, works as a powerful bulwark to ensure that the men who make policy at the state and national level will be responsive to local interests and indeed will develop their policies so as to maximize noncentralized government and local control. Beholden as they are for reelection to their states and localities, American elected officials serve as living indicators of the existence of noncentralization.

The right of legislators to intervene into the administrative branch on behalf of their constituents, whether public or private, gives additional opportunity for myriad interests in the United States to express their needs and gain some satisfaction for them. The late Morton Grodzins has called this the "multiple crack" in American government; crack in two senses—a wallop against the system and a fissure through which the system can be penetrated. The existence of the multiple crack allows people who fail to gain satisfaction at one level of government or through one branch to try their chances at another.

Regular intergovernmental consultation means that policies are rarely formulated by one level of government alone. Rather, they are formulated federally, that is to say, by a sharing of the policy-making process among governments and governmental agencies. In this way, state and local interests are protected at the federal level and national interests are protected in the states and localities.

Finally, the system of grants-in-aid allows the larger governments to utilize their superior revenue raising powers to provide funds for the smaller governments to use to develop and implement programs in the public interest. This system, inaugurated in the earliest days of the Union, serves to vitalize the smaller governments at the least cost to them. At one and the same time, it has been a powerful bulwark against centralization and a means to implement national policies on a nationwide basis.

THE CYCLE OF GENERATIONS

The great principles and mechanisms of American federalism have remained constant over most of the 177 years since the ratification of the Constitution, to form the basic character of the American political system. Only the manner of their expression in political action has changed. The way in which their expression has been changed follows a pattern which can also be traced through American history; one which helps us understand the way in which they and the governmental institutions they support are likely to change in the future.

The rhythm of social change in America and elsewhere is best measured on a generational basis. Over the course of some 25 to 40 years, men pass through the productive phase of their life cycles then leave the stage of history as new men arise to take their places. While this changing of the guard is a continuous matter, the pattern of human relationship is such that the change is felt cumulatively as a generational one, in the Biblical sense. Each new generation of men to assume the reins of power in society is a product of different influences and is shaped to respond to different problems, heightening the impact of the change and encouraging new political action to assimilate the changes into their lives. The perceptive student of American history will note that the important changes in American politics have come on a generation-by-generation basis with great regularity, beginning at the very beginning of settlement on these shores. If he wishes to get some sense of the "timetable" for future change, he is encouraged to cautiously extrapolate from past generational trends. The accompanying chart outlines the cycle of generations and their relationship to governmental change over the past century and projects both ahead to 1980.

We are presently moving into the last third of a generation which began in the years immediately following World War II (between 1945 and 1948). Nineteen eighty is likely to come either at the very end of the present generational cycle or the beginning of the next one. Our generation, emerging after depression and World War, has had to confront three great problems. We have had to deal with the cold war and the end of colonialism, the problem of integrating the Negroes into American society and the problems attendant on the metropolitanization of the country.

THE CYCLE OF GOVERNMENT ACTIVITY IN THE LAST CENTURY

Year	Critical Elections	Active Periods of National Reform	Periods of Intensive State Activity
1877			
	GOP 1892 1896 GOP	1891 - 1895 Aborted Reform Period	
		1901 - 1907 Square Deal	
1913		1913 - 1917 New Freedom	
	GOP 1928 1932 Dem	1933 - 1938 New Deal	
1945		1946 - 1949 Fair Deal	
	Dem 1956 1960 Dem	1961 - New Frontier and Great Society	
1966			
1980	Dem 1984? 1988? ?	? ?	

The national response to world problems is and will continue to be a continuous one, varying in intensity from year to year, to be sure, but remaining the primary item on the agenda of the national government. On the domestic front, we are now approaching the end of the concentrated period of national legislation which occurs in every generation. The spurt of legislative activity embodied in the "New Frontier" and the "Great Society" and concentrated in the past four or five years, is similar to the concentrations of national reform legislation that have occurred in each previous generation since the founding of the Republic, concentrations such as the "New Deal," the "Square Deal," or the spurt of domestic reform legislation in the Lincoln administration. As in previous generations, the four or five year period of concentrated legislation at the national level appears to have come to an end, except for isolated pieces of unfinished business and modifications of the new programs which will continue to occupy Congress. Between now and 1980, then, we will have the task as a nation of implementing the new programs established in recent years.

Because of its peculiar nature as the major impediment to the maintenance of traditional American governmental patterns and institutions, the Negro integration problem will no doubt continue to preoccupy Americans nationally as well as on the state and local level until a reasonable solution is attained. However, we may expect the period of intensive national activity that began in 1954 to taper off and be replaced by intensified state and local efforts, so long as the latter maintain their efforts to deal with the problem.

Even with the spate of federal legislation of recent years, meeting the problems of a metropolitan society has remained primarily the province of the states and localities, though with the very important assistance of the national government to stimulate them. National activity in this field, while administratively continuous, becomes important as new activity only at specific points in the generational cycle when new legislation establishing new programs or revising old ones takes the center of the stage and sets the requisite national patterns for subsequent action at the state and local levels nationwide.

By or perhaps before 1980 we should reach the second stage of legislative activity in the generational cycle, the enactment of legislation consolidating the changes initiated during the reform period and opening the doors to activities that will attempt to meet the problems of the generation that will then be just beginning. Our own generation began with just such consolidationist legislation passed between 1946 and 1949. While one cannot say what kind of new legislation will be enacted by 1980, we can assume that it will have to do with the reform of administrative and legislative procedures and will probably pay considerable attention to problems of intergovernmental relations as well.

Politically speaking, the new programs of each generation have been invariably preceded by critical elections through which the reconstituted electorate—which changes from generation to generation as new people attain voting age and old ones die—determines the basic pattern of party voting for the new era, either by reaffirming the majority party's hold on the public by forcing them to accommodate to new demands and then giving them an extended mandate or by rejecting the majority party as unable to meet those demands and elevating the minority party to majority status. These critical elections, which attain their highest visibility in presidential contests, allow voters, blocs, and interests to realign themselves according to the new problems which face them.

Three times in American history the critical elections have elevated the party previously in the minority to majority status. In the series of elections beginning in 1796 and culminating in 1800, the Jeffersonian Democratic-Republicans replaced the Federalists. In the 1856 and 1860 series, the Republicans replaced the Democrats who had become the heirs of the Jeffersonians and in 1928-1932, the Democrats in turn replaced the Republicans. Between each shift, the critical elections served to reinforce the majority party which was successful in adapting itself to new times and new conditions. Thus in 1824-1828, the Jacksonian Democrats picked up the reigns from their Jeffersonian predecessors; in 1892-1896 the Republicans were able to reconstitute their party coalition to maintain their majority position and even strengthen it. In 1956-1960 the Democrats were able to do the same thing. The old coalition put together by FDR and the New Deal, which underwent severe strains in the late 1940's and early 1950's, was reconstituted and reshaped by Adlai Stevenson and John F. Kennedy to give the Democrats an even stronger majority than before, which made the programs of the 1960's possible.

With this record in mind, it is not unreasonable to forecast a continued Democratic majority through 1980 though with persistant and increasing erosion of that majority as the 1970's wear on. During the 1980's, we may expect another set of critical elections which will very likely elevate a new party to majority status; perhaps a reconstituted Republican party, perhaps some party whose existence is as yet unforeseen. In the interim, the Republican party will no doubt win the presidency once or twice, something that has happened in every generation in the past, by capitalizing on some particular individual with great national appeal. More significantly, it will probably gain power at the state and local levels. Republican governors in increasing numbers across the country, and perhaps to an exceptional degree in the Rocky Mountain states, will be trying to make positive records to strengthen themselves and their party for the immediate future and for long range gains. These vigorous young chief executives will be open to positive programs with political appeal and will seek to actively participate in their formulation.

THE GREAT SOCIETY AND THE PARTNERSHIP

Our present position in the generational cycle has certain immediate implications for the role of the states and their educational agencies in our system of government and may have certain special ones for the Rocky Mountain states. As the Great Society programs begin to take shape in the field as well as in legislation, we can see the way in which they are continuing old traditions of intergovernmental relations and moving into some new areas. As in the past, all governments are deeply and significantly involved in virtually every phase of the Great Society. This is true even of those programs which at first glance appear to be unilateral federal programs or federal-local programs designed to by-pass the states. Through the news media frequently give the impression that all creativity and decision-making are centered in Washington these days, this is most emphatically not so. Indeed, as recent articles in **Time** and **Fortune** have pointed out, one of the major concerns of the present national administration is that the new programs serve to build up the various centers of power in this country. President Johnson has characterized this concern as a new "creative federalism" but it really falls four square within the great tradition of noncentralization. Necessity alone is likely to enhance this concern as both population and programs grow too great for centralized direction. Talk of greater decentralization is even heard in Washington which, though bearing implications inimicable to the idea of noncentralized government, still represents a significant shift in emphasis.

At the same time, the press of new programs involving so many different agencies at each level of government as well as coordination across the levels, has created new demands for better intergovernmental coordination and for simplification in program administration. Some of these demands will no doubt disappear as the new programs become more routinized and those responsible for administering them develop patterns of administration and cooperation that can endure. Indeed, once routinization sets in, many of those with a stake in the programs will find that the very multiplicity of agencies and complexity of procedures serves their purposes better than any streamlining would. Nevertheless, over the next fourteen years, there will be considerable emphasis on improving administration and simplifying coordination if only because the amount of government activity in our society has now reached the point where it is virtually impossible to introduce any new programs without involving so many agencies on every level of government that some sorting out seems to be both necessary and inevitable. The development of computer technology and its application to government will almost certainly have a major impact in this regard.

The burden for this streamlining will fall on all levels of government just as the programs do. Indeed, fragmentation at the state and local level, enhanced as it is by federal grants which frequently allow state and local agencies to develop channels of support that by-pass their general governments, will require at least as much attention as the need for coordination at the federal level. The drive for streamlining may serve, if properly managed, to strengthen the general governments of the states and even of their localities, upgrading their abilities while giving them more control over the activities within their jurisdictions.

Still, as in the past, much of the burden of bringing together the various strands of governmental activity will fall on the local authorities. Following today's conventional patterns of thought which tend to accept bureaucratic principles of hierarchy, we tend to believe that coordination must inevitably come from the top. In fact, the very magnitude of governmental operations would make it impossible for any single center of control to develop at the top even if our system operated as a single pyramid. The empirical evidence has shown time and again that energetic local leaders are best able to ascertain which governmental agencies and programs (regardless of level) need to be coordinated for local purposes and to take the steps necessary to do so. In many cases, local leaders have been able to draw federal or state agencies that have proved to be uncoordinable at the top together into effective local partnerships. In doing so, they reflect the administrative benefits of America's traditional patterns of political "interference" in administration. There is good reason to believe that the nation's policy makers will discover the viability of this non-hierarchical pattern of controlling bureaucracy over the next half generation and begin to consciously make use of it in new ways.

Dealing with administrative difficulties will be only one aspect of the fulfillment of current programmatic innovations over the next half generation. The shape of the programs will also be subject to refinement and development, partly by remedial action at the congressional level and to a great extent, through implementing action at the state and local levels. If present trends continue, the shaping will emphasize more and more planning, greater equalization of public benefits, and great emphasis on collective action.

This conference is one example of the new emphasis on planning. Not only will the requirement for planning to qualify for federal aid grow, but there are likely to be greater efforts to implement the plans that are produced. It is unclear whether these efforts will be successful, at least partly because so many of the plans that are prepared, while meeting the symbolic demands placed upon them, really do not reflect the basic values and fundamental interests of the American people.

One of the elements that may promote greater implementation of plans is the quest for equalization which is part of the Great Society's theoretical foundation. As of now, there is still a coincidence between the policies of those who seek this equalization within the framework of the traditional American desire to provide equality of opportunity for all and the aspirations of those who believe that we must strive for something approaching equality of condition instead. However, there is a tendency built into certain of the Great Society programs that supports the notion of equality of condition going beyond simple provision of equality of opportunity, and, increasingly, public discussion is being couched in such equalitarian terms. This is certainly the case in the realm of education. The issue will be joined as the new programs move toward fulfillment and the outcome will have decisive consequences for the role of government in American society.

Finally, the notion of collective action, which is closely related to the drive for equality of condition, is likely to be pressed by unofficial and some official spokesmen for the new programs. I use the term collective action advisedly, but it would not be entirely amiss to use the term collectivism to describe the more radical versions of Great Society policy. Again, there is a tension between those who advocate collective action in the cooperative spirit that falls with the American tradition of individualism and partnership and those who are willing—even eager—to move toward real collectivism in order to secure their equalizing and planning goals.

Emphasis on planning for good or ill means a concomitant deemphasis on market decisions or on letting nature take its course. This is not to say that planning cannot be used in conjunction with free decision-making; indeed many planners have concluded that it is best used to aid "nature" or "the market," not to try to replace them. But the thrust of many leading supporters of planning today seems to be away from that kind of planning toward the notion that all decisions should be pre-planned and in line with some overall plan.

By the same token, the thrust for equalization makes the maintenance of legitimate distinctions and differences more difficult. This not only operates to limit the choices of individuals and groups but also the possibilities for state and local diversity. It is always difficult to separate the setting of necessary new standards from the drive for standardization, to determine what is necessary and what goes beyond necessity. This difficulty is enhanced when there is a lack of concern for diversity. This will be a recurring problem for the next half generation, particularly in regard to state and local differences within the federal system. In major fields like education, public welfare, and employment security, we see the drive for standardization going full force today as the leading spokesmen for the new programs in those fields argue that differences among the states are detrimental to the national welfare. Coupled with this is the notion that local distinctiveness or uniqueness is to be valued only where it does not extend into policy areas. States and localities could possibly lose the right to opt out of national programs, changing the old system whereby they were simply encouraged to opt in.

It should be recognized that the aforementioned possibilities may remain more theoretical than practical. For example, whatever the possibilities, the states and their subdivisions have never chosen to opt out of the great federal grant programs created since the New Deal or even earlier, primarily because enactment of those programs has itself reflected the existence of a national consensus spread nationwide. There is no reason to believe that this will be any different in the future.

At the same time, the very multiplication of federal aid programs available opens up many more choices for the states and localities. There are already so many grant-in-aid programs available from Washington that most states, if not all, are picking and choosing among them. It is true that the great grant programs covering highways, public health, and now education, are universally accepted and utilized but the myriad of smaller programs are being selected by the states and localities increasingly on the basis of their own overall policy decisions.

Beyond the question of simply participating in the programs, the states and their local subdivisions increasingly determine how much federal money they will use, often not taking all available for them because they are unwilling to divert their own resources from other programs which they consider to be of higher priority to match the federal grants fully. In this way, the states and their subdivisions have actually developed greater flexibility within the framework of the grant programs now than in the past. In some cases, this has led to counter-pressures for federal grants that do not require local matching in order to virtually insure the states' participation on the assumption that they will willingly take something that does not cost them anything. There may be increasing pressures along these and similar lines in the political arena.

To 1980 and Beyond

Within the policy framework projected above, we can make certain specific projections for the immediate future:

(1) *All governments will continue to grow*—in size, expenditures, and scope of activities. With the possible exception of two decades in the middle of the 19th century, government has grown consistently in all three categories since the establishment of the Republic. There is nothing on the horizon to indicate that this trend will be reversed. On the contrary, as the role of government in our society grows greater, so governments must continue to grow. For the moment, it seems as if governmental growth is primarily federal growth, but appearances are deceiving. One of the important discoveries of the new thinking about federalism is that, since the sum total of power in American society is constantly growing, government can grow without increasing its relative share of that power and the federal government can grow without decreasing the power available to state and local government.

We are presently in a period of dramatic growth in federal activity, accompanied by a certain growth in federal expenditures. This growth period, however, has not extended to the field of federal employment which has remained more or less stable for nearly half a generation. The 2.6 million workers employed by the federal government is actually 100,000 less than were employed in 1946. Moreover, federal growth is accompanied by state and local growth of equal magnitude. While the federal budget is increasing, so are state and local budgets, to hold the relative federal and state-local shares of governmental expenditure nearly constant. (Within the states, on the other hand, state expenditures are growing markedly in relation to local expenditures). State and local employment rolls are increasing even more rapidly, up 4.7 million since 1946 to 8 million today.

So long as the press of world affairs requires the federal government to devote something like 50 percent of its budget to paying for current military expenditures and another 20 percent to paying interest and costs from past wars, it is unlikely that spectacular federal growth in the domestic field will continue for more than brief periods. On the contrary, the major growth in government over the next half generation will continue to take place at the state and local levels as it has since the end of World War II. The states and their localities presently account for two thirds of the total governmental expenditure for domestic purposes and are likely to continue to do so unless there is a radical decline in world tensions. This may be obscured by the great growth in actual dollars appropriated by Congress that we can reasonably expect. Fiscal experts are predicting an annual federal budget of $175 billion by 1976. If such a figure is reached—and it does not seem in the least implausible—it will be paralleled, no doubt, by annual state-local expenditures of close to $125 billion.

As governments grow, administrative decision-making will continue to occupy an increasingly important role in our lives. Legislatures will continue to set broad policy goals in their legislation and to prescribe the outlines for administrative regulations. Both of these activities are likely to become even more significant in shaping the administrative decisions, primarily because legislatures will also work to devise means to oversee the administrative agencies and check their discretionary activities in crucial ways. Congress is already discussing potential reforms along these lines and the state legislatures are being encouraged to do the same by a growing number of legislative reform groups. The next fourteen years are likely to see an intensification of the drive to improve and strengthen legislatures just as the last half of the previous generation was devoted to the development of administrative techniques to handle big government.

Within the bureaucracy, there will be greater emphasis on the use of trained professionals. Routine administrative operations are being increasingly taken over by computers so that the percentage of skilled specialists in the overall civil service at all levels of government is likely to increase. Increase in expertise will inevitably strengthen the administrative branches vis-a-vis the legislature unless the legislatures follow through with programs presently under discussion to acquire experts of their own. At the same time, increased expertise at the state and local levels will not only improve the quality of their governmental services but will put the states and localities in a better position to negotiate with their federal counterparts. Not only will these professionals share the same professional values and long-range aspirations, with a consequent easing of communications, but they will also enable their governments to negotiate from positions of greater strength. This has been true of established programs in the past whereby the states and localities have gained greater control over cooperative programs whenever they have developed greater expertise to handle them. Certainly the field of education provides a superb example of how this is so. Today the real repository of educational expertise is at the state and local level. As long as this remains the case, federal aid will be of an assisting variety rather than a threat to state and local autonomy.

(2) *Sharing will be equally important in the future and will even seem to increase.* Since intergovernmental cooperation is already pervasive, it is difficult to talk about an increase in sharing. In fact, the amount of sharing will grow in absolute terms as government activity increases without changing the basic degree of sharing. There will no doubt be changes in the respective roles of different governments and government agencies in specific cases, and new forms of sharing are likely to develop. Regional arrangements are beginning to loom large on the governmental scene ranging from such long term organizations as the Appalachian Regional Commission to this Conference. This new regionalism is promoting new kinds of cooperation in at least two ways; an increase in subnational planning and programs to deal with problems involving more than one state and the involvement of both the federal government and the states in joint policy-

making at the very beginning of new programs. Various approaches to regional cooperation are likely to be tried with increasing frequency over the next half generation, with varying degrees of success.

The character of sharing over the next half generation is more difficult to forecast. One could simply conclude that old patterns will continue with minor adjustments. There are, however, some problems, well-nigh perennial ones, which make the issue somewhat more problematical. It is entirely possible that the widespread recognition of sharing will lead to the use of sharing devices as a means to achieve de facto centralization. If the smaller governments are forced into a position where they must cooperate without really participating in decision making, simply on the grounds that cooperation is expected of them, sharing will be formally preserved without achieving the goals for which it is intended.

In addition, there is the question of direct federal-local relations and even more vital, that of federal-private relations. One of the characteristics of Great Society programs has been the increased emphasis on federal aid to anybody. Thus the federal government is not only developing more programs in which localities can deal directly with Washington to gain assistance, but is revising older programs to allow selective direct federal-local relations where none existed before. Though there are some tendencies to the contrary, it is likely that such relationships will continue to grow in the immediate future.

In a more radical vein, traditional concepts of federalism are being challenged by notions of pluralism whereby great national associations or corporations with powerful means to influence Congress are given responsibilities that might otherwise have been allocated to state or local governments. In some cases, there is every justification for this. In others, the issue is unclear. For example, the use of private industries to run Job Corps centers under federal contracts may or may not be the best way for the federal government to provide assistance to impoverished youth who need additional training. Federal-private relations are also a form of sharing and unquestionably help to perpetuate noncentralized government. At the same time, they may alter the shape of the system if they proliferate over the next fourteen years. There will be, almost certainly, pressures for their proliferation, particularly since the large corporations that have grown great as a result of federal defense spending are beginning to seek alternative ways to continue to draw upon the federal treasury for their profits in an effort to lessen their dependence on defense contracts. In one sense, this is all to the good, since it will make future disarmament efforts easier on the economy. However, if these efforts are not fitted into the federal system, the states and localities may suffer from them.

(3) *The states will have to act constantly and with greater vigor to maintain their traditional position as the keystones in the American governmental arch.* The continued central role of the states is no longer a foregone conclusion within the framework of American federalism. While it is not seriously possible to conceive of the states not playing a major role, the significance of their role will depend to a very great extent upon their responses over the next half generation to the challenges which confront

them. Now that the federal government is meeting little public objection to its involvement in the range of domestic activities and direct federal relations with the localities are becoming equally accepted, it is possible that the role of the localities will be emphasized at the expense of the states. However, the very thrust towards regionalism indicates that sheer federal-local relations will not be sufficient to handle the dispersal of power and operational activity which is considered desirable in this country. The localities cannot confront the powerful federal government alone, nor can overall policy be made in Washington for the country as a whole. Moreover, the states, by their sheer existence, have developed concrete patterns of politics and culture which infuse their localities with unique ways of doing things. Hence, they do not stand at a particular disadvantage in defining a positive place for themselves in the new federalism. But, in order to do so, they will have to function like general governments and indeed, like central governments. It will no longer be possible for them to rely simply upon their role as conduits funneling federal aid to their localities or local requests to Washington, nor will they profit by acting as simply another set of local governments. Rather, their strength lies in the fact that they are general governments with central government responsibilities toward their local subdivisions.

The governors of the states show every indication of recognizing this and of seeking to capitalize on it. Such recent actions as the Interstate Compact on Education, which is a clear attempt on the part of the governors to gain some measure of general control over educational programs within their states that have previously been highly fragmented, is one good example of this new recognition of their role. The Appalachia program, which channels decision-making through the general organs of state government rather than through the specialized agencies, is another. The political situation of the next fourteen years which will encourage Republican governors to make records in their states is likely to stimulate this kind of response. Democratic governors will be forced to respond in kind if only in self defense.

The states will have additional advantages in defining their position because of the nation's population growth. The sheer population size of the country is making the dispersion of political and administrative decisions necessary and desirable now, in the way that the problem of territorial size made such a dispersion necessary and desirable in the past. At the same time, the constant growth of population in the fixed number of states offers each state greater opportunity for internal viability. One need only look at the States of California and New York to see how this is so. States of some 18 million people, they are more populous than all but a few of the sovereign nations of the world and have larger budgets than all but five of them. California maintains an educational plant larger than that of any country with the exception of the Soviet Union. Such states are able to draw upon many kinds of skills found within their borders simply because they have enough people to produce a variety of talents. While they may never become as large as their giant sisters, sheer passage of time will enable most states to reach a stage in population growth that will give them greater flexibility as well as more money with which to function, thus adding to their potential for self-directed action. Even today, the Rocky Mountain states have populations equal to or greater than 29 sovereign nations.

(4) *Localities will have to struggle for policy—as distinct from administrative—control of the new programs.* Despite the fact that federal-local relations are increasing and are likely to increase, the localities are not assured that these relations will continue to emphasize local decision-making with outside financial and technical assistance as in the past. The evidence is that the present pattern will be continued. Nevertheless, the localities will have to compete against the pressures for excessive equalitarian leveling and collectivist action that could make local control a relatively hollow achievement. These pressures will continue to be directed toward eliminating the policy-making powers of local government, particularly in the realms of housing, zoning, and urban development. The growth of expertise at the local level could offset these pressures unless the new urban professionals themselves identify with these centralizing goals.

In their efforts, the localities would be wise to place increased reliance upon their states. The major pressures for direct federal-local relations that bypass the states come from the nation's largest cities, ones whose populations equal or exceed the populations of many states, and who consequently have sufficient self-sufficiency and expertise to work directly with Washington without being at a great disadvantage. As the nation's population decentralizes within the metropolitan areas and within the belts of urban settlement that are forming in various parts of the country, more people will be living in smaller units of local government. Since the chances for local consolidation have diminished and indeed, the value of such consolidation has become incrasingly suspect, there will be relatively few local units capable of dealing directly with Washington, simply by virtue of their lack of appropriate personnel. The states will provide assistance in most cases for a certain price, namely a "say" in local decisions. While this price is not likely to be great—the states are also committed to the principle of local control—it will give the localities additional need to define their positions as well.

(5) *The Rocky Mountain area will enter a period of great governmental growth.* Within the context of nationwide change outlined above, the Rocky Mountain states will face some special problems. By and large, these states, among the least populated in the Union, have had less reason to adapt themselves to the new growth of government in the past and consequently will have more to do in the immediate future. The new programs of the Great Society are tailored primarily to the needs of the Eastern states. This in itself is not unusual. The Eastern states represent the nation's "main street" and have, with few exceptions, constantly maintained the greatest influence in Washington. This automatically forces the states of the West and the South to undergo greater adjustments in response to reform periods than might otherwise be expected. The reform periods of the previous generation, both the New Freedom and the New Deal, were exceptions in this regard, since they served as much to redress the balance between the Northeast and the South and the West as to enhance the power

of the first section. The Great Society follows more traditional lines. Thus, the states of the Rocky Mountain area are less prepared to make use of many Great Society programs than their more populated and more heavily industrialized sisters. Nevertheless, these programs come with a virtual mandate for nationwide implementation. The next fourteen years, then, will see great adjustment in the Rocky Mountain area, primarily at the state level, but at the local level as well.

At the same time, the demands for increased expertise to enable the states to fill in their proper role in the system will fall particularly heavily upon the Rocky Mountain states. Drawing from smaller populations with fewer establishments prepared to train local experts and with the greater gap to overcome, the Rocky Mountain states will be stretched to the maximum to develop the quality of administration that will give them their rightful place in the nation's governmental system. If this is true of the states, it is even more true of the localities. Traditionally, the localities of the Rocky Mountain region, like those of the trans-Mississippi interior generally, have served to provide young professionals with seasoning before they are hired by the larger cities on either coast where they bring their careers to culmination. While this often means that the localities in the interior get the advantage of the most energetic young people, it also means that they lose those people when they reach the peak of their influence in national councils.

The Rocky Mountain states possess one major advantage, however. They have learned how to live within the framework of a federal system in which the federal government plays a very active role. As public land states created through massive federal assistance three or more generations ago, they learned how to carve out autonomous positions in a system loaded heavily in favor of the federal government, hence they are not confronted by a new phenomenon when they find heavy federal involvement in their affairs. On the contrary, they can capitalize on techniques for living with that involvement which they have perfected in such a way that federal aid benefits them rather than interferes with their processes of internal government.

Finally, it is quite likely that the migrational patterns of the country will serve to enhance the position of the Rocky Mountain states by the end of the period under discussion. At the present time, the heaviest migrations, while still tending westward, serve to increase the power of the Pacific Coast states more than those of the Rocky Mountain interior. However, just as in the last century, the Pacific Coast states were settled first before men turned to the interior for opportunity after the 1860's, so may we expect men to turn to the interior once again after the 1960's. If the proper governmental base exists to provide the institutions necessary for economic growth, then men will come to this region to make opportunities for themselves, thus creating larger population complexes in the Rocky Mountain West, aiding those states and localities in their drive for proper roles in the federal system.

What of the years after 1980? By 1980 Americans will be on their way to discover new problems for government to deal with. While it will take a decade or more for those problems to find their way onto the national stage as programs, the states and localities of the nation will be apt to confront them or at least to formulate and refine them in the years of the 9th decade of this century. It is hard to forecast what those problems will be. It is possible that the irresistable momentum of planning and government activity will continue to stimulate a drive for more planning and more government intervention into the lives of the citizenry. Or it may be that Americans will seek solutions which call for limiting or shifting government's role. The combination of social and technological developments as yet unforeseen will be a decisive influence here. Certainly, one of the primary tasks of state and local educational institutions during the next half generation is the development of a new generation that will be able to consider and define those new problems.

SOME IMPLICATIONS FOR EDUCATION

There are some clear implications for education from the foregoing analysis. More educational time will be government supported in the future. This means, on one hand, that state and local governments will support more years of schooling, perhaps more hours of schooling, as well. Moreover, there will in every likelihood, be more federal aid to education over the next fourteen years. This aid may follow present patterns of grants for specific programs and needs, if only because there is a strong reluctance in Congress to appropriate federal funds for general aid to education without tieing those funds to some particular program deemed to be in the national interest.

At the same time, if some plan for distributing federal revenues to the states automatically and without strings is adopted, this could well take up the role of increased federal allocations for education. It would undoubtedly serve the same purpose because as education needs grow greater, the states are more likely to appropriate any unallocated funds to those needs without formally being required to do so. Moreover, since educational expertise is concentrated at the state and local level, there is no serious problem as to the use of those funds. They will be used properly without necessarily having federal requirements attached to them.

It is also fairly clear that future increases in expenditures for education will have to come from some level above that of the local community. Most localities are already spending some sixty percent of their total tax dollar for educational purposes, starving many other necessary local services in the process. Thus, they have every reason to seek outside aid for increased educational expenditures and even to reduce the share of their budgets devoted to education at the present time. This aid could come from either the states or the federal government, so far as they are concerned.

Federal support for education will continue to open doors for government aid to non-public schools. We have already seen how this is so. We have also seen that, for the moment, the decisions as the extent to which non-public schools will be assisted, are to be made at state and local levels. State constitutional restrictions plus local reluctance to extend that aid are leading to mounting pressures at the federal level to force them to assist the non-public schools. These pressures will continue to mount and are likely to force a crisis in federal-state relations and more important, a crisis in intracommunity relations as states are confronted with these pressures and the counter-pressures they are sure to evoke.

Perhaps the greatest new development on the policy front to be expected within the next half generation is the shifting notion of who controls public educational policy. Two trends are evident here. On one hand, there are the proponents of a national educational policy set in Washington and those who advocate the maintenance of the present system, whereby educational policy is set on a state and local basis. If local control of educational policies is to be preserved, the states will have to step in. There are already strong signs that they are doing so, but in order to do so, a second problem is encountered and this is the struggle between those who are professionally involved with education and the generalists in state government. Undoubtedly, the conflict within the next half generation will not only be between proponents of federal control and state or local control but between generalists and specialists. We may see the specialists seeking ostensibly federal control in order to preserve their powers under the present system which favors the professionals while generalists will be arguing for more state control in order to increase their role in educational policy-making.

Finally, and in a somewhat different vein, the increasing complexity of American government means that better education in the political processes of this country—what we have called in the past civics—is absolutely necessary. Schools at all levels must develop means to convey some sense of the functioning of the American system to their students, not along the simplistic lines of the past, or for reformist purposes as so frequently has been the case in recent years, but to give them an understanding of a very complex system of government so that they may function as intelligent citizens within it.

The Rocky Mountain states will be particularly affected in two ways. In the first place, they will be forced to develop stronger institutions of higher education than they have been able to develop in the past. Your states have had notable successes at the elementary and secondary levels. For years you have had an enviable reputation for good schooling below the college level. However, the very limited size of your populations has prevented any one of the Rocky Mountain states from developing the kind of higher educational plant that is needed to provide the brain-power now required within the region. There will be great pressures on you and your governments to do something about this and greater opportunities as your population grows.

In the second place, nonpublic education has played a much smaller role in the Rocky Mountain states than it has in big cities east of the Mississippi River. The pressures to extend assistance to nonpublic schools, then, will represent more of a departure from past patterns than in the East. Should there be federal requirements along this line, the adjustments will be more difficult.

The next half generation promises to be as eventful as the previous one —indeed, as the entire 20th century has been to date. Its very eventfulness makes prediction well-nigh impossible and forecasting very difficult. At the same time, the very complexity of our century makes some degree of planning necessary. Looking at government's role in the future, one must tread a sharp line between uttering simple banalities and predicting beyond reasonable knowledge. This becomes possible only because our political system has shown a tremendous ability to adapt itself to radical changes while changing relatively little in its own right. In a century of change, our political system has served as a rock of stability. There is no reason to believe that it cannot continue to do so provided we understand it and use it wisely.

CHAPTER 7

Non-Government Organizations
In American Political Life

GRANT MCCONNELL*

If we are to attempt to look into the future, it is wise, the present being no more than a transient moment, to look back into the past. For this
reason I wish to take my text from a book written more than a century and
a quarter ago:

> Americans of all ages, all conditions, and all dispositions, con-
> stantly form associations. They have not only commercial and
> manufacturing companies, in which all take part, but associa-
> tions of a thousand other kinds—religious, moral, serious, futile,
> extensive or restricted, enormous or diminutive. The Americans
> make associations to give entertainments, to found establishments
> for education, to build inns, to construct churches, to diffuse
> books, to send missionaries to the antipodes; and in this manner
> they found hospitals, prisons, and schools. If it be proposed to
> advance some truth, or to foster some feeling by the encourage-
> ment of a great example, they form a society. Wherever, at the
> head of some new undertaking, you see the Government in
> France, or a man of rank in England, in the United States you
> will be sure to find an association.

These are the words of Alexis de Tocqueville, who came to the
United States from France, stayed six months, traveled to the far west
(that is to say, to the Mississippi River), then returned to write his collection of observations. His journey should have yielded no more than a
slight volume of prejudices and banalities; instead it produced a master-
piece. The excerpt just quoted is hardly even a sample, yet anyone coming
across this passage today can only comment, thinking of what he sees about
him in everyday American life, "How true." But when it is recalled that
the American life which was observed by Tocqueville was that of the year
1831, two further reflections arise: this man saw deep into the latencies of
America, and among those latencies was a high propensity among Americans to organize themselves—formally and pretentiously, but also in-
formally and casually.

*Professor of Political Science, University of Chicago; Rhodes Scholar (Oxford) 1938. Ph. D.
University of California, Berkeley; taught political science, University of California 1951-57, University of Chicago 1957 to present. Principal writings: *The Decline of Agrarian Democracy; Steel
and the Presidency, 1962; The Steel Seizure of 1952; Private Power and American Democracy* (1966).

ORGANIZATIONS IN THE AMERICAN CULTURE

Tocqueville had two aims, a lesser and a greater. The lesser was to study what might with some fashion be called "the American character"; the greater was to study democracy itself, where, as the great tide of the modern era, it might carry not just Americans but all the world. Understandably then, he related the American trait of forming associations both to the general qualities of American life and to the nature of democracy. What he meant by democracy was, very simply, equality. And a passion for equality was what, beyond all else, distinguished Americans from peoples that had appeared before in history. As to the propensity for association, this in turn he saw as the direct outcome of equality: "If each citizen did not learn, in proportion as he individually becomes more feeble, and consequently more incapable of preserving his freedom single-handed, to combine with his fellow citizens for the purpose of defending it, it is clear that tyranny would unavoidably increase with equality."

These, then, are the terms in which one of the primary problems of American political life has come down to us. Although from time to time there have been dissenters from this formulation, Tocqueville's is the frame of reference within which the dominant development of American political thought has taken place. As we attempt to look ahead, it is useful to ask whether this manner of thinking will serve as well for the time that lies before us.

There can be no doubt whatsoever that the readiness and enthusiasm of Americans for associations which Tocqueville saw so long ago is with us still; it is probably an even more pronounced trait today than it was then. Certainly it is safe to say that America today is far more richly endowed with associations and organizations, if for no other reason than that the nation is larger and vastly more complex. First of all there is the modern corporation, certainly one of the greatest social inventions of all time. A very large part of our economic life is organized and directed through this form; something more than a half of it by a few hundred of the largest corporations. There is no need to attempt to list them, their names are proclaimed at the tops of the tallest buildings in Denver, Chicago, New York and in every town and hamlet of the land; they scream at us as we drive into each village and city; they enter our homes with thousands of labels and an infinitude of televised jokes, songs and "messages" that we raptly absorb day after day and night after night.

Vitally important as the corporation is to our livelihood and well-being, it is only one of a variety of organizational forms existing outside the institutions of formal government and yet which do much to set the pattern of our lives and even—in a large sense—to govern us. Once again to refer to the obvious, America is the land of the private and voluntary association; I am certain that nobody here is not a card carrying member of at least one of these bodies. Some of us belong to professional associations, to trade unions, to recreational groups, to civic clubs, to churches; certainly many of those here must be officers and leaders of such organizations. Despite this inevitable personal familiarity with the phenomenon which so struck Tocqueville, probably each of us is not really aware of the vast extent and diversity of its current manifestations. A statistical tabulation of all the associations and organizations of the United States, if it were possible to make one, would be a very large figure indeed. Just how large is difficult to say, for every day new associations are being formed and others are disappearing. Some are national while many are local and regional. Some have very limited aims while others have very general commitments. However, if we take just the national organizations listed, each with just a few lines about its address, officers and membership, in *The Encyclopedia of Associations,* we find ourselves with a volume of roughly the heft of The Gutenberg *Bible* or, more appropriately perhaps, the United States *Budget.*

The startling fact, however, is the sheer range of concern reflected in the organizations which are national and have acquired offices and postal addresses in their own corporate names. Here are a few taken at random from a recent listing: The Academy of American Poets, the National Council for Accreditation of Teacher Education, the Afghan Hound Club of America, the American Association of Retired Persons, the American Sunbathing Association, the Associated Ship Chandlers, the Congress of Racial Equality, the Federation of Tax Administrators, the Honorable Order of the Blue Goose, the National Association of Shellfish Commissioners, the Society of Nuclear Medicine, the Union of Petroleum Workers, the Concrete Pipe Association, the Dude Ranchers Association, the Women's International Bowling Congress, and the Society of Systematic Zoology.

It is easy to laugh at some of these titles. Some are clearly meant to be taken more seriously than others. Yet, with even the most astonishing we should probably reserve judgment; some which seem frivolous in our eyes may turn out to be the defenders of values about which some of our fellow citizens feel passionately. Beyond this, some of the organizations in the long roster of American associations—whether we sympathize with them or not—have become established powers in national life. They are potent realities and in one way or another they must be taken into account; they cannot be wished away or ignored. If you take a short walk away from the White House in the national capital you will pass by the entrances to the office of many associations which are important forces in policy formation. Thus, immediately upon crossing Lafayette Park, which faces the White House, you see the headquarters of the Chamber of Commerce of the United States. Just a few steps away, in a newer and equally imposing structure, is the home of the AFL-CIO. These buildings, like others which may be seen a little further off, are solid, abundantly marbled, and—more to the point—fully peopled. But, in case you are not free to fly to Washington to take the walk I suggested, take a stroll here in Denver; it is just a short distance to the headquarters of the National Farmers Union. It is just as imposing; in one way it is more so; I shall never forget the view of the Front Range I once had from the top floor office of Jim Patton, the longtime President of the Union.

Considering the development from the time of Tocqueville's visit to America on down to the present, then, it seems reasonably safe to predict that in the next few decades private and nongovernment associations will be important factors in our common social and political life. Some organizations will decline and some will disappear. Others, however, will arise and some will thrive and grow powerful. The quality that is, and has always been, so important a part of the American and which impels us to organize and associate for more ends than any of us individually can conceive, will persist.

IN PRAISE OF THE PRIVATE ASSOCIATION

With the making of this prediction, a very safe and easy one, things become more difficult. From this point on, there are many uncertainties and to attempt to say very much about the future developments in this area leads us into the realm of prophecy; and unfortunately there seem to be few authentic prophets among us. These uncertainties are the product of all the complexities which everyone sees and feels. More specifically, they are the result of the emergence of a number of inter-related problems of increasing importance to life in America. Quite possibly, some of these problems will gradually be solved, or even turn out to be non-problems. On the other hand, it is more likely that some of the problems will grow in seriousness and give us increasing trouble whether we face them squarely or not. At the present time, we do not seem to be facing up to them and their implications; on the whole we are more inclined to marvel at our own achievements and to say how fortunate we all are. If we are to have any degree of control over our common destiny, however, we need to confront these problems and decide what it is we want.

The first of the problems which can be expected to give us trouble as time goes on lies right here, in our own ingrained ways of thinking. It is a very curious thing that there is no well articulated body of doctrine about the place and role of all these many thousand associations in America. There are many discussions about corporations and business firms, and about these there is, indeed, a very sophisticated doctrine deriving from classical economics. Obviously, however, this doctrine does not apply very well to churches, fraternal societies, recreational groups and to many others. It does not even offer a very satisfactory account of trade unions. Yet, it is fairly clear that all of these different forms of organization do have something in common and that a purely economic explanation will not reveal it.

There is also a now fairly extensive body of literature discussing private groups and associations. Some of this is legal and relates to the impressive position accorded these associations by the courts; freedom of association is now virtually one of the fundamental liberties guaranteed under the First Amendment to the Constitution. More of the discussion, however, bears on the way in which these associations fit into the political order. This discussion cannot be said to offer a coherent and well-developed doctrine and must be pieced together and filled in here and there to present such doctrine. It does nevertheless represent a set of beliefs which are very much common property. These beliefs are what we must examine.

One of the first advantages which we generally perceive in the great array of private associations of the land applies especially to the corporations and business forms which organize the work and livelihoods of most of us. This is their efficiency. Instead of having a gross, complicated and unwieldly single organization—the government, to do everything and to direct our every step, we have a multitude of specialized organizations which enlist and order our energies to a multitude of ends. Somehow the results are not chaos, but a meshing of these energies and ends to a degree that never fails to astonish when the system is examined as a whole. Without undertaking to make decisions at some central point on what kind of goods and how many of each shall be made, we somehow find the decisions are made and that in the process the nation grows richer. It is all quite miraculous, as Adam Smith observed many years ago. And as we make comparisons with other ways of organizing these matters, we see that we have escaped a host of clumsy follies. While there are indeed efficiencies of large scale organizations, there are also great inefficiencies of delay, paperwork, bureaucracy and a multiplicity of supervisors supervising supervisors who supervise supervisors. Although we think of this mainly in regard to economic activities, the advantages in efficiency apply to other ends as well. Thus in recent years, for example, we have turned to firms like Xerox, Litton and IBM not just for office machines and electronic devices but for the objectives of social improvement as well. Each of these firms operates schools for job training under the poverty program; the assumption is that they will do this better than ordinary schools run by public bodies.

A much more important part of the argument than this is that the great array of associations insures—or perhaps constitutes—democracy. This is a very simple-seeming statement and it is often made as though it were a direct perception. Some people, indeed, seem to define democracy as the existence of such an array. Most enthusiasts for the private association, however, refer to other values even when the defense of their own particular groups appears to be the strongest motivation. Thus, to take the most familiar example, businessmen often speak of liberty and democracy in general terms when they are attempting to fight off governmental intervention in their own immediate affairs. Use of this generalized argument, however, is not peculiar to business and the existence of particular motivation of interest does not in itself invalidate the argument.

This general argument has several parts. The first of these is that the private associations provide self-determination and self-government. When the association regulates its own affairs it is free of external rule and by this very fact is democratic. This proposition is the same whether seen by a private group or a new nation. Moreover, the private association is inevitably smaller than the nation of which it is a part. As a result, its officers are closer to and more understanding of the needs and desires of its members than some far-off government bureaucrats; thus it is more responsive. A related but different contention is that since the private associations are small, they can have debate and discussion which are impossible in a large organization; thus they have the democratic advantage of a town meeting.

These arguments which many of us find persuasive shade into another set. The first of these is that a large number of private associations in a society present so many barriers to mass movements and the development of totalitarianism. Since a general conquest of power would have to defeat or assimilate all, or at least most, of the private associations which share in power as things are now, we are much safer from something like the Nazi or Communist movements than we would be without them. This argument was foreshadowed by Tocqueville, who understandably did not imagine these apocalyptic threats of the twentieth century: he saw the multitude of associations as protection against majority tyranny, and as safeguards against the evils inherent in the American's passion for equality.

These arguments, in turn, merge into others of a still different character. The central point here is that inside a small association, an individual can find community and a sense of relation with his fellow man and need not feel alone or helpless. In the private association, the individual enjoys fellowship and can rediscover meaning for his life and work. In this setting he is not alienated. Thus, he and his fellows are unlikely to engage in activities that might disrupt society and they can be brought into line when necessary. The private association thus brings order and discipline into the general pattern of things.

Some Difficulties

This summary of the case for the array of private associations in our general social and political system is admittedly sketchy and incomplete. It does not do justice either to the eloquence or the passion with which parts of it are sometimes presented. Nevertheless, most of the case will sound familiar, I suspect. Perhaps it will sound so obvious as to be beyond question. Although it has been necessary to piece it together here from a variety of sources, the case is of long standing and only a few items in it can be said to have a recent origin. So there is a fairly strong temptation to treat it as dogma and as part of the democratic creed to which we are dedicated. Unfortunately, however, if we are to be prepared to face the problems which are likely to grow serious in the future, we must question it.

The first item, efficiency, is the easiest part. Given a particular end, a definite job to get done, it should be possible by engineering and other factual studies to discover what the best size of organization is. Certainly such studies would have their difficulties, but they ought to come reasonably close to a trustworthy answer. We should expect, moreover, that with different ends and different jobs different answers would emerge. The real difficulty arises, however, when there are several ends to be attained or when the end is uncertain. Thus, what does efficiency mean when a contractor is to build a road and also preserve natural beauty? Or when a private school educates a child? Do we really know what the ends of education are and do we agree upon them?

The rest of the argument is where the greatest difficulties lie. To begin with, note that there is a large divergence in the benefits seen in a system of many private associations. On the one hand, the private association is celebrated as the guarantor of freedom; on the other hand, it is hailed as the provider of discipline and order. Thus, at times the labor union, the farm organization and the trade association are seen as something like the New England town with all the neighbors gathering to govern themselves. But thus also, the union is seen as the preventive of wildcat strikes and other forms of "irresponsible" action; the farm organization is praised for preventing the rise of "bolshevism" among farmers; and the trade association is seen as the means of avoiding "cutthroat competition." Unfortunately, liberty and order, as these examples may suggest to some of us, tend to look in different directions and sometimes even to be in conflict. Certainly a degree of order is necessary if freedom is to have meaning, but the two emphases are very different.

If there is an ambiguity (and sometimes a conflict) here, there is an ambivalence and a deep one between the emphasis upon liberty on the one hand and "belonging" and fellowship on the other. I have no doubt that both liberty and a sense of fellowship are qualities profoundly desired by many individuals of the present era. Neither is easy to come by, but regettably they are even more difficult to achieve together. The point was very elegantly put by E. B. White in the opening sentence of a wry and lyrical piece he once wrote about his favorite city, a city from which he has had to escape to the Maine countryside from time to time: "On any person who desires such queer prizes, New York will bestow the gift of loneliness and the gift of privacy." Loneliness and privacy are all too evidently the opposite sides of the same coin. By the same token, "belonging" and submission to restrictions also go together. Probably many of us have had the warming experience of having neighbors rally to give help in time of personal crisis, quite probably the same neighbors whose spying gave them not only information about the crisis but knowledge of other matters which we might have wished to keep private. And privacy is very close indeed to freedom. As the saying goes, you can't have it both ways.

We are entitled, then, to ask just what values have our many private associations stood for in fact? In the first place, we have to take account of the vast diversity among all the associations of the nation. Common sense alone suggests that there are great differences between groups that include The League of Women Voters, the United States Steel Corporation and the International Brotherhood of Teamsters. Certainly on the score of efficiency we know that things differ from one business firm to another. It is similar on other scores within the range of all forms of association.

Granted this range of variation, however, there are some large general points that need to be made. The first of these relates to the much vaunted self-government of private associations. It is not sufficient to say that they are self-governing; we must ask *how* they govern themselves. This is a question which seems to be asked rather infrequently, indeed to ask it is sometimes regarded as hostility. This is itself an interesting and illuminating fact. It suggests that associations regard themselves as having no problem of internal government; their members all share the same interests and to question their unity—or unanimity—is an act intended to weaken or destroy the organization.

While it is impossible to offer any iron-clad generalization about the internal governments of private associations, some tentative comments are possible about those associations which can be said to have membership and which base the legitimacy of their systems upon that fact. This excludes hierarchical churches and modern corporations, which cannot be said to have a membership in any clear or meaningful sense.

The striking general fact which emerges from studies of these private governments—for that is what they are—is that they generally lack the constitutional restraints which we have learned to regard as essential in our public institutions of government. Thus, the elementary matter of a bill of rights, which has been at the heart of the American constitutional system from its beginning, has no counterpart in the system of any private association I know. The constitutions of many associations list the privileges of members as distinguished from non-members and give many statements of ways in which members may offend and for which they may be fined, suspended or expelled; they have bills of obligations but no bills of rights *vis a vis* the organizations themselves. They do not have any genuine semblance of checks and balances to limit the exercise of leadership power. Typically, the highest governing body of a private association is the convention, which is analogous not to be a legislature but to be a general assembly of the members in a town meeting, however approximate this may be. Accordingly, the constitution has no particular sanctity and can be easily amended.

The judicial systems of these associations—and here it should be remembered that the important associations exercise powers and enforce rules often more important to the lives of their members than some of the acts of public government—are rudimentary and end ultimately in a vote of members in general meeting. Offenses punished in this way may be very vague, "speaking ill" of the organization or slandering its officers, for example. The powers of leadership are often extreme and unchecked. Indeed, these not infrequently effectively include the power to preside and run the conventions, to make rules, suspend constitutional provisions, revoke the charters of local chapters, decide appeals and so on. The organizational machinery, the office files, the association journal, appointment of the association's bureaucracy, the calling of meetings, these and other matters of great practical importance are in the leaders' hands. Yet, with only one clear and well-known exception, the International Typographical Union, competitive party systems such as those we have learned to be essential to operation of our public democracy are lacking in these governmental systems. Indeed, factionalism and competition for office are generally deplored in the strongest terms and sometimes are actively suppressed.

While this general pattern is rather commonly known, its importance tends to be dismissed. There are usually several grounds. First, the private association is not important. Certainly many such organizations are not; but some are, and the original argument is that the private association is important. Second, the aggrieved member, unlike the public citizen, has the choice of resignation. This, however, may be a hollow recourse if the association controls the right of entry and continuance in a way of livelihood that may have required many years of training, such as a skilled trade or medicine, for example. It will be hollow to the extent that the association itself is important and has no rival to which recourse may be had. On this score it should be noted that associations reserve their strongest hostility for rivals; in the labor movement, for example, "dual unionism" is a cardinal sin. The third response is that in a private association there are no legitimate differences of interest or opinion; everyone has joined because he shares the interests of his fellows. Yet, this contention is plainly contrary to fact. No collection of human beings has a complete identity of interests. Some individuals are older than others, they are of different religions, races, and inevitably opinions and tastes. Unanimity is a myth in the most cohesive organization, yet enforcement of it is all too frequently attempted.

The point here is not that all of our private associations are tyrannical or that their leaders selfishly exploit their members, although in some instances such statements may be justified. It is rather that their governing institutions and modes of operation often do not adequately reflect the diversity of interest and will among their members; it is also that sometimes they do not serve the principle of liberty well. We can expect this to be a continuing problem in our common life.

TIES WITH GOVERNMENT

In itself, the problem of the manner in which "self-government" of private associations is conducted may not seem seriously important to everyone, although I think that on the grounds already indicated it is a matter for real concern to our general society. It becomes much more evidently important, however, when we confront another problem, the relationships that have come to exist between some of our associations and units of public government. At many points these relationships have become very close and there is every sign that they will not disappear.

The problem here involves many things that are very familiar to us, but also many others that are not. It is at once so mundane that we tend to overlook it; but it is also one involving some fairly abstract considerations. Let me begin by putting it in the most lurid possible light: much of government and public policy in America has been captured by narrow interest groups spearheaded by some of the private associations we praise so highly. That is to say, significant areas of policy and important public agencies have been isolated from influence by the general public and have concurrently been subjected to the preponderant influence and often the complete control of very narrow constituencies. In the process, the distinction between what is public and what is private (even when it comes to real property) has been made indistinct, and the basic American values of liberty and equality have fared ill. The large consequence is a more rigidified political and social system than the open society we like to believe we have.

Without qualification or explanation, statements such as these cannot help leaving an impression of being too strong or even mystifying, particularly since they relate to quite ordinary phenomena. Once more, accordingly, let us cast back into the past. In 1933 at the very depth of the Depression, Congress passed the National Industrial Recovery Act. It was one of the most remarkable experiments in government this country has ever seen. It was a monumental failure and when the Supreme Court gave it the *coup de grace* nearly everyone was relieved, including most of its original enthusiasts. Yet, the underlying ideas were not new; in one sense they were traceable back to Tocqueville and beyond; in another sense they were simply the development of the ideas which had been urged with great fervor by Herbert Hoover. They were the singular property of neither Democrats nor Republicans.

The first of these ideas was that industry should be self-governing, since this was the way to freedom. More than this, each industry should be self-governing, the entities having self-hood being taken as given. Next, industry and government should cease their traditional conflict. Coercion should be avoided; this would be achieved by simply putting government at the beck and call of industry. In practice what this meant was that at the invitation of the government (the NRA) committees representing particular industries met, drew up "codes of fair competition" which the government benevolently validated and then enforced. A particular theory of what was wrong with the economy was involved but that is not at issue here. The "representatives" of the particular industries were selected from or by the existing trade associations, but where such associations did not exist, the government helped in their establishment.

Although the intentions were excellent the results were alarming. With the compulsive authority of government tied to the already existing (or in some cases the newly created) power of the associations, dissident firms and individuals found themselves subjected to serious coercion and discrimination. Moreover, the interests of many people were simply left out; these—particularly those of consumers—fared badly. The bureaucratic confusion became enormous and the end came none too soon. The statements that this was a form of fascism which had been brought down were excessive, but there was an underlying point.

Nearly everyone now is able to see the error of the NRA. Yet essentially the same set of ideas has been in operation in a very large variety of fields. Concurrently with the NRA the Agricultural Adjustment Administration sought to give powers of government to the particular industry involved, agriculture. This time administration was to be turned over to local committees which, however, came under the organizational aegis of local Farm Bureaus, units of the major farm lobby. Labor was to be "cut in" in the same manner by governmental help in organization of its unorganized. All this, it should be emphasized, was nothing new in principle. The government under President Taft had called the original organizational meeting of the Chamber of Commerce of the United States, and the government under President Wilson had actively financed and directed the organization of the local farm bureaus that ultimately joined together in the American Farm Bureau Federation.

The death of the NRA did not spell the end of the development I am tracing. Much the same thing was undertaken in a great variety of areas but with much variety of device. In one sense this was an extension into the growingly vital zone of administration of what had come to be accepted in the making of legislation: the accommodation of one organized interest group after another according to the behest of whatever spokesmen most insistently presented their claims as representative. Thus, to take but one example, there was (and is) the National Rivers and Harbors Congress, an impressive association of local chambers of commerce, construction firms and other businesses, and public officials, all of them banded together for putting through regular rivers-and-harbors bills. These bills have always included some projects of great value, but they have included others of more dubious character as well, and have had the coherence only that by log-rolling each claimant could get what he wanted. Washington cynics have always regarded rivers-and-harbors as a good working definition of the pork barrel.

When World War II drew close and the great mobilization of American industry got under way, the same ideas were brought into play. Using precedents from the NRA as well as some from World War I, many devices were developed for coopting the power of established private associations for disciplinary and other purposes. Let us be clear; this was probably the most effective available way for getting the urgent production of war material in the shortest time. It involved the same process of drawing in trade associations, creating industry committees and then giving their advice public sanctions. This method was supplemented by government hiring of WOCs (without compensation)—"dollar a year men"—from business firms which supported them and to which they ultimately returned. In a time of crisis and given a set of limited and fairly visible ends, the devices were justified and it was probably not vastly important that discrimination and compulsion occurred or that the democratic niceties were not too well observed.

With peacetime, however, the process of heavy involvement of private groups and organizations in doing the work of government—both in the making of policy and in its administration—continued. Now, however, the clear-cut goal of winning the war was not present and what was being asked, however obscurely, of the associations and other private representatives was that they should govern, that they should make the basic choices which in a democracy we like to think are those of the general public itself to make. Thus, the Department of Commerce has had the curious structure of the Business and Defense Services Administration, which has relied heavily on private direction from interest groups; the Department of the Interior the help (or direction?) of the National Petroleum Council; the Treasury has had the American Bankers Association Government Borrowing Committee, the Investment Bankers Association Government Securities Committee and various others. The advisory committees of the Defense Department have been, as befits the weight of that Department, legion. Among the independent regulatory commissions, the influence of the relevant private associations has probably been greater. The basic idea of the Securities and Exchange Commission to this day is that the exchanges, which are intrinsically private clubs, should regulate themselves, with the Commission looking on. Thus recently, when grave questions were raised about the over-the-counter market, the solution proposed was to require all securities dealers to belong to one of the dealers' associations and to have the associations do the regulating. The Senate Banking Committee, the exchanges and the National Association of Securities Dealers all heartily concurred.

A similar pattern is probably even more pervasive within the states. Both policy and administration tend to be highly fragmented in most states, with many offices being elective, administrations being highly fragmented, and legislatures being acutely sensitive to the demands of obscure lobbies. There are many examples which might be drawn here, but one of the most striking categories is licensing. At first glance, it is tempting to assume that state governments have been greedily grasping for control over the right to follow almost all trades and to regulate all professions. Yet the reality is that the impulse for this regulation has generally come from the organized trades and professions themselves. And the regulation has very generally developed under the watchful eyes of the regulated groups themselves. Indeed, sometimes the private associations of the regulated, such as the medical associations and bar associations of some states, are formally the regulating bodies exercising state powers. The advantages—over and above the maintenance of standards for protection of the public, as virtually all of these groups assert their purposes to be—include protection of the job market and effective disciplining of dissidents within their various ranks. The pattern has widened to include cemetery salesmen and cosmetologists; the garage mechanics are now beating at the doors of legislatures for their own licensing. Similar systems are to be found in many other areas of governmental policy in the states as well.

This list of policy areas in which the work of governing, both deciding and administering, is to one degree or another effectively in the hands of narrow interest groups and their organizations is very diverse. Only a small selection of such examples, moreover, has been possible here. A complete list would be very long indeed. Given this condition, how are we to view it?

THE LEFT OUTS

Perhaps the very length of the list suggests that everybody is—or at any rate could be—included. Here is the way everybody can get his cut and all be happy. This is a very widespread and popular view; it has increasingly come to be dignified with the word, "pluralism." This is the American system and, since it has worked here, it is what we have to teach to benighted underdeveloped parts of the world. Unfortunately, there are some difficulties. First, not everybody is included and it is exceedingly doubtful if everybody could be included. There are numerous groups of this kind in America: the Puerto Ricans, the Mexicans, and the people of Appalachia are examples. The most conspicuous category of the excluded, however, is the Negroes. The problem confronting Negroes is, admittedly, highly complex and involves many facets of American life, from basic psychological dispositions, a tragic history on down to the minutiae of organizational arrangements in schools, neighborhoods and business firms. Yet, one of the very most important facts of the situation is that Negroes have been largely powerless. It is unnecessary today to dwell on either the injustices or the dangers to the large society. We have recurrent reminders from Harlem, Woodlawn and Watts, as well as from smaller cities such as Rochester and Bakersfield. Attempts are made by some civil rights organizations to cut Negroes in by organizations such as have sufficed for other groups. Yet this is working but slowly and one of the results is the rise of other organizations which seek to found themselves on black nationalism and still others which tend toward pure violence.

Another group excluded from taking advantage of the supposed opportunity to organize and be dealt into the game is the poor. Today we are probably most aware of the urban poor. Certainly their lot as it is to be seen by anyone willing to wander out of the good middle class districts and to leave major arteries of traffic is one of despair and often of more than quiet desperation. It might be added that today the areas of the poor— "pockets of poverty" does not describe them—often are Negro ghettos. But there is also the category of the rural poor. Like the other poor, these tend to be hidden from sight and easily ignored. They too have never been able to organize for the representation of their own interest— if indeed poverty can be regarded as a common interest. With prosperity we have undertaken a national program to deal with poverty. The Office of Economic Opportunity has commendably sought to enlist the energies of the poor in their own salvation. Yet, the attempt to organize the poor, in effect to treat them as just another interest group like labor, agriculture or the legal profession, has failed, as might have been predicted. The benefits of "pluralism" are not available to everyone. By the same token those who do share in these benefits do so to very unequal degrees.

The second difficulty is that, just as the interests of some categories of people are not readily included in the system by which policy matters are given over to private, organized groups, some kinds of values are not easily incorporated into the pattern. In general these are the values which, although shared by great numbers of people, are not strongly preoccupying for many. One example is the interest of consumers. We have been able to suppose that where competition prevails in the market, this interest is protected. Yet, when monopolistic conditions exist—that is, where strong organizations have taken over or divided the market—this protection fails. And consumer organizations have not had notable success in responding.

Another example is the value of clean water and clean air. Although everyone may suffer from pollution, to deal with it through a politics organized about private asosciations and to act as though this were simply another interest is to accept a very great disadvantage. We have, indeed, made a start toward dealing with pollution, but hardly anyone would be willing to say that the achievements have been great. Still another example is also one on which we perhaps have made a start: the preservation of areas of natural beauty such as those with which this fortunate part of the land is so well endowed. The conservation groups have labored valiantly—and sometimes stridently—on behalf of the public interest in this value, but the contests are unequal and the public losses are many. We have only to look at what has happened in many of the finest parts of the West for evidence. In general, then, a pattern of devolving government and public policy to narrow organized groups tends to favor hard, concrete and material values, and to discriminate against general and non-material values.

One of the presumed advantages of a pattern of politics which is all divided up among a large number of interest groups and their organizations is that it prevents extremism. Plainly, this is desirable. Compromise and moderation are necessities if a nation of this scope and diversity is to remain. So far as averting the rise and growth of mass movements, the expectation is probably justified; a multitude of power centers is a barrier. If we were seriously threatened with such mass movements perhaps we would do well to see to the bolstering of our many associations. Only the hysterical, however, claim that we are in imminent danger of being swept off behind some such movement or another.

In the meantime, there is reason to doubt whether some of our policies as produced by our "pluralistic" way of turning policy over to these groups are as moderate as we might assume. The reason is that when government and policy making are divided up into pieces to be influenced or controlled by the most directly and immediately concerned associations, with barbers licenses controlled by the barber's union, medicine regulated by the medical association, road-building by the contractors, and so on, the policies are unlikely to be checked and moderated by other interests. Indeed, log-rolling can often result in mutual support for the full demands of each of a long list of interested groups. This is not a condition in which an invisible hand nicely balances and counterbalances one interest against another, however much we would like to assume that it works this way.

Sometimes it even happens that groups which struggle with each other manage to produce effects that are anything but moderate. One of the most striking examples is the history of industrial relations in the steel industry since World War II. Regularly during this period, the organized steel industry and the steel union have engaged in titanic struggles usually accompanied by real bitterness. Typically, the union has sought higher wages while the industry has had the goal of increased prices. Repeatedly, because of inflation, war, or the deteriorating condition of the national balance of payments position, the government has been involved. The very nearly consistent pattern throughout this period has been a settlement of each contest in which the union gets greatly increased wages and the industry gets prices increased to cover the increase in wages and something more as well. In these contests, one of which involved the largest strike in American history, the public not only suffers the disruption caused by the contest but pays the cost of settlement as well.

There is also a problem which has been discussed in part already: many of our most important associations do not give good protection for their members against the associations themselves. There is more to the problem than the relationships between leaders and led, however. When the exercise of—or even the heavy influence over—the functions of government comes within the hands of private associations, the manner in which the associations operate becomes very important indeed. Yet, the tendency where this occurs is to be informal and "flexible." This has many desirable features, but it is also a tendency toward favoritism and arbitrariness. One of the essential checks upon public government is that it is required to operate according to law. There are prescribed procedures and definite limits as to what it may do. This restraint, of course, implies the bureaucratic evils of red tape and buck-passing; escape from these is often a motive for turning to private associations for the performance of public functions. Nevertheless, it is always worth recalling that law itself is the best guarantee of freedom we have. The gains of informality may not be worth their cost.

A New Generation

It is impossible to foresee which of these problems will loom greatest in the years to come. Nonetheless, it is likely that we shall be concerned with all of them in one degree or another. Whether we recognize it or not, we are struggling with them today. To the dismay of many individuals who are part of the Depression generation, those whose major formative experience was that grinding ordeal, there are large numbers of our fellow citizens who do not see the lessons of the Depression as taking precedence over everything else. The simple attainment of economic security, for example, is not the heavy preoccupation it has been for many of the rest of us. Whether rightly or wrongly, this has been shoved into the background of the thinking of much of today's youth who are such a large proportion of the population. The simple accumulation of more and more goods and larger and larger bank accounts or stockholdings also seems a less and less worthy goal to an increasing number of the new generation. The signs of this are to be seen in the numbers of men and women in their twenties who join the Peace Corps, who go to work among the poor or who seek to fight the battles of civil rights. Some of them are proposing and attempting to apply methods that are naive, ill considered, or downright weird. Yet their evidence is not such that we can ignore it.

What it indicates, I believe, is that in a substantial degree some of the old preoccupations have lost their urgency by any realistic assessment. With unemployment now at the four percent level the fear of losing a job is not as rational as it once was. The fear of future poverty is also much less vivid to those who never had to worry whether the economic order were about to fall apart. Conceivably today's young are mistaken, but conceivably also they are right. In either event, however, we have to consider that although the Depression-born preoccupations may have deserved a position of greater urgency, perhaps they are intrinsically less important than some of the goals that are now emerging into visibility.

There are several ironies in this situation. One is that the newly discovered goals are really not so new at that; they were objectives even of the Depression-influenced generation. Social justice, civil rights, the ending of poverty, the making of a less ugly world—all of these are firmly in an old American tradition. It is no less than annoying that the new zealots should treat them as their own peculiar discovery. At the same time it is probably fortunate.

The other irony is that many of those who are just now becoming engaged in struggle with the nation's ills see their enemy as "the power structure." What is meant by this is seldom clear. The reasoning, however, seems to be that since simple demands for all the things that are plainly right do not accomplish their achievement, something is standing in the way and actively blocking it; that something must be a secret and massively united "power structure" operating with superb direction, all in great secrecy.

Actually, of course, there is a secret. It is that this "power structure" does not exist. Instead, there is a great myriad of power structures which are simply those honorable and decent organizations which have grown up for the achievement of the goals of the past, mostly directed to the economic security of this group or that. Many of these have peculiar access to or control over units of government and in a multitude of different ways they operate to guarantee the old achievements. Nevertheless, when a union of workers in the building trades will not accept apprentices who are not from families with existing members in the union, when a public vocational school will not admit students for such a trade if they cannot get into the union, when medical training is precluded for students who have not been to the right kind of school, when a public agency listens closely to a few extractive industry spokesmen and is deaf to conservationists, even when a pleasant neighborhood organizes itself to make sure that it will be held for "our kind of people," it is understandable that the conclusion of a massive "power structure" should be drawn.

Yet, American political life is not a conspiracy. Americans, as Tocqueville observed, have shown vast initiative in banding themselves together to act energetically on problems as they come up. One problem after another has fallen to this approach. One group after another has been admitted to the list of those who are entitled by their organized self-help to take a slice of the cake. Moreover, most of the accommodation of these organized groups by government has been made in the belief that government should respond to the wishes of the people so far as these can be discovered.

Whether the myth of the "power structure" is ever finally exploded or not, the sense of outrage which is so plainly rising among substantial segments of the population will fall more and more upon the associations which have had to struggle in the past for their own place in the sun. There is a danger that those which have drawn their lines of defense tight under the pressure of old and probably obsolescent fears and which have established heavy discipline and close ties to particular agencies of government, agencies which have been isolated from other influences, will come under very heavy attack. If this occurs, it will be an unfortunate outcome, for the associations have been the means by which a vast amount of American achievements have been made. A large part of American society consists of these societies. They cannot allow themselves collectively to become a closed society. And they cannot fail to yield the substance of the fellowship which is so often promised in their name and which so many of our contemporaries are seeking.

Ultimately, then, we must watch several problems as regards the many private associations and the system which they compose. First, as Tocqueville noted, the many private associations are and have been responses to and against the impulse toward equality that is so ingrained in the American character. This conflict will continue in the future; it may become more serious. And last, the pattern of associations as we have known it in America so far has worked best for material goals. Will it work as well for others?

BIBLIOGRAPHICAL NOTES

This paper is based upon the research and analysis appearing in my *Private Power and American Democracy* (New York: Alfred A. Knopf, 1966). Attention is also called particularly to the recent volume by Corrinne Lathrop Gilb, *Hidden Hierarchies, The Professions and Government* (New York: Harper and Row, 1966). The opening quotation from De Tocqueville is from Volume II of *Democracy in America* (New York: Alfred A. Knopf, 1945), p. 106. Most national associations of the United States are listed in *The Encyclopedia of Associations* (Detroit: Gale Research Co., various editions). Data on these associations are also regularly collected by the U.S. Department of Commerce. The role of private associations as barriers to totalitarianism has a broad literature; a good introductory discussion is William Kornhauser, *The Politics of Mass Society* (Glencoe, Ill.: Free Press, 1959). The quotation from E. B. White is from *Here Is New York* (New York: Harper and Bros., 1949), p. 9. I have discussed the problem of the internal government of private associations in "The Spirit of Private Government," *American Political Science Review*, vol. lii, no. 3 (Sept., 1958), pp. 754-770. The classic statement of this issue is Robert Michels, *Political Parties* (Glencoe, Ill.: The Free Press, 1949). The relationship of democracy in the largest sense to private associations is discussed in *Private Power*, especially in chapters 4 and 10. For a differing and older view, however, see David B. Truman, *The Governmental Process* (New York: Alfred A. Knopf, 1951).

CHAPTER 8

Urban and Metropolitan Development

WILLIAM L. C. WHEATON*

The United States is going through a profound secular change as a result of urbanization and population growth. The facts of urbanization are clearly established. Between 1950 and 1960, 80 percent of the United States' total population growth occurred in our metropolitan areas. It is estimated that in the next fifteen years our national population will grow from 193 million to 244 million people.[1] This increase of 51 million people will require that we build new urban areas roughly equal to all of the urban areas in the country in 1940. In short, during the next fifteen years, we must build about as many cities as were created in the first 200 years of this nation's existence. The population of the United States is moving to cities, and primarily to metropolitan areas.

Within this great urbanization process the internal changes are equally important. Most of our larger central cities have stationary or declining populations. Fourteen out of the fifteen largest metropolitan centers lost population between 1950 and 1960. Suburban areas accounted for a large share of all urban growth. Their populations increased by 50 percent in the last decade and will certainly double again in this decade.[2] Thus the central cities are losing population and virtually all urban growth is occurring at the fringes.

METROPOLITAN AREAS IN THE INTERMOUNTAIN STATES

It is essential, however, that we distinguish between these great national trends and the trends which are occurring in the metropolitan areas of the Intermountain states. The region has 14 metropolitan areas, all of them relatively small when compared with the national picture. These metropolitan areas contained 40 percent of the region's population in 1950, 50 percent in 1960, and it is safe to say that they will contain 60 to 70 percent of the region's population by 1980. Of these metropolitan areas only two, Denver and Phoenix, are among the 50 largest of the country and only five, adding Salt Lake City, Tucson and Albuquerque, are among the largest 100. The region contains, in short, average or smaller-sized metro-

*Professor of City Planning and Director, Institute of Urban and Regional Development, University of California, Berkeley; member Board of Governors, National Housing Conference; U.S.A. representative to United Nations Committee on Housing, Building and Planning; co-author (with Martin Mayerson and Barbara Terrett) of *Housing, People and Cities,* and (with Martin H. Sussheim) of *The Cost of Municipal Services in Residential Areas.*

[1] U.S. Bureau of the Census, *Current Population Reports,* Series P.25, "Illustrative Projection of the Population of States: 1970 to 1985." U.S. Government Printing Office, Washington, D.C., 1966.

[2] U.S. Bureau of the Census, *U.S. Census of Population: 1960,* Vol. 1: Characteristics of the Population, Part A, Number of Inhabitants, U.S. Government Printing Office, Washington, D.C., 1961.

politan areas and includes none of the great megalopolitan regions which so dominate our national thought today.[3]

For this reason, it is essential that we understand that the Intermountain region is not faced with some of the great dramatic problems characteristic of the New York-Washington region, the Chicago region or the California-West Coast region. None of the cities of this region will be faced in the next fifteen years with the massive problems of high-speed rapid transit now facing larger metropolitan areas. None of them now has huge and almost unconquerable slums, crying out for emergency treatment. None of them faces the problem of hundreds of thousands of low-income groups lacking education, job skills, and the other requisites to effective participation in our society. None of them contains sub-cities of one-half million members of a single minority group. None of them faces insuperable obstacles to the early achievement of civil rights, effective access to education, or effective access to job opportunities. None of them faces the prospect of losing ½ million white people and having them replaced by one-half million Negroes within a 15-year period—something which has occurred in some major metropolitan centers.

This point deserves emphasis because too often we read the national publications about these dramatic problems and become deluded into believing that our cities or our metropolitan areas face identical problems. In fact, this is not the case. Let me illustrate this point. Five years ago I visited with the planners and public officials of a great mid-west metropolis which then had 1½ percent of its population Negro. That city was acting in the same fear of this problem that now characterizes Washington, D. C., Baltimore or Philadelphia, where nearly half of the central city population is Negro. They were concerned that massive transfers of population would upset their residential neighborhoods. They were concerned that tens of thousands of underprivileged children would upset the balance of their schools. In fact, these problems did not exist and could not exist for at least a generation in that metropolitan area. Their attitudes on these problems were clearly irrational. Washington, Baltimore and Philadelphia have gotten along comfortably for half a century with 20 to 25 percent Negro population without ever really realizing that they had a problem. But this metropolitan area believed it had a major problem when in fact it had only a minor and entirely manageable problem.

Because metropolitan size is so important, I think it is essential that this point be clearly understood. The metropolitan areas of the region are small in size: two in the half-million to million category; three in the 250,000 to 500,000 category; five in the group above 100,000 and four in the group below 100,000. Seven of them are characterized by extraordinarily high growth rates, the balance by comparatively normal growth rates. The growth rates are particularly notable, however. We have some national estimates which project probable sizes for some of the region's metropolitan areas in 1980. One presents such national estimates with reservations, but they do illustrate the potential.[4] They surely illustrate the growth

[3] See Table 1 at end of Chapter.
[4] See Table 2 at end of Chapter.

problems that the region will face in the next fifteen years. During that time, and assuming that the region's present virile growth continues, the population of Denver, Salt Lake City and Colorado Springs will double according to the best predictions we have available. The population of Phoenix, Tucson and Albuquerque may increase by two and a half times, and the population of Las Vegas may increase by three times. All of the other metropolitan areas of this region will maintain comfortable growth rates in the range of 30 to 60 percent during the next decade.

What will these cities, then, be like in 1980? Denver, Salt Lake and Phoenix may then be the size of Houston or Baltimore or Cleveland, with no more pressing urban problems than those which face cities of such size today. Tucson, Albuquerque and Las Vegas will grow to the size of Phoenix and Salt Lake City, with comparable problems. The smaller metropolitan areas of the region will grow into size ranges of other metropolitan areas within the region so that we can go to look at our sister cities of the region to see what kinds of problems we may face. (See Table 2.)

Viewing these cities, an extraordinary fact emerges—cities in these size ranges are viewed by city planners all over the world as ideal-sized cities. The present plans for Southeast England call for the creation of several new cities in the population size 250-500,000 in order to create an ideal environment for future population growth. Paris plans to build six new cities around the present metropolitan region, each of which will contain 300,000 to 400,000 people to accommodate new growth. Planners consider cities in this size as capable of having an ideal combination of job opportunities, cultural opportunities, prospects for self-regulation and democratic government, and prospects for a reasonable level of urban services at relatively efficient costs.[5]

For this reason I would characterize the Intermountain states as a magnificent opportunity area in which we could demonstrate in the next fifteen years something like the ideal environment for urban life. Many forces and influences converge to create this possibility. It will not occur automatically, but it could occur with vigorous civic and governmental leadership, popular support and understanding, and adequate planning.

The region presents these possibilities for another reason. The deterioration of the conditions of urban life in our larger metropolitan areas proceeds at a fairly steady rate as they attract more and more people. Open space is eroded, conditions of air and water pollution intensify, residential areas become more crowded, slum areas expand, traffic congestion increases, the costs of municipal services rise. Offsetting these disabilities, of course, the great megalopolitan areas of the East, the Midwest and the West Coast offer unusual employment advantages which enable them to continue to attract population. They are the site of major corporate activity, cultural development and the like, and they will continue to grow. But their comparative advantage over the smaller metropolitan areas of this region will also diminish to the extent that the newer and smaller metro-

---

[5] Cf. Frederic J. Osborn and Arnold Whittick, *New Towns, the Answer to Metropolis,* McGraw-Hill, New York, 1963.

politan areas, more favored by climate, natural terrain and size, may be able to maintain their amenity.

Thus, the growth of the region hinges largely upon the ability of its metropolitan areas to offer qualitatively better environments, qualitatively better standards of living, and qualitatively higher standards of amenity. This has been the force that is largely responsible for the region's rapid growth in the post-war decades. This will be the major force affecting the region's rate of growth in the future. Note that it is the high amenity cities of this region—the ones offering the most attractive environment—that have been the extraordinarily rapid growth cities of the region. Without exception this is true. The older industrial cities of the region have enjoyed relatively slower growth rates.

What must the metropolitan areas of the region do to maintain this comparative advantage? First, I think it is clear that they must accept and indeed embrace the desirability of growth and change. Growth is not always easy. We pay, sometimes, very high prices for growth and change —high prices in the form of new highways disrupting former countryside, new shops and stores competing with the existing ones, progressive loss of access to the countryside, disruption of older neighborhoods and business districts. Nevertheless, growth presents opportunities for adaptation to changing circumstances which are not available in stagnant or slowly growing communities. Business can adapt by building new shopping centers or offices. The school system can adapt as it adds to the school plant and curriculum. Government can adapt as tax revenues rise. Under conditions of stagnancy all of these adaptations become much more difficult.

Growth, however, requires extraordinarily high rates of private and public investment. In urban areas we have to invest $10,000 to $15,000 per capita in physical resources, the housing, schools, stores, factories, police and fire stations, hospitals and the like, necessary to maintain even minimum standards of urban services. Further, we have to invest from $7,000 to $15,000 per capita in human resources—in education, recreation and the other services required to equip a person to participate effectively in modern urban society. These extraordinarily high investment requirements, however, are offset by later extraordinarily high productivity. The child of this generation may reasonably expect to earn at least twice the amount of the reasonable expectations of the person of the last generation. Our current average family income of about $7,000 per year is expected to rise to the vicinity of $12,000 by 1980 and probably to $15,000 within a few years thereafter.[6] The investment in physical facilities and in human resources pays off, in short, at an enormously high rate.

Growth also requires a willingness to accept change—change in the social order; change in business activity; change in public services; change in political values. To the extent that the public does not believe in the future and is unwilling to accept change and its costs, we face serious impediments to growth. Let us identify then a few aspects in which growth

[6] National Planning Association, *Looking Ahead*, Washington, D.C., 1966.

and change are necessary if we are to realize the future urban opportunities of this region.

ASPECTS IN WHICH GROWTH AND CHANGE ARE NECESSARY

Metropolitan Area Governments

First among these is surely the establishment of metropolitan area governments or policies. Some of our older metropolitan areas have as many as a thousand local governments, the accumulation of a hundred years of political history and of slow growth both in urban population and in urban services. Under these circumstances of multiple governments, no effective local government is possible.[7] Each municipality or each special district, each school board, each county, has so little power, so little resources, that it is unable to deliver services in any meaningful way to its population. As a result, education falters, transportation services fail, health services are not established, welfare services are deficient and zoning and other land use controls utterly fail. No one of these ineffective government units can preside over its destiny. The major policy determinants of its growth are external to its jurisdiction. It becomes a cog in a vast machine of autonomous but ineffective local areas.

Under these circumstances, political responsiveness breaks down. We may elect our own local officials and know them, often through face-to-face relationships, but they are powerless to respond to our needs—indeed, no one can respond to needs, sometimes of great urgency. The democratic faith begins to falter because democratic institutions malfunction. This leads people in turn to seek out separate enclaves within which they can isolate and protect themselves from what they regard as the uncontrollable forces of the market and the ineffective forces of local democracy. Differentiation of sub-areas begins to develop in an acute form. Rich communities arise with very high standards of education and other services, and these contrast sharply with neighboring poor communities with intolerably low standards of education and other services. People and communities forget their economic and social dependence upon each other. Walls are built between communities and eventually metropolitan area consensus begins to break down.

We need not discuss here in detail the cures for these problems of metropolitan area government. In Toronto and London, however, federal forms of government have been established in which purely local functions may be conducted by purely local government while the more important metropolitan functions such as transportation, land use control, the location and development of industry and higher education are performed by a metropolitan area-wide government. In our smaller metropolitan governments, systematic annexation can achieve the same end. In still others the transfer of municipal functions to the counties may provide an appropriate means. But whatever the form of metropolitan action, it is essential that some area-wide government be empowered to maintain mini-

---

[7] John C. Bollens and Henry Schmant, *The Metropolis, Its People, Politics and Economic Life,* Harper & Row, New York City, 1965; Robert C. Wood and Vladimir Almendinger, *1400 Governments,* Harvard University Press, Cambridge, 1961.

mum levels of basic services for the metropolitan area as a whole and be empowered to plan for its future effectively. To the extent that we fail to achieve such systems of overall policy control, we will surely see a further weakening of local government, the progressive transfer of responsibilities for local functions to the state and to the national government.

Effective Machinery for Conflict Resolution

A second major requirement for metropolitan growth and change is the establishment of effective machinery for conflict resolution. The civil rights movement is one of the most dramatic examples of urban society's need for machinery to resolve problems of cultural conflict. Our present deep concern with problems of poverty and the underprivileged minorities is not merely a conflict about race, though that is a real one. It is also a conflict between classes and a conflict between cultures. We have always had fairly vigorous conflict between age groups. When we neglected the care of the aged, they blew up a storm about Medicare, Social Security, old-age pensions and the like, until society recognized the existence of compelling human problems it had hitherto neglected. We may well be embarking upon a period of equally dramatic conflict with youth, whose impatience—and it is a traditional impatience—with our failure to solve grave social problems leads them to adopt forms of action reflecting that impatience. We may be sure—indeed, we may hope—that youth will persist in calling our attention to the disparities between our democratic premises and our very indifferent delivery, both in achieving a more effective democracy at home, and a more effective peace abroad.

Within the metropolitan areas of the Intermountain states you have an opportunity to resolve these problems more expeditiously and more fully than in other regions, in part because the problems have not risen to levels which require drastic or emergency action, in part because the scale of metropolitan areas permits greater public involvement in the dialogue and greater public recognition of the existence of pressing problems affecting other groups. If a metropolitan area can establish the tradition of residential integration when its Negro or Mexican-American population is very small, the problems of racial residential segregation need never arise. If in 1940 the City of Chicago had established a policy of permitting each Negro family to locate in a residential block in accordance with its ability to pay, there would not now be the festering sore of three-quarters of a million Negroes almost entirely concentrated in a single area, isolated from the rest of the population. A dispersed pattern would have imposed upon each block the responsibility for accommodating to and welcoming one or two Negro families in the income and class groups who desire integration. This surely would not have been a serious obstacle to the dominant white population. Instead a pattern of residential segregation was established and enforced largely by private market mechanisms, but with the support of government. As a consequence those able to move out of the ghetto were denied the opportunity, and ultimately expressed the resentment and hostility which their treatment properly evokes. Further, the whole community itself has been grievously afflicted as old neighborhoods of whites have felt compelled—indeed, been forced—to evacuate their neighborhood to make room for hundreds of thousands of newcomers to the city who are denied access to any but the older areas and perforce were compelled to occupy areas already occupied by others. This disastrous policy has now created problems virtually impossible to solve, but which might easily have been avoided through farsighted community leadership, rational analyses of the alternatives and the judicious exercise of public power and private influence. I say we must establish the machinery for facing these problems now if we are to prevent them from becoming far worse in the future. Their solution today is comparatively easy. Tomorrow it will be far more difficult.

Maintenance of Comparative Amenity

Next on the agenda of growth is the maintenance of the comparative amenity of the metropolitan areas of this region. Let me mention a few items of urban growth and development that should command your attention and efforts. In all metropolitan areas the preservation of open space is increasingly urgent. What was once a purely local problem now demands national attention. Growth necessarily requires the conversion of land from rural or natural use to urban use. But in the process, if we permit scattered, unplanned and non-contiguous growth, we destroy the open character of four to ten times the amount of land which is actually needed for urban use. We invariably also destroy some of our most precious scenic and agricultural areas because these are attractive to scattered development. We make it more costly ultimately to acquire the public open space in the form of parks, playgrounds and school sites which we will later need. We make it impossible for private landowners to preserve agricultural and grazing land which has no foreseeable urban use.

In other countries, particularly Britain and the Scandinavian countries, the fringes of the metropolitan area are rigorously controlled to preserve the rural, the scenic and the farming areas until they are actually needed for contiguous urban growth. As a result, one can drive out of the city and into the country and enjoy it, where in the United States one drives out of the city and into what has been called a "slurb"—a partially urbanized area in which the countryside has been effectively destroyed. To secure control of open space we need substantial expansion of planning powers and wholly new methods of regulating the location and timing of development. We also need substantial new incentives through taxation and otherwise for the preservation of land in agricultural and other open uses.

Control of Air Pollution

Nationally we are also recognizing the growing threat of air pollution. Where once the problem was almost exclusively one of industrial air pollution, now it is becoming increasingly one of automobile air pollution. By 1980 we will probably have 120 million cars on our highways—one car for every two-and-one-half people. In the larger metropolitan areas this number alone, without careful regulation, could constitute a fatal menace to public health. We must be prepared to pay a modest price to prevent further calamitous pollution of the air. In some cases this means that we must forego industrial development unless the industry involved is prepared to guarantee effective control of the pollutants it might generate. When all communities are eager to secure the jobs and the tax base provided by industry, all are powerless to demand performance from new industry. To prevent municipal rivalry in the degradation of the air, then, we need at least statewide regulation and ultimately we may need federal standards. In the field of automobiles, California is now moving toward requiring a primitive form of pollution control on all new vehicles. The standards are too low; indeed, it appears that technologically we still do not know how to impose a higher standard. It may well be that during the next generation we will shift to other forms of vehicular power in order to prevent a growing public health menace. Or we may be compelled to restrict the area of the use of automobiles in order to preserve public health.

Control of Water Pollution

Water pollution is not a general problem in the region as yet. But unless preventive action is taken now it will slowly and inexorably become a major one. Again, the establishment of standards of water treatment and water quality control will add to the cost of urban development while it raises urban amenity and enhances the region's competitive position vis-a-vis other regions which have allowed this problem to accumulate to intolerable levels. This region's failure to deal effectively with Lake Tahoe is evidence of our inability to grapple with these problems in a decisive way. That beautiful lake is on the way to destruction if controls are not imposed. Lake Erie has become a virtual cesspool in which animal life is rapidly dwindling, fishing is largely gone and recreational use is on the wane. There are some estimates that within twenty-five years Lake Erie may begin to congeal—be too thick to sail on but not quite thick enough to walk on—if present rates of pollution continue. The Cuyahoga River in Cleveland is an officially declared fire hazard—certainly only the first in such a series until we are prepared to take far more drastic steps in preventing river, streams and lake pollution. Again, we are dealing with largely metropolitan and occasionally state problems—problems which may expand to unmanageable levels unless they are treated at an early date.

Providing Adequate Housing

In older metropolitan areas the problems of substandard housing and slums are of awesome proportions. In New York City more than ¼ million substandard dwelling units, inhabited by ¾ of a million people, will require for their elimination more than the total amount proposed by President Johnson for the whole nation, in his recent Demonstration Cities Message. Those slums are the result of combined public and private neglect. They also result from the failure of the metropolitan area to provide an adequate housing stock for its expanding population, thus enforcing the overcrowding of the poor in densely developed areas.

The present housing stock of metropolitan areas of this region is relatively new and is at relatively low densities. There are a few intolerable slums which deserve to be eliminated. There is a large stock of housing of moderate age which must be conserved or rehabilitated if the cycle of slum creation is to be prevented. And there is a large and expanding need for more new residential construction to accommodate the expanding population. If we can build an adequate supply of new housing in all price ranges, not merely for the rich, but also for the poor, not merely for those who are already in our metropolitan areas, but also for those who are newly arrived, we can avoid the generation of vast slum areas and we can also preserve the older stock and the older neighborhoods. But if we do not build new housing for the low-income recent arrivals, they must occupy the older stock and the inhabitants of that older stock must move elsewhere and see their former neighborhoods become crowded and begin deteriorating. With population growth, in short, we face the challenge of providing new housing for all new arrivals or seeing the accelerated obsolescence and decay of older neighborhoods. The recently adopted rent certificate plan and some of the new formulae for low interest rate mortgage loans for private non-profit construction offer a challenge to the homebuilding industry and to inventive civic leadership. But each community must set for itself a target of providing adequate housing for its expanding population or face the generation of inadequate housing.

In the housing field too, we should note the emergence of new kinds of needs with which we have dealt inadequately in the past. Between 1960 and 1980, the aged in this region will increase by more than 300,000. We are seeing the emergence of many new types of housing for the aged— whole new communities which provide health and recreation services and which contain the smaller units more suitable to the requirements of those with declining physical powers. Some of these communities may become social disaster areas in the future when their present healthy populations reach the stage where they require more intensive care. The suburban area which encourages the construction of such communities now, because they pay good taxes and impose no school costs, may be courting disaster a few years from now as extraordinarily high levels of health care become necessary to serve them. We probably need a more balanced disstribution of housing facilities for the aged, both to provide a higher level of amenity and enjoyment for them now, and to make sure there is an equitable distribution of future municipal burdens. In addition, we have largely failed to solve the problem of housing for the aged poor, who surely are entitled to equally advantageous special facilities.

During the next ten years, the number of young families will multiply rapidly as the millions of children born in the period 1945-50 become of marriageable age and form their own families. The 1960-1980 increase will exceed 600,000 young people. Most of these new families will not have the income required to buy the expensive homes presently produced by the building industry. A vast market for smaller, lower-priced houses thus must be met, through the more efficient operation of the building industry, through the construction of a steadily larger supply of rental hous-

ing and through the modification of municipal regulations which now tend
to limit the construction of low-priced homes. Doubtless some combination
of these factors will be utilized to serve this need.

Industrial Area Planning

Industrial area planning is another field for metropolitan concern.
In recent years we have begun to see the development of planned industrial parks on a widespread basis. The competition between communities for industry, however, has too often led them to abandon standards
in the location and design of industrial districts rather than to seek improved standards. To the extent that we can secure metropolitan collaboration in planning and industrial location and employment, we should also
be able to raise standards so that almost all industry can be a good neighbor
and we can then slowly eliminate the scattered and obsolete factory districts which now afflict almost every metropolitan area. Such planning
will also enable our cities to adopt affirmative forward-looking programs
through redevelopment and land bank powers so that each may attract to
a high-amenity environment those industries which are susceptible of being drawn into the metropolitan region.

Central Business Districts and Shopping Centers

Central Business Districts also present a challenge to the future. They
have important functions to perform for the whole metropolitan region
through the provision of sites for central shopping, specialty shops, public
and civic buildings, and region-serving cultural and educational facilities.
Despite the decline in the relative importance of central business districts in the last quarter of a century, they remain an important tax resource in most metropolitan areas. But in the main, our central business
districts are almost wholly obsolete, filled with structures designed to serve
past needs, congested with automobile traffic, unattractive and lacking in
amenity by almost any standard. Most central business districts today are
not competitive with suburban shopping centers on the fringe. Their
economic stagnation in the face of vigorous suburban competition is testi-
mony to their obsolescence. In Denver we have a small but dramatic il-
lustration of the potential for reconstruction in the Mile High Center
Buildings. During the next fifteen years, if central business districts are
to survive as viable economic entities, they will have to be substantially
rebuilt and along dramatic new lines which can accommodate automobiles,
buses, and the pedestrian, and become genuinely attractive places for public
and private business. We have a few examples of such reconstructions already, in Hartford, New Haven and Philadelphia, and in smaller communities like Rochester.

Our newer metropolitan areas are also beginning to suffer from obsolescence in neighborhood shopping centers. While they still contain tawdry
and obsolete string shopping streets, vestiges of the streetcar era, they also
contain small shopping centers which were quite modern in the 1930s, but
have been rendered obsolete by the more advanced designs and mer-
chandising skills of the 1950s and 60s. A recent estimate indicated that

nearly half of the very large number of shopping centers in one of the cities of this region were in a state of constructive decay and required extensive replanning and modernizing to remain competitive. It is reasonable to assume that many of those districts should be rebuilt in the next 15 years to create attractive neighborhood centers—hopefully to incorporate functions such as post offices, libraries, churches, health centers and other activities which any genuine neighborhood should contain.

Community Facilities

Community facilities are a major contributor to the amenity of a region. We have mentioned parks and shops, and we must also identify others. Most important are schools at all levels, for education will become our largest single industry in the future, education for youth, in the middle years and for the aged. We face marvelous opportunities to develop life-long education campuses, which can be real community centers. We are already facing major requirements in medical and health facilities. One can foresee new types of health centers, which combine the features of hospitals, nursing homes, and motels for the ambulatory recuperating cases. These are only a few of the community facilities that should be of concern; churches, recreation centers, utility services and others should be added—all the way out to underground wiring. If we are to compete in amenity we must literally plan for high quality all the way up and down the line.

Highways

Finally, the dominant feature of every American city is highways. Today in the American image the term "highway" or "expressway" is almost synonymous with the concept of blight, for a new highway quickly generates an endless stream of inharmonious gas stations, restaurants, hot dog stands, used car lots, factories, stores and billboards. The American people have come to assume that this is inevitable and that the construction of a new highway will automatically generate the same kind of hideous mess that characterized the last generation's highways. This need not be the case at all. The scenic highway can be something of remarkable grandeur, drama and beauty, opening up new vistas of the countryside or the cityscape, enabling us to see things which were never exposed before. If we can have scenic highways in the best parts of our interstate system with controlled access, the preservation of views, the preservation of the natural landscape, and attractive treatment of the man-built landscape, why cannot we do it everywhere? The dramatic, impressive and joyful entrances to cities today are almost accidents of terrain or some small group's dedication to beauty. Consider the Golden Gate entrance to San Francisco, a natural accident, which man enhanced, or the lakefront entrance to Chicago, a product of human effort. But all our city entrances could be made great experiences if we cared, if we insisted on a high-quality performance, if we controlled the highway environment, if we demanded that all highways become scenic highways. We should long since have stopped building mile after mile of depravity and we must do so if we are to realize the urban future which is possible.

PLANNING BETTER CITIES AND METROPOLITAN AREAS

Building competitive amenity then involves attention to each aspect of urban development—to open space, air and water pollution, housing, industry, business districts and highways. It also demands that we raise our standards in everything else we build; that we stop building homes and stores and business districts which are obsolete and backward-looking when built, and that we think more of building something which will still be functional and attractive a generation hence.

If we are to attain the true promise of American urban civilization, however, we must reach further—we must begin to think and to experiment with the building of wholly new cities. Some of these will be remote from existing metropolitan areas on new sites which offer some unusual advantage of site or climate, or some new opportunity for industrial development. The region has already seen the emergence of several new amenity cities built around recreation resources. It has one or two built around new technologies, and there will be more. We must devise ways of planning these new cities from the start so that they become models for the future, not replications of the obsolete past. Other new cities are needed as satellites to existing metropolitan areas to attract part of their growh and to provide models for future development. When I speak of new cities I do not mean merely a new tract, however large. I refer to a city of 50,000 people or more containing its own homes, factories, shops, schools, parks, and other facilities, a balanced and complete community in every sense.

Almost every country in the world except the United States has a systematic program for the planning and construction of new satellite cities. Those of Sweden and Finland offer a standard of living and amenity which far exceed anything found in the United States. We might pause to wonder why relatively poorer countries have achieved such distinction and why no example of this type exists in the United States. The President has urged upon the Congress the authorization of aids for new city building, but no state has yet taken the initiative to begin planning and building such cities or to facilitate private efforts to do so. Until we can demonstrate in living new communities that America can equal the best of Europe, the American people will remain unconvinced by promises about the future. We need a hundred demonstrations to awaken public interest in this field.

I have dwelt upon four aspects of metropolitan development which seem to me to be among the most important we face in the next fifteen years. These are the acceptance of growth and change, the need for metropolitan government, the development of means for dealing with cultural conflict, and the maintenance of amenity in the urban environment. There is one more aspect of urbanization that must be stressed: the maintenance and cultivation of diversity. Metropolitan areas contain rich and poor, skilled and unskilled, the educated and the illiterate, black and white, the ethnic and the "wasps," the devotees of popular culture and the classicists. They also contain those who prefer a high degree of urbanity, those who prefer a quieter, more suburban life, those with a high tolerance for change, and those with a lower tolerance, those who prefer anonymity and those who seek community. The essence of urbanism is diversity. In all of our planning we must constantly search for forms which nurture and cultivate these competing and sometimes conflicting values, which provide space and facilities for each, which provide for each cult its cathedrals.

Growth and change are fundamental to the American way of life. The nation was founded and the West was developed by people prepared to invest their lives and their fortunes in the future, by people with a Utopian vision. Some of these visions were religious; others were secular. But secular or religious, they were founded upon the faith that the current generation's efforts and investments could and would build a dramatically better future for succeeding generations. What has happened to our society that this vision has become so attenuated? Why are we prepared to invest only when we can see a 20 percent return or a ten-year payout? What has happened to the men who were prepared to invest in futures they knew would not be realized for half a century? Why are we obsessed by fear of change, hostility toward the new, resistance to the future?

Here it is clear, I believe, that we need some radical new concept of urban education which will lift the popular vision of the future, dramatize it, analyze its costs and benefits, to enable the public to grasp the vision of the enormous potential of our economy. We need an Urban Extension Service to introduce the public at large to new things, just as the Agricultural Extension Service served so fruitfully to introduce the farmer to new methods and ways of life. President Johnson's recent message on cities has challenged us to such a vision, to "set in motion forces of change in great urban areas that will make them the masterpieces of our civilization." We cannot do less than to accept that challenge.

TABLE 1

Population of Metropolitan Areas in the Intermountain States, 1950 and 1960.[1]

Metropolitan Area	Population and Year 1950	1960	Rank in Size 1960 In U.S.	In Region	1950-60 Growth %
Denver, Colo.	612,128	929,383	26	1	52
Phoenix, Ariz.	331,770	663,510	37	2	100
Salt Lake City, Utah	274,895	383,035	62	3	46
Tucson, Ariz.	141,216	265,660	96	4	88
Albuquerque, N. Mex.	145,673	262,199	97	5	80
Colorado Springs, Colo.	74,523	143,742	154	6	92
Las Vegas, Nev.	48,289	127,016	169	7	163
Pueblo, Colo.	90,188	118,707	175	8	31
Ogden, Utah	83,319	110,744	180	9	32
Provo-Orem, Utah	81,912	106,991	186	10	30
Boise, Ida.	70,820	93,460	197	11	32.3
Reno, Nev.	50,205	84,743	200	12	69
Billings, Mont.	55,875	79,016	203	13	41
Great Falls, Mont.	53,027	73,418	206	14	38
Total	2,113,840	3,441,624			

[1] U.S. Bureau of the Census, *U.S. Census of Population: 1960.* Vol. 1: Characteristics of the Population; Part A, Number of Inhabitants. U.S.G.P.O., Washington, D.C., 1961.

TABLE 2

Estimated Growth of Intermountain Metropolitan Areas, 1960-1980.

	1960	1980
Denver[1]	929,000	1,780,000
Phoenix[1]	663,000	1,556,000
Salt Lake City[2]	383,000	625,000
Tucson[2]	265,000	672,000
Albuquerque[2]	262,000	629,000
Colorado Springs[2]	143,000	279,000
Las Vegas[2]	127,000	444,000
Pueblo[2]	118,000	186,000

[1] Ira S. Lowry, Metropolitan Populations to 1980: Trial Projections, The Rand Corporation, Santa Monica, 1964.

[2] Jerome P. Pickard, Metropolitanization of the United States, Urban Land Institute, Washington, D.C., 1959.

CHAPTER 9

The Industrial Relations System

JOSEPH W. GARBARINO*

It is difficult to strike the proper balance between humility and arrogance that is appropriate to an attempt to describe the outlines of the American industrial relations system a decade and a half in the future. The wisdom of humility is suggested by the experience of a noted labor economist who remarked in his presidential address to the American Economic Association at the beginning of the New Deal in 1932 that he could see " . . . no reason to believe that American trade unionism will so revolutionize itself within a short period of time as to become in the next decade a more potent social influence than it has been in the past decade." On the other hand, the forecaster's confidence can be bolstered by the quite notable display of prescience provided by Daniel Bell, whose delineation of "The Next American Labor Movement" in the April 1953 issue of Fortune has been borne out surprisingly well by subsequent developments. Ten years ago a collection of experts gathered at Michigan State University also compiled a record that has stood up well up to the present time.[1] Fortunately, the degree of success achieved in these undertakings is known only long after the event, and, since a certain element of boldness is conducive to reader interest, I shall attempt to be selectively speculative in identifying potential changes.

It is something of a paradox that both the failure and the relative successes cited resulted from the use of the same standard forecasting techniques, an extrapolation of the trends of the recent past. This suggests that the very success of the more recent attempts makes still another application of essentially the same procedures more hazardous. The American industrial relations system has been quite stable in its general outlines since the end of World War II. In the face of dynamic social, economic, and technological changes in the United States and in the world at large, an extension of this stability fourteen more years into the future seems potentially risky. Economists' habits of thought can be illustrated by Alfred Marshall's use of a Latin aphorism roughly equivalent to "Nature does not move by jumps" on the title page of eight editions of his classic *Principles of Economics*. In spite of Marshall's impressive authority, certain "jumps" may well occur in the period under discussion, but, in general, I shall rely on the identification of broad trends and their extension to 1980. Depending on the rate of change of these trends, however, their cumulative effect on our institutions could be very substantial.

*Professor of Business Administration and Director, Institute of Business and Economic Research, University of California, Berkeley; author of *Health Plans and Collective Bargaining* (University of California Press); *Wage Policy and Long Term Contracts* (Brookings Institute) and of numerous research monographs and articles.

[1] Jack Stieber (ed.), *U.S. Industrial Relations*, Michigan State, 1958.

BASIC CHARACTERISTICS OF THE INDUSTRIAL RELATIONS SYSTEM

The United States is firmly committed to recognizing the right of employees " . . . to organize and bargain collectively through representatives of their own choosing" over most of the economy as the cornerstone of employer-employee relations. Legislative enunciation of this policy and its administrative implementation began over three decades ago. Over that period the union movement grew from a membership of about three million to seventeen million. This multitude is organized into some 180 "national" unions based largely on industrial or broad occupational categories, with the great bulk of these unions united into a single federation, the AFL-CIO. Although the national unions individually and through the federation are active in political affairs, largely as *de facto,* and occasionally disgruntled, allies of the Democratic party, their principal interest and main source of strength lies in their collective bargaining relationships with employers. Bargaining structure is usually described as "decentralized" meaning that the control of bargaining policy is in the hands of the national unions or their regional or local subdivisions. Compared with labor-management agreements in other countries, the contracts that result from bargaining are relatively detailed, cover a broad and growing range of subject matter, are typically renegotiated every two or three years rather than annually, and almost invariably include a system of private third party arbitration of disputes that arise during the term of the contract. One of the features of the system that often escapes public notice is that employers are highly organized on a local and regional basis and that possibly half of all employees are working under contracts negotiated with groups or "unions" of employers.

Although some of the fastest growing unions in recent years are to be found in white collar employment, and despite the fact that white collar workers outnumber blue collar workers, no more than one of every seven union members is a white collar employee, and it is estimated that only about ten percent of all white collar workers are union members.

Having sketched the system as it currently exists, in the next sections we take up in turn: (1) automation and industrial relations, (2) the future of unions and collective bargaining, (3) some issues in bargaining, and (4) the role of government in industrial relations.

AUTOMATION AND INDUSTRIAL RELATIONS

Any projection of the future of the economy and society in general, and of industrial relations patterns in particular, should face the "automation" issue directly at the outset. The great bulk of the widely read literature on the impact of automation (read cybernation, computerization) has called for rapid, massive adjustments in our economic and political institutions to deal with the presumed effects.[2] If the more gloomy forecasts are close to being correct, the role of work and the worker in society will have to be redefined. Except insofar as they continue to exist as

---

[2] For a succinct statement of this position see *The Triple Revolution,* a statement prepared by a committee of social scientists and journalists and printed in the New York Times, March, 1964.

vaguely anti-social protective devices for an aging in-group, unions and collective bargaining are seen as either inadequate or irrelevant to the new problems. Once the discussion moves beyond the level appropriate to the "journal of opinion" article, the assessment of the importance of automation becomes controversial and the opposing arguments become highly statistical and probably unmanageable in public discussion.

The general public would probably be surprised to discover that there appears to be a sizable majority consensus among professional economists that the current rate of technological change is, at most, only moderately higher than that of the past and that no major acceleration is anticipated. A leading economist (and a participant in this conference), for example, remarked in a recent lecture, "The nonsense that is talked about cyber-culture and the hooting and hollering about automation at a time when substantial segments of the economy are technologically stagnant or even deteriorating is another tribute to a major intellectual default on the part of the economics profession."[3] The recent report of the National Commission on Technology, Automation and Economic Progress, a representative body of distinguished citizens, states on its first page, "Our broad conclusion is that the pace of technological change has increased in recent decades and may increase in the future, but a sharp break in the continuity of technical progress has not occurred, nor is it likely to occur in the next decade."[4] (This may sound remarkably like a long version of "Nature does not move in jumps" to the reader, but the thirteen members of the Commission included only one professional economist.)

In view of the importance of the issue, perhaps a path can be traced between superficiality on the one hand and serving up an undigestible lump of statistics on the other by stressing a few major points.

First: The rate of increase in productivity, usually defined as the increase in output per man hour in the private economy, is our best measure of the pace of technological change as it affects labor demand. The first warning about "cybernation" was issued by Norbert Weiner in his book, *Cybernetics,* published in 1948, some eighteen years ago. The coinage of the word *automation* is usually attributed to a Ford Motors executive and dated around 1951. It is true that over the period 1960-65 annual increases in productivity averaged 3.6 percent, while for 1947-1960 the average was 3.3 percent.[5] But this is hardly the record of an eccelerating technological explosion, however, particularly when it appears that the rate of increase during 1965, the last year of the period, was the lowest of the past five years. The reader would be right to protest that this evidence is not conclusive since the productivity index is a crude measure, but on the other hand, there is very little systematic evidence that has been put forth by backers of the claim that a really large scale automation problem exists in the economy as a whole.

[3] Kenneth E. Boulding, *Proceedings,* American Economic Association, May 1966, p. 12.

[4] *Technology and the American Economy,* Report of the National Commission on Technology, Automation, and Economic Progress, USGPO, 1966, p. 1.

[5] *Economic Report of the President,* 1966, USGPO, Washington, 1966. Calculated from data on p. 245.

Unfortunately, even if the prophets of automated doom turn out to be exaggerating the revolutionary character of change, there could be a major employment problem ahead stemming mainly from demographic factors on the supply side of the market.

Second: The increase in the number of jobs that will have to be provided by 1980 if we are to reach relatively full employment depends on two factors: the number of persons in the population in 1980 who are aged fourteen or more, and the percentage of this group who are classed as being "in the labor force," defined as being employed or unemployed and seeking work.

The percentage of the fourteen-plus population which is either at work or looking for work is referred to as the "labor force participation rate" (LFPR). Obviously, as of 1966 there is little that can be done to influence the size of the 1980 population of 14 years and over. The census estimate that there will be some 35.6 million more Americans in this age group in 1980 than there were in 1965 can be accepted as accurate. But perhaps developments that can be foreseen or induced will reduce the LFPR, that is, the percentage of the total labor force for which the economy will have to provide jobs. The first proposals that spring to mind are the familiar ones of encouraging early retirement and longer periods of education, both examples of adjustments in participation rates that have been occurring for a long time.

It is sobering to realize that the very substantial reduction in participation rates for the elderly and the school age population that have taken place in the past have been very largely offset by the increase in the participation of women in the labor force. (Although male participation rates dropped from 84.7 to 78.3 percent between 1947 and 1965, the LFPR as a whole dropped only from 57.4 to 56.7.) Because of the increase in the proportion of the population that will be in the middle-age groups in 1980 and because of a projection of a continuation of the upward trend in women's participation rates, the forecasted LFPR for 1980 is actually higher than in 1965 (58.3 percent or 1.6 points higher). Translated into numbers, the combined effect of the larger population and the larger proportion of that population that is expected to be in the job market, means that a net increase of about 22.5 million more jobs will be needed by 1980 if we are to achieve a 4 percent unemployment level. This would mean a 30 percent increase in the number of jobs available in 1965.

The job creation problem can be put into perspective by noting that the 30 percent increase needed over the next fifteen years corresponds to a 22 percent increase that actually occurred in the fifteen years from 1950 to 1965.

Third: The answer to the job creation problem proposed by the Kennedy administration and concurred in by the Johnson administration has been to concentrate on raising the rate of economic growth since growth creates jobs, and there are a multitude of uses to which the increased production could be put.

Just as the five years since 1960 have been years of higher-than-average growth in productivity, so have they been years of above-average growth in total production. Using gross national product (GNP) in constant prices as a measure of growth in production, the average increase in real GNP for the past five years has been just over 4.5 percent per year. This is a substantially higher rate of growth than we have experienced for the postwar period as a whole, or for that matter, for any extended time period. If we were to achieve the difficult feat of maintaining that rate of growth until 1980, what would the unemployment situation be like at that time?

A fairly reliable answer to this question can be arrived at by a simple rough calculation. In 1965 each employee (including the armed forces) accounted for $8131 of GNP. As productivity has increased over the years this figure has increased in spite of the fact that the average employee has worked fewer hours per year. Over the 1960-65 period, for example, the compounded average annual increase in GNP per employee was 2.9 percent. If the average GNP per employee continues to increase at that same rate until 1980, every employee would theoretically be producing about $12,463 worth of goods and services and the resulting total GNP would be about $1,213 billions in constant (1958) prices at full employment.[6]

If we are lucky enough and wise enough to be able to maintain the 4.5 percent annual rate of growth of GNP until 1980, we would be producing about $1,180 billions of GNP and the overall unemployment problem would be of minor proportions.

On the other hand, if our growth rate falls off to a 4 percent average (still a historically high rate), GNP would reach only about $1,100 billions or about $117 billions short of the theoretical potential. In the absence of other changes, this would imply an unemployment rate of about 13-14 percent instead of the 4 percent target.

The extrapolation of exponential rates of growth into the future is obviously a fascinating but highly speculative exercise. Depending on your judgment of the probabilities, you can come to either an optimistic or a pessimistic conclusion.

Optimistic version—If we extend our 1960-65 growth rates in both production and productivity to 1980, the labor supply and demand situation would be one of approximate balance with a relatively minor unemployment problem.

Pessimistic version—If total production increases at a slower rate and/or productivity increases at a more rapid rate than in 1960-65, substantial changes in our manpower policies and our industrial relations practices will be needed.

---

[6] This GNP figure results from multiplying the $12,463 of GNP per employee by 96 percent of the civilian labor force plus an estimated 2.7 million men in the armed services. The other 4 percent are assumed to represent a "full employment" level of unemployment.

Labor Market Adjustments

Even if one opts for the optimistic version, a continuous effort, intelligently directed, will be needed to make the labor market adjustments necessary. In an economy as dynamic as these rates of change imply, individual companies and industries, the various geographic regions, and the various occupational categories would be experiencing changing fortunes and would have to display a high degree of adaptability.

At a minimum, a more sophisticated manpower policy than we have had in the past would have to be developed. A particular burden would be placed on the educational system to provide both general basic skills of a transferable nature and specialized training or retraining to a large segment of the adult population. More and earlier information about labor market trends and changing job requirements would be needed. Our systems of employee benefits, both governmental and private, would have to be designed to encourage mobility of workers between companies, occupations and localities. New types of benefits such as relocation allowances probably will be developed. Many of the mechanisms introduced under the various manpower development and training programs of the recent past will be even more necessary in a dynamic high employment economy, although the private sector can be expected to do a larger part of the total job under the stimulus of relatively tight labor market conditions.

If the pessimistic version of the future turns out to be the correct one, then the problems of adjustment will be painful and accompanied by major social stresses.

In that case, the basic problem will then appear to be a need to develop policies to reduce the supply of labor services to match existing demand. This problem can be analyzed in terms of two concepts already introduced: the labor force participation rate and the average work year per employee.

Many proposals to reduce the supply of labor are directed at lowering the LFPR of a given population. The leading examples are earlier retirement and extended schooling. Let us analyze each of these in turn.

Early retirement. Many unions (for example, the West Coast longshoremen) have bargained for progressively lower retirement ages in their pension plans. This approach may be a solution to the job problems of particular unions, companies or industries, but its effectiveness for the economy as a whole requires some qualification. As long as the desire for more income is high and the decision to participate in the labor force is a free and voluntary one, "retirement" need not mean withdrawal from the labor force. An extreme example is provided by the military. Military retirement policies have always featured early retirement for reasons that need not concern us here. In the last several years, large numbers of military personnel who remained in service after World War II have been retiring after 20 or 30 years of service. Probably relatively few of these men have left the labor force. If these men or any other retired person are unemployed by our census definitions, they appear in the statistics as such. Indications of the widespread desire of the population as a whole to continue working after "retirement" is provided by the continuous pressure to raise the income limits placed on persons receiving Social Security benefits. As retirement ages are dropped, the percentage of retirees who actually leave the labor force will certainly fall and this policy will become increasingly ineffective as a method of reducing labor supply. To complicate the matter further, as wages rise, jobs become less onerous, and working hours fall, workers are encouraged to remain in the labor force and other persons are encouraged to enter. This is certainly a major reason for the rise in participation rates for women.

Longer schooling. Lowering the LFPR by encouraging more schooling will probably be more effective than lowering the retirement age. This policy has some interesting overtones. Michael Harrington has pointed out that one of the ways we have kept unemployment down has been by greatly expanding a new "occupation," that of graduate student. For a number of reasons, including the competition for good students and the early age of marriage in recent years, a growing proportion of our university students have been converted into a special kind of "employee." In one graduate school at Berkeley a recent study found that each Ph.D. candidate was being provided an average income of $3,000 per year from one source or another in addition to tuition and fees. (Incidentally, the school in question believes it is "below the market" in this respect.)

This is not a frivolous example. It illustrates the willingness of society to provide income to persons to pursue what is regarded as a socially desirable activity or role. This principle has been extended in the antipoverty program and may be pushed further. There are serious proposals for a "negative income tax" payment and somewhat less politically acceptable, if not less serious, proposals for the government to serve as an "employer of last resort" or to provide a substantial minimum income as a civic right. These are put forth primarily in the context of the poverty problem but insofar as they provide jobs or reduce the LFPR they also reduce the unemployment problem.

Reduction of the Work Year. Turning to the reduction of the labor supply by the reduction of the average work year, the Bureau of Labor Statistics has estimated that the average civilian employee worked 1999 hours in 1964.[7] This figure has been dropping steadily by between .3 and .4 percent per year. If we assume a rate of decline for the future of .35 percent, by 1980 the average work year would be about 1895 hours.

In the past this figure has been cut by a reduction in the work day, the work week, by providing paid holidays and by more widely distributed and longer vacations. Peter Henle has estimated that between 1940 and 1960 the average full-time worker had his work year reduced by 155 hours. Of this total 75 have resulted from a shorter work week in one form or another, 48 from more vacations, and 32 from more holidays.[8]

---

[7] *Technology and the American Economy,* p. 12.

[8] In E. O. Smigel (ed.), *Work and Leisure,* College and University Press, New Haven, 1963, p. 198. Henle's estimates referred to paid vacations and holidays, but this probably does not effect the general magnitude of the estimates.

All methods of reducing the work year have been employed in recent years. In the construction industry, long the bellwether of the shorter
work week, the 35 or 36 hour week has been appearing in collective
bargaining contracts while in other areas more paid holidays and longer
vacations have been more prominent. The so-called "sabbatical," a vacation of 13 or more weeks at intervals of several years, is the most notable
innovation. From Henle's data it appears that the average worker in a
metropolitan area worked about 40 hours a week, had about 6.5 holidays
and a vacation of 1.3 weeks in 1960-61. It does not seem unreasonable to
suggest that by 1980 the average work week might be down to 37 hours,
holidays up to 9 and vacations averaging 2 weeks. If this came to pass
then, all other things being equal, the work year would be about 10 percent shorter than in 1964.[9] This work pattern is hardly a Utopian vision
requiring major upheavals in our ethic of work and leisure, as evidenced
by the fact that today a substantial minority of the labor force has already achieved this schedule. The importance of this conclusion is that
it means that a falling off of the overall growth rate to 4 percent would
still be compatible with about 4 percent unemployment in this situation.

It might be argued that a shorter work year would increase the number of multiple job holders or "moonlighters" so that the analysis over-
estimates the reduction in labor supply that would take place. This does
not seem a valid argument for several reasons: (1) a person looking for
a second job is not counted as unemployed; (2) recent studies indicate
that only five percent of the work force are currently "moonlighting;" (3)
these workers seldom hold regular second jobs but work relatively few
hours at part time extra jobs often in shortage occupations; (4) both employers and unions discourage the practice.

To sum up: Both collective bargaining and legislation in coming years
will be used to reduce the labor supply by reducing the length of the
average working lifetime and by encouraging earlier retirement and longer
schooling, and through reducing the average work year. Even considering
the qualifications noted above as to the effect of some of these tactics,
their overall result will produce an approximate balance between labor
supply and demand in 1980. This conclusion requires that the economy
continue to grow at about 4 percent annually, a historically high rate, but
one that is below that of the last five years. It requires that we lower the
retirement age and raise the average school leaving age moderately and
that we accelerate the reduction of the work year by adopting something
like a 37 hour week with about 9 holidays and 2 weeks vacation on the
average. These adjustments will not be accomplished without political
and economic friction, but they are essentially a continuation of long
standing trends and do not seem unrealistic. Our political and economic institutions do not require revolutionary redesigning to accomplish these
results.

It is important to emphasize that the discussion in this section does
not mean that there are not major adjustments needed to accommodate

---

[9] The 10 percent figure was arrived at by assuming that the 3 hour reduction in the work week
would cut the year by 150 hours, the extra holidays by about 19 hours and the extra vacations
another 26 hours. The total is 195 hours or 9.75 percent of 2000 hours.

the labor market changes. In particular, the flood of new entrants into the labor force creates difficult problems as does the concentration of unskilled minority groups into highly visible urban pockets of underemployment. The point is that the difficulties are not solely or even mainly a result of an unprecedented technological revolution.

Insofar as productivity indexes measure the progress of automation, the pace of change is not substantially higher than that of the pre-cybernated era. The shifts in the industrial and occupational mix of the labor force to emphasize service industries and white-collar occupations are extensions of trends that go back as far as we have statistics. The adjustments needed are dramatic because it is probably relatively somewhat more difficult and because, in a growing economy, they involve large absolute numbers.

In considering the problem of adjusting the character of the labor supply to meet changes on the demand side of the market, educational policies loom large. While this emphasis is in the main justified, too much can be read into the inverse correlation that exists between levels of education and employment rates. These differences are of long standing, but they need not imply that raising the educational level at the lower end of the distribution will reduce these unemployment rates to those characteristics of the upper end. We have always used the educational system as a screening device for access to jobs. Given a choice between similar applicants with different levels of formal education, most employers will choose the one with more education. In a loose labor market, he will eventually set standards that may eliminate the less educated without individual consideration. Unless there is an adequate number of jobs, someone will also be at the end of the line.

The escalation of educational requirements may lead to a demand that the screening be accomplished by other means. The point is that too much must not be expected from remedies proposed for structural problems unless the basic buoyancy of the economy is assured.

THE FUTURE OF UNIONS AND COLLECTIVE BARGAINING

Discussions of unions and collective bargaining obviously belong together in the same section, but I believe that it is also important to point out that they can be two separate phenomena. To the average American, the word "union" conjures up an image of an organization such as the Teamsters, the United Auto Workers or the Plumbers union. In other words, the union movement in the United States has historically been predominantly a blue collar movement. Collective bargaining is identified with the union movement, but, considered as a decision making process, collective bargaining is of more general significance. Many aspects of international relations and of race relations, for example, involve directly analogous bargaining processes. More to the point, many occupational associations not usually thought of as unions are increasingly engaging in what is essentially a collective bargaining process. The medical association and the teachers associations come immediately to mind. In short, although unions are the most prominent practitioners of collective bargaining, they are by no means the only ones and it is important to distinguish between the future of the union movement in its traditional guise and the future of collective bargaining.

The State of the Unions

In the 1953 *Fortune* article cited earlier, Daniel Bell commented that " . . . U.S. labor has lost the greatest single dynamic any movement can have—a confidence that it is going to get bigger." Since that time a large body of a "literature of crisis" has been accumulating. The general theme has been an elaboration of Bell's view that the unions had entered a period of stagnation characterized by unimaginative leadership, a defensive, vested interest mentality, a failure of nerve in the arena of social reform, and an erosion of their present membership base coupled with an inability to expand into new territory.

In addition to the indictment of the mental attitudes or the social conscience of the leadership, the case for stagnation has rested on the twin facts that the industrial and occupational groups which American unionism had been successful in penetrating were largely already "saturated" and that these sectors of the economy were declining relative to the largely unorganized sectors. Although even the most confirmed of the pessimists agrees that the union movement of the future will be large in absolute numbers, unless they break into new occupational and industrial territory, they are destined to decline in relative influence and importance. The Bureau of Labor Statistics reports that white collar workers first out-numbered blue collar workers in 1956 and have widened their lead ever since. In 1962 the Bureau estimated that there were about 22 million potentially organizable white collar employees but calculated that only about 2.3 million of these were union members.[10]

The changing ratio of white to blue collar workers reflects the combined action of two factors. First, even within what are thought of as predominantly blue collar industries the "nonproduction" workers are a growing proportion to total employment. For example, in manufacturing as a whole, nonproduction workers rose from 16 percent of all employees in 1947 to 26 percent in 1965, a more than 50 percent increase. In primary metals the rise was from 13 to 18 percent; in transportation equipment, from 19 to 29 percent; in machinery, from 21 to 30 percent.[11] There is no reason to expect a reversal of this trend which apparently is one of long standing.

The second factor at work is a faster-than-average rate of employment growth in industries in which white collar workers make up a larger percentage of the labor force than in industries dominated by blue collar workers. The outstanding example, of course, is government at all levels. This trend is also expected to continue. The following table presents projections of employment increases by industry to 1975 along with estimates of the percentage of union membership in each industry. These

---

[10] *Monthly Labor Review*, May 1964, p. 506.

[11] *Manpower Report of the President*, USGPO, Washington, 1966, p. 201.

data indicate that the industries that are expected to experience above average increases in employment are those in which union penetration is, in general, below average.

Projected Changes in Employment by Industry; 1964-1975 and Degree of Union Organization, 1962

Industry	Percent Change in Employment 1964-1975*	Percent Unionization 1962**
Nonagricultural Total	30	32
Mining	—2	54
Contract Construction	37	83
Manufacturing	14	49
Transportation and Public Utilities	12	85
Trade	33	10
Finance, Insurance and Real Estate	26	1
Services	43	13
Government	54	13

(The four industries with greater-than-average increases in employment were 30 percent unionized in 1962. The four industries with less-than-average increases in employment were 48 percent unionized.)

*Technology and the American Economy, op. cit., p. 29.

**Calculated from membership data in Monthly Labor Review, May 1964, p. 507 and employment data from Manpower Report of the President 1966, p. 198.

This sort of analysis provides the basis for the stagnationists' argument that the expansion of unions may have reached its peak, and an erosion may even be in prospect. The present day labor movement is likely to be hard put to make major inroads in organizing a labor force that includes growing percentages of white collar workers, persons with higher average levels of education, and a larger proportion of women and part-time workers. (In 1963 there were 6.8 million voluntary part-time workers, a one-third increase over 1957.) In addition, management is increasingly sophisticated in dealing with employee relations.

From the union point of view, this is a depressing prospect, but the picture is far from being all black. Some unions have shown substantial rates of growth in recent years, and these unions are located in expanding sectors of the economy. The unions with the highest percentage rates of growth recently have been unions of government employees (Federation of Federal Government Employees, the State, County, and Municipal Employees, the American Federation of Teachers, the Post Office Clerks and the Letter Carriers); and unions of service workers (Retail Clerks, Hotel and Restaurant Workers and the Building Service Workers). Although their percentage increase is not impressive because of their huge present membership base, the Teamsters' absolute growth has been impressive, and this aggressive, flexible, and strategically located union is represented in a remarkable variety of industries and occupations. It has a foothold in several growing areas of the economy, including some white collar groups.

An important new factor that suggests further growth in unionization outside traditional industrial boundaries is a tendency to extend the governmental recognition of "the right to organize and bargain collectively" to government workers of all kinds, to employees of non-profit institutions and possibly even to agriculture. In addition to making explicit the right to organize, legislatures are showing signs of providing the election machinery to determine questions of representation that the Wagner Act introduced into labor relations in 1935. The difference between facing the need to win recognition as bargaining agent by economic pressure, actual or potential, and winning a representation election is very substantial. This is particularly true when the target of an organizing campaign is a group of relatively high status persons or a group of women. During the Kennedy administration, the federal government adopted a policy that made the organization of its employees easier. Some municipalities have adopted official labor relations machinery (examples are New York and Philadelphia), and some states have begun to extend their labor relations acts to cover non-profit organizations (New York). The importance of this last move for the burgeoning medical care industry is obvious. The California state legislature is under pressure to provide machinery to implement collective bargaining in agriculture as well as in the state service. The nationwide collective bargaining ferment among teachers' organizations needs no emphasis.

Those analysts who dissent from the stagnationists' view do so on two different grounds, an appeal to history and to international comparisons. Looked at over the long run, American unions have grown in spurts interspersed with periods when they rested on a plateau or even may have regressed somewhat. The bursts of growth were not predicted or perhaps predictable. The dissenters believe that there is an excellent chance of history repeating itself. More important, the experience of most of the industrial countries of Western Europe indicates that there is nothing in the psychology or the sociology of the occupational groups that make up white collar employment that precludes their organization. Although figures are highly tentative, it appears that the percentage of union membership of white collar workers in these countries ranges from around 30 to about 65 percent, compared to the American rate of 10 percent. The significance of this comparison is sometimes challenged by arguing that the European countries have a more clearly defined class structure, and that this tends to encourage group identification on economic grounds. This point might be argued either way. In some European countries the class consciousness of the blue collar workers expressed itself early in politically oriented unions allied with socialist parties. Typically, the white collar groups have been more conservative and have hesitated to collaborate with the blue collar unions on political grounds. In some countries, such as Sweden, completely separate white collar union federations have been organized, at least partly to avoid the political commitment implied in working with existing blue collar unions. In other words, it is possible that class consciousness and a tradition of political unionism in the earlier manual unions might well have militated against white collar unionism. Significantly, it appears that in these countries the strategic core of white collar unionism is found among government employees.

Striking a balance between the stagnationists' position and the dissenters, I predict that by 1980 the blue collar union sector will be somewhat larger in absolute numbers, but somewhat smaller as a percentage of all employees than at present. I would expect that white collar unions will have increased their penetration of their potential market to double its present level or to 20 percent.

Supplementing this growth, or possibly even substituting for it, will be an increased level of bargaining activity that will be undertaken by "professional" societies and associations. The boundary between employee associations and unions will be much more blurred than at present, but it is not really important whether organized employee activity is the product of organizations calling themsleves "unions" or by other more prestigious titles. The teachers at all levels, the health professions, the governmental employees, the engineers and other relatively high status occupational groups will choose to be represented by more than one type of organization. The associations will increasingly look and behave like unions in any event. To come back to international comparisons, in Sweden the professional associations, including doctors, lawyers, and university teachers, have formed a federation of their own and publish a pamphlet forthrightly entitled, "Swedish Professional Associations as Trade Unions." Whatever the formal nomenclature, the differences in the objectives and the tactics of the teachers' or the nurses' associations and the corresponding union groups will be no greater than existing differences between various blue collar unions today.

In brief, collective bargaining as a process of making decisions about employee relations policies will extend well beyond the confines of the union movement *per se* to include the occupational associations. By this statement, I mean that a sizable fraction of these latter groups will carry on formal negotiations with their employers through professional representatives at regular intervals, with the results being embodied in written agreements covering a wide range of conditions of employment. These agreements will be reached under pressure of threats of collective action, including the threat of concerted withdrawal of services, i.e., strikes.

Some Collective Bargaining Issues

It is obvious that this section cannot attempt to cover the entire range of possible collective bargaining issues that can be expected to arise over the next decade and a half. We shall confine the discussion to the identification of some dominant themes that appear to be of special importance and interest.

Wage increases will of course be a regular focus of bargaining. Perhaps for our purposes it will be enough to suggest the probable level of money wages that is likely to prevail in 1980 on the assumption that trends of the past fifteen years continue for the next fifteen. In this event, present manufacturing average hourly earnings of $2.50 would rise to about $4.50, present construction wages of $3.68 would rise to about $7.50. Specialty trades in construction such as the plumbers, will probably reach $12.00 an hour or more. New college graduates are likely to be entertaining offers in the range of $1000 a month. At the rate of increase that has prevailed since 1951, the 1964 average annual salary of classroom teachers of about $6000 would jump to over $12,000 by 1980. Even if prices were to rise by 25 percent over the next fifteen years (a highly likely prospect), these increases would represent a very sizable increase in real earnings. The pessimist skeptical of the relevance of compounded rates of growth is reminded that the same range of predictions made in 1950 about 1966 would have seemed unrealistic to many persons.

Of greater intellectual interest are two other major issues:

1. Changes in the form of compensation.

The next collective bargaining innovation may well be a push for the replacement of the hourly basis of pay for blue collar workers with a weekly salary. A minor trend in this direction has been in existence for some time, but unfortunately there is no straightforward measure of the shift. The earlier data cited on the increase in the proportion of all employees accounted for by nonproduction employees in manufacturing (from 16 percent in 1947 to 26 in 1965) is probably a good approximation of the change from wages to salaries as a measure of payment. The steel industry has reported that its salaried employment rose from 11 percent in 1940 to 21 percent in 1958.[12] This shift is primarily the result of the growing importance of white collar occupations, which are more commonly paid a weekly salary, rather than a change in pay systems for specific workers. There has, however, also been some shift toward weekly pay for production workers. IBM some years ago announced that it was placing virtually all employees on salary. Some of the large chemical companies have been moving more slowly in this direction. In general, the tendency exists in automated, continuous process industries and for highly skilled workers.

The United Auto Workers has announced its intention to move in this direction and it is rumored that the 1967 contract bargaining will represent a serious attempt to achieve this goal. Actually the unions have been closing in on this objective for years by negotiating guaranteed full day pay if asked to report, guaranteed weeks, and by combining unemployment compensation with supplementary unemployment benefits under the name of the guaranteed annual wage.

A different version of a change in the form of compensation is the trend toward taking a larger part of total compensation in "fringe benefits." This includes various insurance-type benefits such as pensions and health and welfare benefits as well as holidays, longer vacations, and various savings, stock purchase, and profit sharing plans. The Chamber of Commerce estimates that fringes of all kinds amounted to 84 cents per hour in industry as a whole in 1963, or 28 percent of payroll. This compares with

---

[12] American Iron and Steel Institute, *Charting Steel's Progress*, 1959 edition, p. 55.

22 cents and 15.5 percent in 1947.[13] These figures may be on the high side, but the trend is probably fairly accurately represented.

This movement could slow its pace, but it is not likely that it will. The percentage of total compensation represented by fringes is considerably higher in most other industrial countries. France is reported regularly in the business press to have a fringe ratio of over 50 percent of total compensation. There are advantages to taking more income in this way stemming from the benefits of group insurance for various contingencies and tax advantages as workers' incomes rise to the point where progressive income taxes begin to be a factor.

2.   Job security and job rationing.

In the United States the industrial relations system has developed two important mechanisms to provide job security, loosely defined as the recognition of the right of a particular worker or group of workers to a job or a group of jobs.

(a)   In some types of labor markets an element of job security is provided by partial or complete control of entrance to the job market by unions, hiring halls, or other devices operated singly or in combination. In effect, in markets of this type, a judgment is made about the number of "regular" jobs likely to be available in the long run and the number of workers recognized as having a "right" to a job in this market is limited to create a certain relationship between demand and supply. The purest example of this process is provided by the operation of the West Coast longshore hiring hall. In this case workers are classified into groups with differential claims on jobs, and the jobs available for each class are rationed by being parceled out among the eligible workers by rotation.

Arrangements such as these are found in a variety of occupations, but the rationale for them is clearest in what are called "casual" labor markets. (Briefly, a casual market is one in which jobs are of short duration, with different employers and usually with relatively low skill requirements.) In casual labor markets such as agriculture and longshoring there is a tendency to generate a "surplus" of workers in periods of general slackness of employment. Under these circumstances, the available work tends to be divided among a group of workers so large that average annual earnings per worker falls below some concept of a "social minimum wage." In the eyes of at least some analysts there are social reasons why this result should not be accepted. They would prefer to limit the size of the work group to raise annual earnings and solve the income problem of the excluded workers another way. A full discussion of the issues involved in this situation is impossible. The crux of the matter involves these questions: Who determines how many workers are to be admitted to the eligible group? How are the individuals included to be selected? How is the available work to be shared among those in the group?

Left to themselves, labor markets which come to be controlled by those persons already in the market tend to produce situations in which the number admitted to membership may be kept too small, at least in the

---

[13] U.S. Chamber of Commerce, *Fringe Benefits 1963*, p. 27.

opinion of some observers, and in which the group tends to be dominated by a particular social class, or a particular ethnic or racial group. Note that the labor market involved may be that of company executives, university professors, government departments, military officers, or physicians as well as those of manual or white collar workers.

The limitations placed on the closed shop by the Taft-Hartley Act, the concern with admission to apprentice programs by civil rights organizations, with the effect of admission tests to universities, with the criteria for selection for management training programs, and recently even with the criteria for the selection of university presidents reflect a growing concern with the problem of job rationing.

In the future, the ways in which managerial groups and employee organizations in all types of institutions deal with the problem of access to jobs are going to be under continuous scrutiny. In industrial relations, the problem will be particularly acute because long established company and union practices will be challenged, and hard won rights to job security of those presently employed will be put in question.

One of the probable results will be that the use of the level of formal educational attainment as a rationing device will be the subject of increasing criticism, although it is very hard to propose a more acceptable method of selection.

(b)   The most familiar and the most pervasive method of providing job security is seniority. As it now operates seniority is based on continuous service with a single employer and thus it is found in different types of labor markets from those already discussed. Seniority is not workable as a job security system in industries such as construction, longshoring, maritime, and entertainmnt because the employer-employee relationship is typically not a long term one. Although it raises many of the same problems already noted, they are less severe. In labor-management relations in the future, the demand to raise the level of security provided by long service will be stronger than it has been in the past. "Total job security" or a permanent job commitment by a company to a particular worker has already been announced as a goal by the steelworkers' union.

There have already been demands for seniority rights that would be "portable" between plants of the same company, among companies in the same industry, and among industries in the same locality. (In their 1940 statement on tenure, the American Association of University Professors, incidentally, was already calling for colleges and universities to count service in all institutions of higher education toward the award of tenure.) These demands have not been achieved in the past because of management opposition and because they create very serious internal conflicts among union members themselves since relatively short service workers are made less secure as longer service workers are made more secure by expanding the area to which the seniority principle applies.

The final resolution may not take the form of completely portable seniority, but this formulation of the issue is indicative of the growing pressure for the recognition of a "property right in a job." Companies will increasingly have to "buy back jobs" from employees who believe they have acquired a vested, negotiable interest in their relationship with their employer through long service. Retirement plans and severance pay plans are examples of existing devices that are used to liquidate the job rights of long service workers.

In the future more and different benefits of this type will be acquired by high-seniority workers. They will take forms such as company financed retraining programs, either with a view toward reemployment with the same company or elsewhere, and preference in hiring into new job classifications including crossing what are now regarded as distinct occupational boundaries. Relocation and moving allowances, including protection against capital loss in real estate transactions and financial assistance in acquiring new housing, are also likely to be developed. The UAW some years ago proposed that laid-off blue collar workers be given training and preference in hiring for new white collar jobs, and the U.S. Steel Company is reported to have agreed to assist skilled workers involved in a plant shutdown in disposing of their homes if they would relocate in a new area.

The costs of programs such as these will be part of the explanation for the rising trend of fringe costs relative to direct wages. It should be pointed out that a successful policy of encouraging job expansion through economic growth would have the dual effect of minimizing the job rationing problem and making the private sector more willing to bear the costs of retraining and relocation, at least for workers with scarce skills and ability.

STRIKES AND THE GOVERNMENT

As long as public policy encourages voluntary association of employees and recognizes the legitimacy of collective action to advance group interests, there will be a strike problem in some form. In fact, as long as the various levels of government are unwilling to utilize mass coercion by the police or the military, there will probably be a strike problem even if strikes are decreed to be illegal. The experience with the Condon-Wadlin Act in dealing with strikes of public employees in New York State is evidence of that. The potential use of some kind of "ultimate weapon" in the form of a concerted withdrawal of cooperation is regarded as being essential to a bargaining system, even though it may be rarely used. As long as the possibility of a deadlock in negotiations exists, sometime, somewhere, a strike or its equivalent will occur.

If we compare the number of strikes that actually take place with the number of potential strikes that might have occurred anywhere in the economy, the incidence of strikes is certainly very low. Within that number, moreover, only a not-very-large fraction turn out to be strikes that can not be tolerated by the public without serious cost until the parties struggle to an agreement. Nevertheless, there are strikes that are "public interest" strikes in that they create so strong a demand that some level of government *do something* that the authorities feel bound to respond with positive action.

Small though the number of public interest strikes is, their number is probably growing. In part this is because, in my opinion, the number of strikes that would be classed as public interest disputes by current criteria is likely to grow. In addition, there is some reason to believe that the threshold of tolerance for strikes in general may be lowered.

If the earlier predictions of a growth of organization among government employees, the health occupations, and teachers are borne out, then public interest strikes will be more numerous since these areas are more sensitive in that respect. It also may well be that the public tolerance for strikes is inversely proportional to the level of wages of the groups involved, so that as incomes of potential strikers rise, the general public will be less willing to pay the cost of strikes to achieve still higher incomes. More important, if our full employment-rapid growth policy is successful, inflationary pressures will be substantial. The responsibility of doing something about inflation could mean that wage settlements that may be acceptable to both parties may turn out to be in conflict with governmental stabilization objectives.

It is true that as decision making in industrial relations becomes more politicized, strikes tend to be converted into demonstrations rather than economic battles to the near death. But they still represent disputes that have to be settled, and the milder forms of strikes, as with conflict generally, "escalate" fairly rapidly if no solution is reached.

Although there is more interest in compulsory arbitration at the present time than in many years previously, there is little prospect that a full-fledged system will be adopted. Policy has been evolving slowly toward an extension of the industry panel approach to the problem of crisis disputes. The Railway Labor Act has called for panels that provide voluntary arbitration for the railroads and airlines for many years. In the special cases of the atomic energy and the missile base industries, panels staffed by "professional neutrals" have been introduced. There may be some extension of the standing panels to a few other sectors, but the principal reliance is likely to be on *ad hoc* third party panels that will be used in potential public interest strike situations. Their function will be to delay final confrontations, to provide maneuverability and flexibility for all parties, to suggest the terms of settlements, and to focus all the apparatus of public and political pressure on the parties to reach agreement.

Special efforts will be made to encourage the parties to adopt their own machinery to avoid deadlocks. The government will be careful to avoid the appearance of direct compulsion except in extreme emergencies so as not to expose its own impotence in situations involving large scale defiance. The result will be a confused and often messy system, but once we accept the idea that a dispute settlement system "can't win 'em all" and that, short of complete totalitarianism, some strikes will always occur, a workable compromise may be reached. The result will certainly not be ideal, but if we are lucky, it may be tolerable.

SUMMARY AND CONCLUSIONS

Once again, the reader is reminded that the pattern of events sketched in this paper assumes that no major social or political upheaval will occur during the period covered. Apocalyptic visions can be the basis for interesting predictions, and only a fool would rule out the possibility that one or more might not come to pass. For example, in spite of the conclusions suggested by the data available for analysis, it is hard not to share the general concern with the pace of technological change. Reading of the levels of real income that a successful growth policy implies leaves one wondering if a viable international political system is compatible with the differentials in income among the nations that their realization would make inevitable. Nevertheless, an exercise in prediction must come out on the side of an assumption of continuity, though not necessarily stability.

The picture that emerges from the discussion is one of a nation of employees increasingly engaged in activities in the service sector of the economy, working considerably fewer hours per year, at occupations that are predominantly white collar in nature, and at pay levels that have historically been regarded as those of the economic middle class.

A somewhat, but not very much, higher percentage of these employees will be members of unions or closely allied organizations with the growth accounted for entirely by white collar employees working in government agencies, non-profit organizations, and service industries. Outside the unionized sector, a variety of professional associations will be functioning much like unions in economic matters, though holding themselves aloof from affiliation with the traditional unions.

A larger part of total compensation of employees and of total labor cost of employers will be accounted for by supplements to direct wages. In addition to protecting the worker against risks such as ill health, injury, or old age, these funds will be used to increase the job security of the worker and to minimize the cost of the instability of jobs. The latter movement will be in response to insistent demands for a virtually permanent job guarantee for workers with long periods of satisfactory service. The system of allocating jobs will be under continuous review and attack from various groups demanding free or preferential access to opportunity.

Government will be involved in labor conflict to a greater extent than at present, but not as part of a formal dispute settlement machinery covering the bulk of the economy. Special boards of professional neutrals will be convened to review difficult issues and recommend settlements. An arsenal of techniques for marshalling public opinion and for exerting political pressure for settlements will be in use. Direct government transfers of income will be generally accepted and more widely used than at present.

Perhaps the most important characteristic of the 1980 industrial relations system is that group bargaining will be much more pervasive than it now is. Administrative and managerial authority will be increasingly limited in all types of organizations. The "consent of the governed" principle will be extended to employer-employee relations, and bargaining out of decisions will be generalized over most of our organizations.

Operation of this employee relations system will require a high degree of administrative skill and these skills will be in short supply. Successful industrial democracy, like successful political democracy, requires that both governed and governors work at their job.

In terms of the new administrative skills this system will require, we have been moving in two different directions in the development of managerial techniques. On the one hand is the view that administration can be made into a science or technology. An organization is studied in terms of its mission and structured in a particular way. Information is generated, processed, analyzed, and a formal decision making technique is used to arrive at a policy. On the other hand is the view that administration is a political process in which the implementation of a decision is at least as important as its content. This means securing the active, willing cooperation of employees functioning less as subordinates and more as colleagues. The concept of administration as a technical skill versus the concept of administration as a social or political process is epitomized by the image that the press has created of Robert McNamara as the administrative technocrat while someone like Sargent Shriver is pictured as the model of the administrative politician. Regardless of the truth or falsity of these particular images, the dichotomy they represent is real. The problem of combining these skills in one person or of organizing their cooperation in the same institution is a major challenge. The degree of its resolution will be one determinant of the success with which the employee relations system will be able to adapt to the world of 1980.

CHAPTER 10

Communications

The subject which I have been assigned, the role of communications in the society of 1980, is a particularly attractive one. The year 1980 is far enough in the future so that I will probably not be held accountable for any rash prediction I might make. Yet, it is near enough to make possible fairly realistic speculation.

EVOLUTION OF COMMUNICATIONS

As a starting point in reflecting upon the evolution of communications, I turned to the dictionary, and found not one definition, but many. Here is one that is short and very much to the point. Communications is an "exchange of information." It is also, I might add, defined as a "process by which meanings are exchanged between individuals through a common system of symbols." Still another definition terms communications "the technology of the transmission of information."

I shall not pretend that I chose these definitions at random, for they embrace the major points I should like to discuss.

First, there can be no argument that communications is an exchange of information. But I question whether it is universally appreciated how even this traditional concept is changing.

At first, of course, information was exchanged between individuals at a distance limited by the need to hear the spoken word directly. Later the telegraph permitted rapid communications between widely separated points. In the 130 years since Morse demonstrated his invention, the distance over which information could be exchanged has been increased, first by ocean cables, and finally by wireless methods. Distance limitations have nearly disappeared. In the case of the Mariner IV spacecraft, successful two-way communications were maintained over 134 million miles, so that in contemplating the distance over which we can exchange information, we may truly say, "The sky is the limit."

For many years, advances in communications technology were directed point-to-point systems. With the development of radio broadcasting and later television, the scope was broaden to permit one-way exchange of information with many people.

*Executive Vice-President, Corporate Planning, Radio Corporation of America, New York City (since 1955); a Fellow of the Institute of Electrical and Electronic Engineers; a Director of R.C.A. Communications, Inc., the Electrical Industries Association and of the Business Equipment Manufacturers Association.

In all communications, we make use of symbols. The methods which were originally used imposed restrictions on the kind of symbols which could be employed and the speed at which they could be sent. One hundred years ago, for example, only telegraph code symbols could be transmitted over ocean cables at a speed of about 5 words per minute. Then it became possible to transmit speech—a much more sophisticated kind of symbol. The ability to send television picture information is an even greater advance. Each of these steps represents an increase in the rate of information transfer. At the original rate of transfer over the ocean cable, for example, it would take some 40 hours to send a single television picture frame, which on your home receiver is reproduced in 1/30 second.

The greater sophistication of information content and the higher rate of transfer has imposed greater demands upon communications channels and has required so-called wide-band circuits to which I shall refer later. This trend toward greater sophistication was accompanied by the development of the theory of communications by Shannon and others and this better understanding of fundamental principles has enabled still further advances to be made.

Thinking again of the definition as an "exchange of information," originally the data transmitted was intended to be used as directly as possible by people, with intermediate devices only to convert symbols into such form as they could be interpreted by the human ear or eye.

The computer has introduced new concepts into the field of communications. It is one of the most powerful information handling tools ever developed and today there is a mounting volume of data transmission intended solely for use by computers.

The volume of machine-to-machine communications is so large that it will soon surpass the volume of communications between people over our long-distance facilities. Entire languages have been created, not for man to understand, but for the convenience of computers.

COMPUTERS AND COMMUNICATIONS

You may not, perhaps, have associated computers with communications and yet they participate in the exchange of information and are considered as a part of the technology of the transmission of information. The significance of the introduction of computers into communications systems is that it becomes possible to do more than merely send information over distances. It can be stored, retrieved or processed in various ways. For example, it is possible to interrogate a computer by means of telegraph code signals and to have it respond at a distant point in a simulated human voice. Or code signals can be put in and pictures or diagrams received in reply. In some of the newer systems, we can draw diagrams with a light pen and send such signals to a computer for further processing.

One of the more interesting fields of research is that of the problems of communications between man and machines. Perhaps by 1980, the present complexities of putting information into and receiving data from computers will be greatly simplified.

As in the case of development of simple communications systems, data processing communications was originally a point-to-point affair. Now the scope has been broadened to approach something like a mass communications system in which many users may be connected to a single central information processor. These are called "time sharing" systems but, unlike television broadcasting, they have two-way capabilities in which questions may be asked and responses received by all users of the facility.

The future applications of this new communications capability will touch virtually every aspect of our lives. An example of some of the relevant applications for the sponsors of this conference is in the area of education. For example, the overburdened teacher can be assisted by letting a computer conduct drills. Questions suited to a particular group of students can be printed out by a computer miles away. The student can answer, the machine can evaluate the answers and furnish the teacher with a progress report indicating satisfactory performance or the need for remedial action.

Other systems can serve as libraries, so that those who desire reference information can send in key index data by wire and receive back very promptly the appropriate quotations from available source material. Similarly students can make use of the computational ability of machines at remote points by suitable communications facilities.

In the future we are likely to encounter a higher degree of sophistication—making use of improved man-machine communications involving programmed learning methods in which information can be presented to the student, checks made by means of responses to questions, and the program paced to provide for optimum retention and rate of learning.

The examples which I have cited will illustrate the great diversity in use of communications which has already been achieved and which can be expected to broaden even further in the future.

What made this possible was a series of related advances in the "technology of the transmission of information"—our third dictionary definition. One of the most important of these has been the broadening of the useful radio spectrum by 1,000 times and more. Among the elements that contributed to this dramatic expansion were new concepts in ultra-high freguency transmitting and receiving tubes, and new transmission techniques.

The significance of these technological developments becomes startlingly clear when one realizes that the bulk of today's standard long-distance communications services currently employ techniques that were unknown except on a limited experimental basis prior to World War II. The advances of technology have enabled us to provide wider bands for the transmission of intelligence at high rates and in extremely sophisticated form.

Still another development of immense significance was the invention of the transistor in 1948. This spurred investigation of the electronic properties of materials and heralded the new technology of solid-state electronics, which has resulted in many new and useful electronic elements.

Solid-state components possess several important advantages over conventional tubes. They require less power; the heat problem is reduced; they are extraordinarily reliable; and they are incredibly tiny. An integrated circuit, a new form of combining many elements on a fleck of silicon, can carry as many as several hundred discrete electronic components, and a thimble can comfortably hold enough to provide circuitry for thousands of radios.

The New Era

These minute chips are ushering in a new era in communications based upon extremely compact and reliable equipment adaptable to both sight and sound. They are making possible increasingly flexible terminal and switching apparatus that operates at far higher levels of speed and capacity for all types of point-to-point communications.

It is no exaggeration to say that without integrated circuitry and solid-state electronics, space exploration as we can now foresee it would be totally impossible. A communications satellite, for instance, would be out of the question were it not for compact lightweight apparatus capable of functioning on a very modest power supply.

In another area, solid-state electronics has made invaluable contributions to communications through applications in computer technology. The first electronic digital computer was a huge, room-sized, and by today's standards, slow-witted machine called ENIAC. It employed something like 19,000 tubes throughout its miles of circuitry. By conventional methods, improvement in performance could result only by adding to the already unwieldly number of tubes and miles of wiring. Our modern computers are so fast that the time required to send signals over the wiring between components is a limiting factor in their performance. Light, or electrical impulses travel at such a speed that it takes about one thousandth of a micro-second to travel over a foot of wire. Not too many feet of wire will slow down the action of high-performance equipment.

Newer computers using integrated circuits are quite compact, and, together with the other advantages offered by solid-state circuitry, provide for results which could scarcely have been visualized ten years ago.

The broad technological advances I have discussed—development of wideband systems, solid-state components, and electronic computers—have given us for the first time the prospect of a total communications capability at any point in the world we may choose.

Computer signals can be transmitted to a typesetting machine, an assembly line, or a computer in the next town or half a world away. A television program can be relayed by satellite from one continent to another. Telephone calls can reach across oceans. Teleprinter messages can be exchanged in volume by businesses, governments, or information services anywhere in the world.

Furthermore, all types of information can pass simultaneously through the same channels in the forms of nearly identical electronic pulses. In other words, the technology of the past few years has begun to interact and impose the need for unity upon what has traditionally been a collection of complementary but separate communication services. Eventually, perhaps by 1980, there will emerge a master international communications system, which will integrate the thousands of channels available for the world's voice, telegraph, television, and data services.

Such an achievement will not evolve without effort. For one thing, tradition has operated against it. In our country the services provided by the telephone, telegraph and radio have been segregated by law, by now outmoded technical limitations, and by common usage. Internationally, we are faced with a cat's cradle of national systems, each with its own operating standards, equipment and codes. The extent of international agreement has been upon the allocation and use of frequencies, but not much more.

However, since there is such an obvious need for a unified global system, I feel confident that differences of opinion, both domestic and international, will some day be resolved and that a truly integrated communications network will become a reality.

If this occurs by 1980, a person living in that society will be very much a communicating individual. He could have at his disposal a private telecommunications center which would incorporate a television and tape recording system, a two-way picturephone, a high-speed electronic printer, and a combined computer and display unit.

His center would serve all communications functions from entertainment to the automatic remote transaction of his personal business. His presence would not be required, since the system would perform any function automatically by proper computer programming. His tape decks would record incoming material in both sight and sound for later reply. His newspapers, even his books could be produced by the high-speed electronic printer directly from signals received in his home.

If he were a businessman, a similar center would serve him at his office through a wideband channel appropriately interconnected with all related functions and services. All of the communications used in the daily activities of an individual living in 1980 would thus be provided by a single facility.

When this time comes, personal communications centers will be linked with local and regional centers that would form part of a unified national and international network. Such a system would include cables, microwave systems, and satellite relays. Together, these could form a complex to provide any communications service to any destination. Eventually, perhaps through laser channels, such a facility could reach out to manned space stations, and even to space exploration on the moon and the near planets.

The possibilities I have just described may sound as though I had strayed beyond the bounds of logical possibility into the area of science fiction. However, I assure you that it is entirely reasonable. We are today rapidly approaching a capability of communicating any type of intelligence in any desired quantity over any distance.

PROBLEMS AND PROSPECTS

The promise of such a total communications capability poses two distinct problems. The first is technical in nature, and is directed towards the engineering profession.

Traditionally, our engineering accomplishments have largely been pinpointed at specific objectives. To build a bridge. To establish a communications circuit across the ocean. To develop an autopilot. All of these are useful and difficult achievements, but they are not of the same scale of complexity as broad systems problems. This, however, is precisely the nature of the task confronting engineers when they address themselves to the concept of total communications.

Fortunately, we can draw upon past experience in this area. Telephone engineers have had to think of broad complex networks for many years. Present-day television broadcasting came about through the systems engineering approach. Here, it was not simply a matter of developing a device to receive television signals. It was necessary to create the entire system as a whole—transmission facilities, methods for producing programs, receiving sets, cameras, tubes, and all of the elements needed to enable the viewer to see and hear programs successfully.

Because of our record of accomplishment in systems engineering, I venture to predict that the technical problems of an integrated international communications network will be solved.

However, at the same time, there is a thicket of nontechnical problems that relate to the economic, social, and political consequences of instant point-to-point communication anywhere on this earth.

Let me sound one note of warning. The economic problems are still with us. We can provide communications over vast distances or we can connect great numbers of users to data processors if we wish, but we must remember that the more sophisticated the service, the greater its cost. It is necessary to temper the enthusiasm for unique solutions to problems with the drab reality of whether or not it can be justified economically.

Nevertheless, new technology also reduces costs. Let us for the moment forget monetary limitations and see where the future may lead us.

Imagine if you will, a world where lasers provide individuals with private lines for sound-and-sight communication across any distance, much as we now have telephone access to friends or business associates in the same city.

—A world where microwave channels carry television, telephone, facsimile newspapers, telegraph messages, and computer data into any home or office or educational institution anywhere providing instant access to ideas, to new developments in science and the arts, to shifting social and political viewpoints.

—A world linked together by continental and global networks of computer centers to provide, upon demand, all known and recorded data on any conceivable subject.

—A world where no spot is out of range of transmitting satellites that can broadcast directly to individual television sets and radio receivers in the home.

What will be the consequences of such a world? Will a universal language emerge, perhaps adapted to the needs of communications devices, spoken and understood by all mankind, in addition to their native tongues?

Will developing countries seize the opportunity to use relatively inexpensive satellite broadcasting to erase illiteracy?

What will be the official attitude when one country can televise its programs directly into the homes of other countries?

What type of international agreements can best prevent confusion and garbling of the various communications frequencies?

Will these agreements rigorously protect national interests, or will today's parochial nationalism retreat in the face of a one-world order?

These questions and others like them make up the second great problem area associated with the total communications concept. They are outside the province of technology, and so prediction is less certain. Yet, they will be of vital concern to society in 1980.

The revolutionary advance in communications that began less than a quarter of a century ago cannot safely be considered merely as an improvement in services or the introduction of versatile new electronic gadgetry.

Impressive and sophisticated it certainly is, but its ultimate use is of far greater significance. However it is employed, the communications capability of 1980 can change the course of the world. I hope that mankind will find a way to use it wisely so that the changed world will be a better world with better understanding among all peoples.

CHAPTER 11

Transportation

PAUL W. CHERINGTON*

Transportation is one of the most important functions in the American economy and in our society. All signs point to the likelihood that over the next fourteen years its importance will increase. Today transportation of freight and passengers in the United States costs approximately $120 billion, divided roughly 60 percent for passenger transportation and 40 percent for freight. The transportation system, including its air, rail, highway, pipe-line and water components, can be said literally to tie the country together, both for the swift interchange of passengers between regions, the flow of commuters and shoppers into and out of large metropolitan areas, and for the economical movement of freight.

Our overseas trade moves swiftly and economically by ocean and air. In particular, the airplane has made a trip abroad a commonplace event in the lives of many Americans. Bulk cargoes like grain and oil move at only a few mills a ton-mile.

Yet, there are many who are sharply critical of the U.S. transportation system. While no one really claims that it is not the best in the world, many claim that it is inefficient, unsafe, overbuilt, and badly in need of nationalization. Others claim that segments of the transportation system are technologically obsolete, that managements are backward, and so on. Recently, transportation has come in for new and intensive consideration, both on the part of the federal government and on the part of many cities and states and numerous business firms. In part, this revived attention flows from the criticisms of the existing transportation system, and in part it reflects a growing concern that, particularly in urban transportation, the existing facilities will become saturated. Indeed, in some cases, this is already true.

What, then, can we expect the U.S. transportation system for freight and passengers to look like by 1980 and how is this likely to affect both the social structure and the activities of individuals? What changes will be involved? An examination of these questions is the purpose of this paper.

Our transportation system is a mixture of technology, economics, management, and social and political forces. No one of these factors can be

*James J. Hill Professor of Transportation, Harvard Business School; research in the air transportation and weapons procurement fields and teaching in the fields of Transportation, Logistics and Government and Business; has consulted with the Office of the Secretary of Defense, the Air Force, the Army, several transportation and equipment manufacturers, the Aeronautical Research Foundation of which he was Director of Research, 1955-57, and the Brookings Institution, Washington, D.C., for which he prepared a report on *The Business Representative* in Washington; currently a senior consultant to United Research, Inc., Cambridge, Mass., President of the Transportation Research Foundation, a member of the Board of Economic Advisors to the Governor of Massachusetts and a Director of the Egret Fund.

overlooked in appraising the transportation system or in projecting it into the future. But in many ways it is a given state of technology and the economics and management of that technology which are the real deteiminants. Social goals (safety) or political activities (legislation to raise truck weight limits) serve largely as constraints on the system, although at times their impact is severe. We might well then examine the probable trends in transportation technology and its economics and management over the next fourteen years. In order to do so, it will be necessary to break down the transportation system into its constituent parts and further to subdivide those major components by various modes.

INTERCITY FREIGHT TRANSPORTATION

Today in the United States our carriers—public and private—carry approximately a trillion five hundred million ton miles of intercity freight a year. There are no very good estimates of what this will be by 1980, but some forecasts place the figure at close to three trillion ton miles or about double today's volume. (A ton mile is one ton of freight carried one mile.) This staggering freight transportation operation is conducted primarily by the railroads and by intercity trucks, but pipelines, inland waterway carriers, Great Lakes vessels and coastal tankers also provide a significant portion of the total transportation load. Air freight, although growing at a rapid rate, is still only a tiny fraction of the total intercity freight movement in terms of ton miles, although it is now a business with revenues of some $400 million a year. The basic technology and economics of this segment of the transportation system are deeply rooted. Although there promises to be major changes and advances in the equipment used by the various forms of carriers, there is no evidence to indicate that there will be a drastic change in technology The main evolutionary changes which seem likely to take place can be described as follows.

Rail Freight Transport

Over the past decade the railroads, which perform about 45 percent of all intercity freight transport, have moved increasingly to larger and heavier cars and more recently still to handling entire trainloads of commodities, known as unit-trains. Larger cars, multiple car lots up to and including unit-trains, bring about substantial economies in rail transportation, largely by reducing terminal and switching costs and permitting a higher utilization of cars. These trends will almost certainly continue, and perhaps accelerate, over the next decade or so. Thus, a considerable fraction of coal and ore now moves in unit-train lots. Cars of a hundred tons capacity are by no means uncommon, and there is talk of still larger cars. These, in turn, will require heavier locomotives or more units. But basically the railroad technological developments are apt to be evolutionary. At the other end of the spectrum, railroads have made increasing progress with the handling of containers or truck trailers on flatcars (to FC or piggyback). Piggy-back service was introduced and has grown both to take advantage of the economies of railroad live-haul service and to provide a better less than carload lot service. This traffic also is apt to grow, and to play an increasingly important role in merchandise traffic and the transportation of non-bulk commodities.

Over the last two to three decades, the railroads have lost a considerable share of total intercity traffic (as indicated above they now handle approximately 45 percent of it). It is not expected that even with these new and more economical types of equipment they will be able to recapture a larger share of the total market, but the growing size of the intercity freight market will assure them increased business, and it seems probable that they will be able to maintain approximately their present share.

Furthermore, the series of mergers which has taken place among railroads in recent years will reduce the size and hence the cost of railroads and will permit the carriers to move the bulk of their traffic over those lines which are most economical and least circuitous. In the face of steadily rising general prices, the cost of rail service of the last ten years has actually declined. Part of this decline reflects the loss of high-value high-rated cargo, but a good deal of it reflects the use of technologically superior equipment, requiring less manpower per given unit of output.

Major advances in rail transportation technology, over the next ten to fourteen years, will be in communications and control devices. Computers and microwave systems now permit long stretches of railroad to be controlled from a single point. In the old days the length of a railroad division was typically one hundred miles. Now entire railroads can be handled as one division and even the largest can be broken up into no more than three or four divisions. Improved communications and control techniques are thus apt to centralize railroad management in a limited number of spots and make for faster service, better information on the status of car movements, better coordination of connections, and the like. All of this should strengthen the railroads' position in one of the areas in which it is weakest, namely fast and reliable service. It should also help to increase equipment utilization which is now extremely low and thus an extremely costly aspect of railroad operations.

Heavier cars, faster trains, reduced switching and yard operations, and centralized control are likely to lead to still further reductions in the number of railroad employees. In 1965 the railroads handled their total movements with approximately 650,000 employees. Sixteen years ago, in 1950, railroads handled about the same volume of traffic but there were almost double the number of employees.

Further increases in railroad productivity are likely to take place, partly for reasons mentioned above and partly because of the increased mechanization of maintenance away operations. The familiar railroad section gang of thirty years ago has now largely been replaced by tamping, ballast cleaning, and rail laying machines. There will undoubtedy be continued application of machines to these functions, but there is no basic technological replacement in sight for the steel rail laid on ties on rock ballast; continuous welded rail and cement cross ties may come into wider use, however. In sum, the railroads will be increasingly in the wholesale transportation business and, except for bulk commodities for which waterway or pipe-line transport is not available, rail hauls will tend to become longer.

Highway Freight Transport

Like the railroads, the technological advances in trucking in the period to 1980 are likely to be evolutionary rather than revolutionary. In part they will reflect the gradual evolution of the motor truck in terms of size, carrying capacity, speed and economy, and in part the gradual improvement of highways through such programs as the interstate highway system being constructed largely by federal funds.

In terms of over-the-road equipment, trucks have been getting steadily larger and more powerful over the years. One of the basic constraints on truck size has been the axle load restrictions and width, length and height restrictions imposed by various states. In a good many Western states particularly, the laws have now been altered to permit fairly heavy axle loads and so-called "double bottoms"—two trailers pulled in tandem behind a single tractor. Very few of the Eastern states permit double bottoming, and certain of these states have held down axle loads in order to protect their highways. Gradually, however, permissible loads are increasing. As they do, truck and trailer manufacturers are able to design equipment which will carry more and hence reduce operating costs. Furthermore, the improvement in highways permit faster running times and less loss and damage to cargo in transit.

The rapidity of these advances is really more of an economic and political question than a technological question, but there is no doubt that trucks will be larger, more powerful, and faster in 1980 than they are today. There is a real question as to the length of haul for which they are well adapted. It is sometimes assumed that above two or three hundred miles, rail service, either in regular cars or in piggy-back service, may be more economical than over-the-road operation. These limits, however, tend to be extended in many instances by virtue of the faster service by truck and especially where roads are particularly good and permit high speed truck operation. The outer limit of economical truck transportation is obviously affected by permission to double bottom or load more heavily items which tend to make the truck more economical. Offsetting some of these truck advantages is an increasing trend toward imposing higher user charges and taxes on truck operations. These tend to curtail trucks' ability to compete with rail.

One of the most expensive aspects of truck transportation is terminal handling of cargo and pick up and delivery. The average size of truck shipments is small, and many of them originate in downtown locations. The picking up of a few hundred pounds of freight by a pickup and delivery truck is an expensive operation; so is its handling over the platform at the truck terminal. Even where these terminals have been heavily automated, a considerable burden of cost is still imposed on these shipments. Increasingly truckers must increase the automation in terminals and seek to improve and make less costly pick up and delivery service in order to control the rising labor costs pertaining to these functions. Increasing attention will undoubtedly be given to these problems.

In fact there are three major segments of the intercity trucking business. The first part is composed of common carriers who hold themselvs out to handle virtually all freight by all shippers. A second class is the contract carrier, which is much more specialized, serving a limited number of shippers for specific commodities. Finally, there is a large and broad group of private carriers, some of whom conduct operations for their own freight which closely approximate service which would otherwise be bought from a common carrier. Other private carriers are essentially short-haul or farm-to-market operators. Common carriers are closely regulated by the ICC, contract carriers less so and private carriers not at all, except for certain safety provisions. As a whole, truck transportation amounts to some 500 billion ton-miles a year of which the common carriers handle about one third and the private carriers about 60 percent.

The bulk of the common carrier truck freight is handled by approximately 1200 "Class One" truck lines. There are innumerable so-called owner-operators, a single individual or a family who owns one or a handful of trucks. These trucks can be "trip leased" to either shippers or, alternatively, to common carriers for a single trip. Despite the fierce competition in the trucking industry, these smaller owner-operators have survived and flourished. In part they have been able to do this through the purchase of relatively cheap second-hand equipment. If there should be a major improvement in the technology or economics of new trucks and new trailers, these smaller operators might find it hard to survive. Although less well publicized than railroad mergers, there has been a steady growth in trucking mergers. So far the truck merger movement has not produced economies of scale sufficient either to drive out the small carriers, such as owner-operators. The next 14 years, however, may see this come to pass.

Waterways and Pipelines

Just as the technological advances in rail and highway freight are expected to be gradual and evolutionary, there is nothing on the horizon that indicates that waterways and pipelines, which are now heavily used for bulk products and of course for petroleum and natural gas, will change radically in the next fourteen years. Tows will be somewhat heavier, pipeline pumping stations somewhat larger and more economical, but basically these two modes are not expected to be very different in 1980 than they are today, although their volume of business will be much greater.

A major factor which will affect waterways is the question of user charges and programs for improving both the channels and the locks on their inland waterways. To date, the waterway operators have not had to pay tolls or charges for using the extensive network of inland waterways which has been put in place by the federal government. A proposal is now pending that they be forced to pay such user charges or tolls and that the whole waterway improvement program be carefully scrutinized. The depth of the navigating channel and the number and length of locks on a river are very important for waterway operators. The industry, both common carriers and private operators (of whom there are a large number), have fought successfully for a gradual deepening of the channels, removal of navigation hazards, and the substitution of fewer but larger locks which can accommodate entire tows and thus reduce transit time. Whether or not they are successful in avoiding user charges, there is little doubt that our inland waterway system will be gradually improved over the years.

On the Great Lakes, where the principal cargoes are coal, iron ore, and grain, U.S. flag carriers have been under a severe handicap over the last twenty years in the face of foreign, particularly Canadian, competition. No new lake transports have been built in American yards for approximately a decade. Whether technological advances will permit the revival of this industry or whether as our vessels become obsolete the Lakes traffic will pass to the railroads or into foreign ships is a matter of speculation.

Air Freight

As previously noted, air transportation of cargo is now a tiny fraction (less than 1 percent) of total cargo movement in the United States. This is a sector, however, which is growing rapidly, and in which major technological advances are taking place to the point where some forecasts indicate a ten- to twenty-fold increase in air freight over the next decade. New equipment will greatly reduce the costs of air shipment from a current level of approximately 18¢ to 21¢ a ton mile down to a level perhaps as low as 9¢ to 11¢. Essentially, the technological changes which may make this growth possible consist of very large air transports capable of handling a hundred tons or more of freight together with greatly improved ground cargo handling methods and equipment. The reductions in tariff rates to the extent predicted by many will undoubtedly bring about an increased amount of air freight. But the new rates will still be well above those which prevail for surface transportation. Average truck rates in the country, even for smaller shipments, come to approximately 6¢ or 7¢ a ton mile and for long haul, truckload shipments to considerably less than that. Average rail shipments move with approximately a cent a ton mile, although carload merchandise traffic moves at approximately 2¼¢ a ton mile. Air transportation has its obvious advantage in longer hauls. This is reflected in the fact that current air shipments move an average of approximately 700 miles, rail shipments approximately 350 miles, and truck shipments somewhat below 100 miles. These averages, however, embrace a wide range of shipment lengths.

The large air transports which should make possible this revolution in air freight are primarily derivatives of larger engines and of military cargo airplanes such as the C5A, being built for rapid logistics deployment by the military. But even if these airplanes and improved air cargo handling systems are developed, it is unlikely that air will capture any major fraction of total cargo moving within the United States in the next fourteen years. The costs are certain to be higher and speed of transportation tends not to be too important except for relatively specialized commodities. Air freight can, however, be extremely useful to shippers in extending a market range and in specialized situations. For example, strawberry growers on the west coast recently have been able to move a major proportion of their crop to the east coast at economical rates. The marketing of this commodity in eastern markets would simply not be possible due to perishability by surface. Thus, the growth of air transportation, dramatic as it may be, will tend to focus upon specialized segments of the transportation market. It is hard to forecast just where the growth will occur. In terms of dollar volume, air cargo could easily increase to about 3 billion dollars a year out of the total transportation freight bill by 1980 of perhaps 80 billion dollars. Even this would be a drastic shift from the $350-$400 million level which prevails today.

INTERCITY PASSENGER TRAVEL

We turn now to a consideration of probable developments in the equipment and technological base for intercity passenger movements.

Rail and Other Private Right-of-Way Systems

By 1980 there will be few, if any, conventional intercity passenger trains left in service. The volume of intercity rail traffic service has been declining rapidly over the last few years and that which remains is conducted at a substantial deficit from the standpoint of the railroads. The decline in rail passenger service has been most dramatic in the East, but it is a nationwide phenomenon. The total rail passenger deficit in 1965 was approximately $450 million, constituting a substantial drain on railroad freight revenues. Continued erosion of passenger service in the East should lead to its virtual abandonment by the early 70's. Passenger service in the West, particularly on trans-continental trains, may continue somewhat beyond this, but even here increasing passenger deficits, the obsolescence of equipment, and improved air service is almost certain to spell the doom of conventional rail passenger service.

Recently, federal legislation has provided for a demonstration program of a high speed rail intercity system to be operated in the corridor between Boston, New York, and Washington. Such a program will be commenced during late 1966 and early 1967, and these tests will undoubtedly determine whether additional programs will be undertaken in this area, and whether intercity rail passenger transportation experiments will be extended to other corridors, such as Los Angeles-San Francisco, Chicago-Detroit-Cleveland, Philadelphia-Pittsburgh, and the like. The initial experiments in the Northeast Corridor Study will be conducted with new experimental cars and some of the trains will use turbine power. But essentially they will operate over existing tracks, which are being somewhat modified and improved for purposes of the experiment. Various proposals have been made for radical innovations in ground transportation in the corridors. These extend all the way from essentially a new high-speed rail line (steel wheels on steel rails) to very exotic subterranean systems operated by air pressure or other propulsion devices. The public acceptance of the corridor projects and the relative costs of the various exotic proposals vs.

the cost of increased highway facilities are likely to determine whether these projects are carried through to completion, either in the Northeast Corridor or in other corridors having a high population density.

Numerous articles have appeared raising the question of why the Japanese can have a high-speed railroad between Tokyo and Osaka whereas rail service in what appears to be comparable corridors in the United States is rapidly deteriorating. It should be borne in mind that the population density in the Tokyo-Osaka corridor is several times that of the Boston-Washington corridor, that the income of people living in the Tokyo-Osaka corridor is approximately one-third that of the Boston-Washington corridor while the incidence of automobile ownership in the Boston-Washington corridor is approximately seven times that of the Tokyo-Osaka corridor. Thus, while circumstances in the Tokyo-Osaka corridor are ideal for public transportation, those in the Boston-Washington corridor appear to point to continued heavy reliance on the private automobile.

Almost irrespective of the technology employed in providing rail or other surface common carrier passenger transportation in a corridor, the capital costs are likely to be enormous. Extensive land taking must be undertaken as must the erection of special rights of way, either above or below the ground. Cost estimates for a completely new system between Boston and Washington range between 3 and 13 billion dollars. With strong evidence pointing in the direction of the private automobile, there is natural reluctance and hesitation about embarking on such an expensive project until or unless there is fairly clear-cut experimental evidence that the public will accept and patronize a new surface common carrier system. This is particularly true in view of the fact that air service, despite restrictions of air traffic control and airport delays, will in most cases be able to provide faster service and at fares which are probably not much above any self-supporting surface system which can be developed.

Of the various exotic or quasi-exotic systems which have been proposed for passenger transportation within major passenger corridors, some deserve special mention. One of these is a scheme providing for a wide gauge rail system with flat cars onto which passenger cars would be driven and transported over the route at relatively high speeds (approaching 150 mph). Subterranean systems have already been mentioned. These would be far below the surface and would be built by utilizing the digging, burrowing and cutting techniques developed in the building of missile sites and similar underground defense installations. One of the most intriguing ideas is the so-called ground effect machine, a device which rides from a few inches to a foot or so above the surface, either through a forced blast of air or a captured air bubble. Such GEM's would undoubtedly have their own right-of-way. They might carry automobiles or might have seats for passengers or a combination of the two.

Finally, there is a distinct possibility that by 1980 there will be automatic or semi-automatic highways which can take control of a passenger car either operating on its own wheels or operating on a simple platform and handle its complete trip over a system, freeing the driver from the actual operation of the vehicle between two points on the right of way. It is not clear whether automatic highways will use the automobile's own engine as a power source or will transmit power along with the necessary commands and controls.

Some of these more exotic schemes will require extensive additional research and development. Because of their high capital costs, it is unlikely that they will be installed, even if successfully developed by 1980, except in corridors having a very high density of traffic, such as New York-Boston, New York-Washington, and the like.

Private Automobiles

No matter what technology may bring forth in the way of intercity passenger travel by 1980, it is certain that the great bulk of it will still be conducted by private automobiles operating on a conventional highway system. Of the approximately one trillion passenger miles generated in the United States in 1965, well over 90 percent was performed by private automobiles and there is no reason to believe that this percentage will drop substantially. The technological trends which are likely to prevail in automobile performance indicate that while increased attention will be given to safety, at the same time horse power and speed will gradually increase. In part this will reflect fairly rapid improvements in highways and in signaling and control devices, especially within semi-built-up or built-up areas. There is every likelihood that the Interstate Highway Program, amounting to some 45,000 miles of road, will be extended and continued beyond its current target completion date of 1972. Many segments of the existing system will undoubtedly be enlarged. Automobile ownership is expected to rise from approximately 85 million cars in 1965, or roughly one for every three people, to perhaps 140 million cars by 1980, or roughly one to every two people. In addition, automobile use is likely to further increase from approximately 13,000 miles per car per year at present up to some 20,000 miles per car per year.

What will the passenger car of 1980 look like? With the exception of an increased attention to safety, there is little likelihood that it will be fundamentally different from the 1967 models, although there will certainly be differences in styling. One potential is that some manufacturer will develop a practical and economical turbine engine. On the other hand, the chances seem to be against this eventuality. The present internal combustion engine is relatively simple, economical, and trouble-free. The basic engine itself, for a low priced car, can be produced in quantity at a cost of not much more than $100. It is extremely doubtful whether the turbine engine with its somewhat closer tolerances, even though it has fewer moving parts, can be developed for anything like this small sum. Thus, it is likely that by 1980 we will still be using the gasoline internal combustion engine.

A second possibility is that the car of 1980 will be equipped with communications and electronics gear which will permit external control. Given the relatively slow pace of technological advance in the automotive industry, however, any such developments seem likely to take place after

1980, rather than before. That the 1980 car will be safer seems reasonably assured. It will also be fitted with devices to prevent the discharge of air pollutants and there may well be similar noise suppression devices added to it.

Highway construction on the major intercity roads is similarly not likely to change drastically, although increasing attention will undoubtedly be given to the safety aspects of highways and gradients. Rights of way will permit comparatively high speed operation, with at least today's level of safety. There is no question that in 1980, as today, the private automobile will still be the primary means of intercity passenger transportation.

Buses

The bus has enjoyed a useful but relatively unglamorous position in the American transportation system. Intercity bus travel is comparatively short range and has been static in terms of total volume for over a decade, despite the rapid decline in rail transportation. There is little on the horizon to indicate that this situation will change in the next fourteen years. Bus transportation will undoubtedly be more comfortable; it will probably be quicker; but in terms of intercity travel, at least, it will not play a major factor in the over-all transportation passenger system, accounting for perhaps 2 percent of total intercity passenger miles.

Air

Air transportation of passengers in contrast to surface transportation is likely to show rapid technological advance over the next decade and a half. The jet has already created one revolution in long haul passenger transportation and the smaller intercity jet is beginning to do the same thing for comparatively short hauls. By 1980, furthermore, other technological developments should bring about even more startling changes. The basic developments will follow three lines. One, a supersonic transport; two, very large conventional transports; and three, short take-off and landing aircraft. Each of these systems is well within the state of the art, and each is being actively worked on with varying levels of intensity. Unless unforeseen problems arise, there is little question but that each will be a major element in intercity passenger travel by 1980.

A supersonic transport has been under consideration and development by a federal program for the last seven years. The selection of the contractor to build a prototype for such an airplane should be made early in 1967. This will be a large airplane with approximately 250 seats capable of sustained speeds of roughly Mach 3, or about 2100 mph. Because of noise and other factors, the supersonic will climb at subsonic speeds to its cruising altitude of somewhere between 70 and 80 thousand feet. Thus, for short hauls it will not save any time and will be expensive to operate. But for longer distances, where speed becomes particularly important, there will be an extensive network of supersonic passenger routes, both domestic and international, by 1980.

There are numerous technical problems still to be solved before an SST can be operated commercially; some affect safety and some the economics of the airplane. Included are the noise problem, the sonic boom problem, the sudden decompression problem, and so on. These problems, although severe, are likely to prove soluble. The supersonic will permit coast to coast transportation in approximately two hours, trans-ocean transportation to London and Paris in approximately two and a half hours, and a flight from the West Coast to Tokyo in approximately four and a half hours. These are less than half of current flight times and represent as much of a decrease in flight time as the jet did over the fastest piston aircraft when they were introduced in 1958-59.

At shorter ranges, the SST will have relatively less advantages, but even here there will be a considerable saving in time for flights in the range of 500 to 1500 miles. There is some question as to what the economics of supersonic transport will be, but present indications are that the costs will be no more than 10 percent above current subsonic transports. The British and French are building a joint supersonic transport known as the Concorde. This airplane will be somewhat smaller and slower (Mach 2) than the proposed U.S. SST. The Russians are also reported to be working on an SST.

Another development is the very large subsonic transport, which, like its cargo counterpart, is an outgrowth both of the existing subsonic jet, and the development of engines and airframes suitable for long range large logistics lift. These large passenger aircraft will hold between 400 and 700 passengers, depending on their configuration, and should bring about fares which are 15 to 35 percent below the existing air fares.* They will be made possible by the large engine being developed for the C5A and will be available in service by 1970. There seems to be little doubt that one or more manufacturers will build such aircraft and that the air carriers will purchase them and put them in service.

This airplane, in combination with the supersonic transport, is likely to bring about a real revolution in air passenger transport over the next decade. The day of mass air transportation will be at hand. The question is not so much a technological one as an economic one, namely, will the air traffic control, airport, and ground handling facilities be available to handle both these aircraft and the large number of passengers which they will accommodate. Current facilities and procedures would quickly bog down under passenger loads such as those contemplated. Thus, not only will the airlines have to purchase and put into service these new aircraft, they will also have to give, along with airport authorities, municipalities, and the federal government, increasing attention to the ground environment capable of handling a major influx of passengers.

The SST and the large subsonic transport, when linked together with adequate ground facilities, including airport approach and airport passenger handling facilities, will lead in the next decade and a half to a major revolution in air transportation. In the past, air travel has been largely confined to businessmen and to some tourist and personal travel. However, in any one year, only about 10 to 25 percent of the population has used

---

*There are also "stretched" versions of existing jets, such as the DC-8-61, which will hold up to 250 passengers and which will enter service in 1967.

air transportation and less than half of the total population has ever been on a commercial airliner. The large subsonic transport alone is apt to change this, both in terms of domestic travel and particularly with respect to international travel.

But these two aircraft are not all. For in the next decade and a half we are apt to see developed economical and feasible short take-off or veritcal take-off landing aircraft which will bring air transportation if not to the city's center, at least close to it. For several years we have had helicopter operations in New York (until recently) and Los Angeles and San Francisco. Helicopters, however, are relatively expensive and have never reached the point where they could be economically self-supporting. Once the federal government ceased subsidizing the helicopter operations in those three cities, the trunk airlines essentially took the place of the federal government as a matter of public relations for the attraction of long haul traffic. On the other hand, there is within the state of the art the capability of developing a 40-50 passenger (or perhaps larger) vertical rising or short take-off aircraft which will be attractive for short haul intercity travel since it will permit arrivals and departures close to the center of the city. The introduction of a high lift vehicle will permit rapid transportation of passengers in the range below 300 miles, where the airplane is not particularly efficient, especially where there is extensive surface travel time to remote large airport complexes. The addition of this vehicle, therefore, will round out the air transportation system and should provide a major new impetus to air travel.

There are a number of ways in which vertical or short take-off and landing aircraft operate. One is by tilting the engines; another is by tilting both the wings and the engines; a third is through high lift devices, operated through louvres in the wings much like venetian blinds, which direct the flow and blast, either horizontally or vertically. Which of these various devices will prove to be the most feasible and most economical cannot be foreseen at the present. All are under various stages of development and undoubtedly within the next decade and a half one or another will prove to be decisively superior. In any event, it seems almost certain that within this time period we will have vertical or VSTOL aircraft in commercial service over a large number of relatively short haul segments.

URBAN AND COMMUTER TRANSPORTATION

Thus far we have talked entirely about intercity transportation. It is this type of transportation which accounts for the great bulk of passenger miles. But in terms of numbers of trips, a far more important segment is urban and commuter transportation. This is an area which is receiving increased attention, both by individual cities and by several levels of government. This attention is generated largely by the gradual saturation of our urban highway network, particularly at the rush hours, to the point where it can no longer accommodate additional automobiles.

Basically, there are three modes of urban transportation: the private automobile, the rubber-tired bus either operating on conventional highways or on segregated lanes bordering highways, and rail rapid transit.

Each mode has its vigorous (often highly emotional) advocates. There is no question that given sufficient traffic density, the most economical form of urban mass transportation is the subway or surface rail car. Such cars can handle 80-100 passengers at relatively high speeds and at relatively low cost, during the rush hours. However, there appears to be major passenger resistance to this form of transportation in the United States. The system is comparatively inflexible, often over-crowded at rush hours, lacking in privacy, and basically uncomfortable. In an affluent economy, it is hard to imagine that many people will be attracted to subway or mass rail transit except in a comparatively few very dense metropolitan areas, such as New York City, downtown Chicago, Philadelphia, Boston, and the like, although new subway systems are now being installed in Washington, D.C. and in San Francisco.

Some of the complaints are made against bus commuter transportation, whether it be operated on thruways or on segregated lanes, adjacent to urban-suburban highways. Particularly when buses must operate with private vehicles, their speed is slow and the discomforts, crowding, and lack of privacy make them fundamentally unattractive to the traveling public. Few, if any, cities have been bold enough thus far to set aside special lanes for buses, but this seems a logical development. Under these circumstances, particularly if the level of crowding can be kept down, the buses can be air conditioned, and the service provided with reasonable frequency, commuter bus transportation in segregated lanes will undoubtedly find a major role to play in the future.

Nevertheless, in most cities, the major way of going from the suburbs to the central city will probably continue to be the private automobile. This, in turn, will place increasing strain on additional highway capacity and particularly on downtown parking capacity.

It has long been recognized by city planners that the urban transportation system has a major effect on land use and vice versa. Probably the effect of land use on the transportation system plays a greater role, but there is clearly a feedback effect between land use and transportation. In the downtown area, in most major cities in the United States, we can expect to continue to find a variety of financial, shopping and cultural services which simply cannot be supported in the outlying surburban areas. On the other hand, for a great deal of retail trade, food, clothing, furniture, etc., the suburban areas, particularly where these areas are linked by a system of circumferential highways, are probably optimum. Most major U.S. cities, however, will continue to be heavily dependent on commuter and shopper transportation to the central city. The major impact of this transportation demand will fall during the morning rush hours, but there is likely to be a continued demand for off-peak transportation for shopping and other purposes. Parking private automobiles, at least in single level lots, is one of the most uneconomic uses of central city land which can be imagined. It is surprising, therefore, that there has been comparatively little work done on multi-story, high-speed automatic garages. All of the technology needed for such garages is in existence and the next decade may well see their extensive use in downtown areas.

Another development which could greatly ease the commuting problem is the development of a small commuter car, big enough for one or two passengers, which would be used almost entirely for urban transit. It could be operated either by electricity or gasoline and might be provided with its own right-of-way and parking facilities.

City officials, city planners, and others are increasingly concerned that the demand of urban highway transportation will gradually absorb valuable land and open spaces and that most U.S. cities will eventually come to look like Los Angeles, one enormous system of freeways. With a suitable mixture of rapid rail transit, rapid bus transit, and downtown parking facilities, together with increased control over freeway use (including perhaps user charges at on-peak hours), there is no reason to suppose that the urban transportation problem cannot be handled in terms of either technology or economics. Whether it can be solved from a political and social point of view is an entirely different question.

International Transportation

The large subsonic transport mentioned above and the supersonic transport are apt to continue the revolution which has occurred with repect to international passenger travel over the last decade or decade and a half. As already indicated, the supersonic transport will cut travel times in half, while the large subsonic transport will probably cut between 15 and 30 percent off the current economy fares. It is possible to conceive that by 1980 a round trip from New York to London, for example, will be available for approximately $200 and that a round trip in a supersonic plane taking roughly 2½ hours each way can be purchased for a price of approximately $300-350. The large subsonic aircraft, furthermore, will undoubtedly lead to substantial increases in international air cargo service.

Ocean Shipping

But undoubtedly the most dramatic changes which will take place in international trade will occur in the field of ocean shipping. There are several trends at work here which deserve to be examined.

With respect to passengers, the ocean liner, as we know it today, is increasingly becoming essentially a floating hotel for cruises or cruise-like trips. Blue ribbon trans-Atlantic service will probably continue to decline, and while by 1980 there will still be some volume of service, it will be patronized largely by people who, as an alternative, would go on a cruise or would go to a resort hotel. Particularly with the advent of supersonic transports, and a 2½ hour trans-Atlantic trip, the use of ocean liners for transportation *per se* will rapidly decline. Nevertheless, there will be a considerable volume of cruise service, particularly during the winter months to the Caribbean and southern latitudes, and in the summer to Northern Europe and the Far East.

But the major advances in ocean transportation from both a technological and economic point of view will come in the freight area. Indeed, many of these trends are already apparent, and the next decade and a half will serve to accelerate and emphasize them. Fundamently, the changes will be of three kinds. First, there will be an increasing use of very large specialized bulk carriers; second, there will be a substantial growth in the use of containers; and third, the semi-automated merchant ship will begin to appear. Each of these developments deserves brief mention.

In the 1940's, a 16,000 ton tanker was regarded as a fairly respectable ship. Today, tankers already in service have capacities of 150-175,000 tons, and the Gulf Oil Company has recently ordered tankers for service between the Middle East and Europe of 300,000 tons. These ships are handled with approximately the same size crew as the smaller World War II type ship, and obviously have enormously increased productivity. This is true even though they cannot transit canals such as the Suez and the Panama. The trend towards very large bulk carriers whether for petroleum products, ore, coal, grain or other bulk commodities, is likely to accelerate sharply within the next decade and a half. As liner service for general cargo on fixed routes and schedules becomes somewhat less attractive in terms of profitability, an increasing amount of capital is apt to be diverted to bulk tonnage.

For a variety of reasons, the U.S. merchant marine has been largely driven from the international bulk cargo trade. In part, this is because of union manning and wage scales. But for whatever reason, most of our bulk cargoes are handled in foreign flag ships. Some of these are owned by U.S. citizens but are registered under what is known as "flags of convenience" in countries such as Panama, Honduras, and Liberia. Recently, proposals have been made that we should attempt to recapture some of this bulk carriage. However, at present in order to be registered under the U.S. flag a ship must be built in U.S. yards and U.S. shipbuilding costs are roughly double or more those available in either European or Japanese yards. Furthermore, U.S. flag ships must be manned entirely by U.S. seamen and officers, and the pay of these men and officers runs between three and four times that of foreign crews. Thus, in the absence of substantial construction and operating subsidy, it is hard to see how this bulk carriage can be recaptured to U.S. flag operations. In the domestic trade, such as between the Gulf and the Atlantic coasts, foreign flag vessels are barred, and these are reserved on a monopoly basis to U.S. operators. This traffic, however, at least with respect to petroleum, receives vigorous competition from pipelines.

Leaving aside the question of the registry of the vessel, there is no question that bulk cargo such as petroleum, coal, grain, etc., will increasingly move in very large special-purpose bulk carriers. This will mean, in turn, a need for greatly increasing the channel depths and loading and unloading facilities in ports. It is likely that these very large vessels will serve only a limited number of ports, unlike the present situation, where many ports receive some service.

A second major development in ocean transportation is the trend toward containerization. At the present time, general cargo—manufactured goods, small lots of raw materials, and the like—is handled in cases, boxes, bags, bales, and so on, and each ton is literally handled by stevedores both on the pier and in the hold of the ship. The first step away from this inefficient, expensive and backbreaking task was the use of pallets onto which the cargo was stacked and then the pallet and the cargo were lifted into the hold of the ship. The next logical development which is already taking place at a rapid rate is the use of containers. These containers can be loaded at inland points, moved to piers by rail or truck, lifted aboard the ship, and at the destination port receive similar treatment to an inland destination. The problem of port and customs clearance can be resolved either by pre-examination or through other means. For many cargoes, loading and discharging costs make up a major portion of the over-all transportation charges. Thus, the use of containers will substantially reduce the cost of handling much of this general cargo. Already, complete or partial container ships are in operation in the intercoastal trade between the East Coast, Puerto Rico and the Gulf, between the West Coast and Hawaii, and more recently across the North Atlantic to various European destinations. The use of containers, both because of lower costs, less loss and damage and pilferage, and faster transit times can be expected to increase materially over the next few years. The United States appears to have a short headstart in the container business, but there is no reason to believe that the foreign flag carriers will not be able to catch up with us rapidly in this area.

A third development in the ocean freight transportation field is the use of semi-automated vessels. The typical merchant vessel now has a crew which numbers between 40 and 55, including a sizable engine room crew, deck hands, and officers and crew on the bridge, together with the necessary housekeeping personnel. With the aid of electronics, there is no reason why many of the activities which these crewmen perform cannot be automated. Theoretically it should be possible to sail a ship, once it is out of the harbor and set on its proper course, with no crew at all. No one seriously believes that this degree of automation will come about, but it is possible to substantially reduce crew and manning sizes. Some recent ships have been built to be operated with a crew of no more than 32, but this is only part way to the goal. A fully automated ship should be capable of sailing safely and economically with a crew of no more than 8 or 10. Because of highest labor costs afloat, the advantages of reduced crew size are particularly important to U.S. operators. However, the political problems involved may very well slow down the introduction of such vessels. Essentially, the U.S. liner fleet numbering some 320 subsidized vessels and rapidly approaching a stage of block obsolescence (due to the large number of vessels built during World War II) is dependent upon either subsidy or replacement by largely automated vessels. So far, the political problems surrounding reduced crew sizes have prevented operators and the government from moving into this field aggressively. There is no reason, either technical or economic, why this development should not be pursued much more swiftly than it has been in the past.

Two other possible ocean transport developments deserve mention. One is the development of a small nuclear reactor to drive merchant ships.

The other is the potential development of large ground effect or captured air bubble machines. Partly due to the development of nuclear reactors for submarines, and partly because of the general advance of nuclear technology, it is now possible to develop a small reactor, requiring only a reasonable amount of shielding, which would drive merchant vessels at speeds of 30-35 knots. Steam turbine and other devices can provide speeds of up to 30 knots, but only at severe penalties in terms of fuel consumption. For relatively valuable cargoes and express service on major blue ribbon trade routes, fast nuclear liners might well be an important factor in future ocean shipping.

More exotic is the proposal currently being studied by the Maritime Administration to build a large ground effect or captured air bubble vessel. These machines essentially use the surface effect to ride along just above the ocean surface. Small GEM machines are already in service for passenger service in San Francisco, in Italy, and in various parts of Europe, but nothing approaching the size of a 12-15,000 ton merchant vessel has ever been tried. Undoubtedly experimental work will be undertaken for such vessels, but whether they will prove feasible and economical cannot be forecast at this point. The hydrofoil, although it may be useful for smaller vessels, does not appear to be a practicable solution for any vessel intended to handle a major volume of cargo economically.

REGULATION AND LABOR

This, then is the panorama of the probable technological and economic advances, which will take place in transportation in the next decade and a half. As we indicated at the outset, the extent and speed with which these systems are brought into service will be heavily dependent upon a variety of social and political factors which are quite divorced from basic technological or economic trends. For example, within the United States, major portions of the transportation system including all rail, all common carrier airlines, common carrier highway carriers, and the like, are closely regulated. Generally speaking, there are either legislative or administrative prohibitions against intermodal ownership. In short, the Civil Aeronautics Board virtually prohibits another transportation company from owning an airline and the ICC has laid down fairly stringent rules for the ownership of truck lines by railroad carriers. Rates, and hence competition for traffic, tend to be closely regulated, as are mergers. Thus, many of the changes which might take place rapidly tend to be slowed down by various institutional factors, having little or no basis in either technology or economics.

A major aspect of the problem is the labor situation. In trucking, labor is controlled by the Teamsters Union. This union has been relatively progressive in terms of work rules, but is has exacted a high toll in terms of wages and salaries. It is not uncommon for an over-the-road truckdriver to earn between 12 and 15 thousand dollars a year, although to achieve such a wage he must work long hours and be away from home a great deal. In contrast, railroad labor has been comparatively restrictive in terms of its rules and practices, undoubtedly reflecting the drastic layoffs which the railroads have made over the last two decades. Airlines labor, except for the pilots, is more loosely organized. The pilots find themselves in the enviable position of comparatively restricted work rules and very high rates of pay, at least in the upper seniority brackets. But labor plays its most significant role in ocean shipping, where a variety of craft unions control the masters and mates, the engineers, the seamen, the stewards, and the radio operators, to say nothing of the longshoremen. These unions not only insist on a high degree of job protection but also on wage rates which range upwards from those which prevail for comparable on-shore jobs in the United States. This places the U.S. flag wage bill far above wage rates for ocean-going personnel from other countries and is one of the critical factors in the decline of the U.S. merchant marine over the last 20 years.

CONCLUSION

As we said at the outset, the United States undoubtedly has the finest domestic transportation system in the world. Nevertheless, it is apparent to any casual observer that there are many inequities and rough spots in the system which demand correction. Partly in response to this situation, and partly because of the wide ranging structure of government organizations which have been created over a period of years to take care of transportation on a more or less patchwork basis, the President recently proposed the creation of a Cabinet Secretary of Transportation who would have jurisdiction over all but the regulatory functions. Whether this legislation will be passed during 1966 or in 1967 is still a matter of conjecture, but there seems to be little question but that in due course there will be a separate Cabinet office for Transportation and that it will take over many of the programs and operating functions which now reside in such disparate groups as HUD, Commerce, FAA, Coast Guard, and the like. We can only hope that a department will still further improve our transportation system.

With respect to the Rocky Mountain area states, national developments in transportation over the next decade and a half are almost certain to produce a greater degree of mobility in terms of time and dollar saving. This section of the country with its vast stretch from the Canadian to the Mexican border and from the Sierras to the plains of Nebraska is a vast but sparsely settled territory. Transportation between the major communities and states is essential to the further development of the region. There is every promise in both the technological and economic trends, heretofore presented, that travel and shipment of goods within the region will be easier and cheaper than it is at present.

CHAPTER 12

Expecting The Unexpected: The Uncertain Future Of Knowledge And Technology

KENNETH E. BOULDING*

HOW IS PREDICTION POSSIBLE?

One thing we can say about man's future with a great deal of confidence is that it will be more or less surprising. This phenomenon of surprise is not something which arises merely out of man's ignorance, though ignorance can contribute to what might be called unnecessary surprises. There is, however, something fundamental in the nature of an evolutionary system which makes exact foreknowledge about it impossible, and as social systems are in a large measure evolutionary in character, they participate in the property of containing ineradicable surprise.

Mechanical Systems

In *mechanical* systems which have no surprise in them, we can hardly say that there is a future or a past at all, as the present is a purely arbitrary point. The best example of a system of this kind is the solar system, at least before the advent of political astronomy in the shape of man-made satellites. In the Newtonian system in which the planets are moved by angels, that is, differential equations of the second degree, the system can be moved backwards or forwards in time simply by turning the crank of an orrery. Time is reversible, and what we have is a wholly predictable succession of states of the system. The fact that such a system takes place in time is quite accidental to it. We could just as well set it out as a succession in space, as we do, for instance, when we express it as a graph.

We can express the same thing in another way. If we use the familiar sequence of Monday, Tuesday, Wednesday, etc., to denote successive states of a system, then if the state of the system on any one day depends only on its state of the day before, we say that the system is of the first degree, and it can be expressed by a difference or differential equation of the first degree. If we know, then, the constant relation between today and tomorrow, and we know what the state of the system is on Monday, we can predict its state on Tuesday. Knowing its state on Tuesday we can predict its state on Wednesday, and so on indefinitely into the future.

*Professor of Economics and Co-Director, Center for Research on Conflict Resolution, University of Michigan; author of numerous monographs and articles and consultant to several organizations; most recent book: *Conflict and Defense*.

This is how we calculate compound interest or exponential growth. If a system is of the second order, then the state today depends not only on the state yesterday but also on the state the day before yesterday. In that case we have to know both Monday and Tuesday independently before we can predict Wednesday. If we know Monday and Tuesday, however, we know Wednesday; then we know Tuesday and Wednesday and hence we know Thursday; then we know Wednesday and Thursday and hence we know Friday, and so on indefinitely. The greater part of the solar system can be predicted with equations as simple as this, though comets, I understand, require equations of the third degree, in which case we need to know Monday, Tuesday, and Wednesday before we can predict Thursday. Having Thursday, however, Tuesday, Wednesday, and Thursday gives us Friday, and so on again. As the degree of the system increases, we need more and more initial information about it before the total description of the system and therefore prediction about it becomes possible. As we move towards evolutionary systems, we shall find that the degree of the system increases eventually to the point where mechanical predictions simply break down. If the system, for instance, has an infinite degree, which human history probably has for all practical purposes, exact prediction becomes theoretically impossible; for we could never put enough information into the system to describe it exactly. Even if we knew everything that had happened before the present, a sufficient pattern would not emerge.

Pattern Systems

There are many systems which do not possess the hundred percent predictability of mechanical systems like the solar system, but which nevertheless exhibit partial predictability in greater or less degree. If we put a chicken egg to hatch, we should be extremely surprised if it hatched into an alligator. When we see a kitten, we have a great deal of confidence that it will grow up into a cat, not a dog, if it grows up at all. Similarly, little boys almost invariably grow up into men and little girls into women, though there are a few exceptions to this rule. Similarly, when we see a skeleton steel structure, we expect to come back in a few months and see a finished building; when we see a keel in a shipyard we would later expect to find a ship, and so on over a very large range of human experiences. Probably the most respectable name for systems of this kind would be pattern-systems, as their predictability depends on the perception and recognition of a pattern which has been experienced in the past. We have watched our parents aging, so we predict that we will age ourselves in much the same way. There is a pattern of all human life from the fertilized egg to the grave, even though this pattern may be sliced off at any time by death. In a more frivolous mood I am tempted to call these systems wallpaper systems. Once we have perceived a pattern on wallpaper, we have great confidence in predicting it beyond the corner of the room that we cannot see, even though here too it might be cut off by an unexpected system break such as a door.

Just as astronomy and physics are the principal domain of mechanical systems, so the biological world is the principal domain of the pattern systems. In the fertilized egg there is a genetic blueprint for the creature that will emerge (if the process is not stopped by death), which charts within very narrow limits the growth of the phenotype, and in a very real sense creates the creature. Even if the growth of the creature is interrupted at some point by a nonfatal illness or temporary deficiencies in the food supply, the growth pattern often catches up again once the deficiency is restored. We have a great deal of confidence, therefore, in the stability of these patterns, a confidence which is rarely misplaced. The main uncertainties involved are those relating to the limits of the system, beyond which it cannot recover, for every system of this kind is subject to certain random processes which may lead to death at any time. In the mythology of the Fates, Clotho spins the pattern with great regularity; Atropos snips it at the moment of death (she is clearly the goddess of system break); and Lachesis, who measures it, is a fairly random number. Her measure is a roulette wheel with one mark on it that gives the sign to Atropos, and then—snip!

Equilibrium Systems

A third broad class of systems which admit of predictability may be identified as *equilibrium systems*. These are systems in which the dynamic processes produce a succession of states, all of which are virtually identical. Whatever sense we have of stability in the world is derived from our perception of equilibrium processes. In the short run at any rate, people stay much the same from day to day; the field, the forest, the swamp and the lake reproduce themselves season after season, year after year, in an ecological equilibrium. The stores are always full of commodities, the gas stations full of gas. Cities contain streets, public buildings, churches, schools, and houses, year after year. The university has freshmen, sophomores, professors, deans, and a president; when one goes, another takes his place. When an equilibrium is stable, we have a good deal of confidence that a disturbance will be followed by a movement toward equilibrium again. The sick man recovers, the burned city is rebuilt, the forest comes back after a fire.

An increasingly important class of equilibrium systems is what may be called *control systems,* that is, equilibria which have been deliberately contrived by man. In a house with a furnace and a thermostat we can predict the inside temperature with a great deal of confidence, even though the outside temperature cannot be predicted with any great degree of confidence. In this case we predict the future not because we know it but because we make it. Thus modern economists are not merely interested in predicting the business cycle but in controlling it, and in setting up social "thermostats" which will counteract the random and perverse processes which operate on the economy, just as a thermostatically controlled furnace counteracts changes in outside temperature. Control systems must have what is called "equilibrating feedback." When outside disturbances threaten the equilibrium of the system, it must be capable of detecting and interpreting this information and of setting in motion dynamic processes which will counteract the disturbances. Thus if we want a stable rate of growth in the economy, we must be able to perceive when the rate of growth is slowing down and be able to speed it up, or when the rate of growth is getting too large and be able to slow it down. Similarly, if we want stable peace, we have to have a control apparatus which will perceive the movement towards war and set in motion counteracting dynamic processes.

In the biological world and also in social systems, we often get patterns of succession of short-run equilibrium states, which are generally described as ecological succession. The lake fills up and becomes a swamp, finally a prairie, and then a forest. Many philosophers of history have tried to interpret human history likewise in terms of a succession of states or stages, hunting, pastoral, agricultural, and industrial, though the pattern of human history is not as clear and precise as those we find in the biological world. Insofar as we can detect these patterns of succession; however, we gain some powers of prediction.

Evolutionary Systems.

The patterns of ecological succession, however, do not help us very much when it comes to the great processes of evolution. These involve the processes of genetic mutation and ecological selection in the biological field, and parallel phenomena involving the growth of knowledge and organizations, cultures and societies, techniques and commodities, in the social field. Evolutionary theory is all hindsight; it has practically no predictive power at all. In evolutionary systems, time is not reversible nor is it arbitrary. There are indeed two systems in which time is not reversible; one is thermodynamics and the other is evolution. In thermodynamics, time's arrow points "down," according to the famous and dismal Second Law, by which entropy, that is, disorganization, continually increases, the availability of energy continually declines, potential is continuously used up, and what's done cannot be undone and can never be done again. Thermodynamics postulates a universe which starts off, as it were, with a capital and potential which it is inexorably squandering; and the end of the process is a kind of thin uniform soup in which all things are equally distributed, all at the same temperature, and chaos and old night have returned again.

By contrast, in the evolutionary process time's arrow points "up," towards the development of ever more complex and more improbable forms. Thermodyamically, it may be true that evolution is only just the segregation of entropy, that is, the building up of more and more complex little castles of order at the cost of increasing chaos elsewhere. Nevertheless, the castles of order do get more and more complex, from hydrogen to carbon to uranium, from small molecules to big molecules, to viruses, to cells, to multi-celled organisms, to vertebrates and mammals, to man, to families, to tribes, to nations, and perhaps to a world. If the evolutionary process continues, therefore, it is pretty safe to predict an increase in complexity. The nature of that complexity, however, because it is itself an information system, cannot be known in advance, at least by an organism with a merely human capacity for knowing things.

In practice, the main cause for failures in prediction is a sudden change in the characteristics of the system itself. Such a change has been called a "system break." Death, bankruptcy, and conquest are extreme forms of a system break, in which a complex system at some point simply ceases to exhibit any kind of equilibrium or homeostasis, and disintegrates. Less dramatic system breaks, however, are also common—graduation, a new job, or marriage in the case of an individual, turning points in the economy, the outbreak of war or peace in the international system, sudden changes in birth or death rates in demographic systems, and so on. The growth of knowledge and technology is as much subject to system breaks as other systems. Sometimes, for instance, there is what I have elsewhere described as an "acceleration," that is, a sudden change in the rate of growth of knowledge or productivity. Such an acceleration occurred in Europe about 1600 with the rise of science. It took place in Japan around 1868, at the time of the Meiji Restoration. As we shall see, a system break of this kind seems to have occurred in American agriculture about 1935.

System breaks, unfortunately, are very hard to detect. They are virtually impossible to predict in advance; they are even difficult to detect after they have happened for some time, because in the short run it is virtually impossible to distinguish the beginning of a new long-term trend from a strictly temporary fluctuation. Thus suppose we had a sudden increase in the birth rate which persisted for four or five years; it could still be argued (and was!) that this was only temporary. A change has to be established for a considerable time before we decide that it is permanent, and even then it can fool us.

PREDICTING KNOWLEDGE AND TECHNOLOGY

The Problem of Predicting Knowledge

The growth of knowledge is one of the most persistent and significant movements in the history of man, and, one might almost say, in the history of the universe. It is perhaps stretching the word to regard the whole evolutionary process as essentially a process of the growth of knowledge, but if we think of knowledge as a capital structure of information, that is, as an improbable arrangement or structure, we see that it is this increasing improbability of structure which characterizes the whole evolutionary process. Even the chemical atoms have "know-how" in the form of valency —carbon knows how to hitch onto four hydrogens, but not onto five. The gene unquestionably represents know-how in the form of a blueprint for the creature which it builds, and human and social development is ineradicably bound up with the growth of human knowledge, that is, with images inside the organism which correspond in some way to the world without.

Of the various processes which we have identified as permitting prediction, the growth of knowledge is least like a mechanical process and most like an evolutionary process. Mechanical projections of trends in growth rates in a system as complex as this are to be treated with the utmost reserve, though the concept of a rate of growth of knowledge which has some stability, at least in short periods, is by no means absurd. We can perceive also a certain acceleration in the growth of knowledge, that is, the rate of growth increases all the time. Thus knowledge is like a sum of capital which accumulates at continually rising interest rates. Even though the absence of any measure of the total stock of knowledge makes quantitative statements about it more akin to poetry than to mathematics, in a poetical sort of way we can hazard a guess that human knowledge perhaps doubled in a hundred thousand years in the paleolithic, in five thousand years in the neolithic, and perhaps every thousand years in the age of civilization until the rise of science. In many fields of science now knowledge seems to double about every fifteen years. It is this enormous increase in the rate of growth of knowledge which has dominated the history of the last two or three hundred years, in all aspects of human life, politically, economically, and in all forms of human organization. The domination of the world by European culture, for instance, is almost a byproduct of what may have been an accident, the fact that the mutation into science first took place in Europe.

The growth of knowledge, however, has been a subject of many interruptions and even reversals, and it would be very unwise to predict that just because knowledge has been growing at a certain rate in the past, it will continue to grow at the same rate in the future. It would be still more unwise to predict a constant rate of acceleration. We could say pretty safely, however, that the probability of growth is greater than that of decline, and that of acceleration is greater than that of deceleration.

A number of pattern systems can be detected in the growth of knowledge, especially in the spread of knowledge through education. The growth of knowledge has two aspects which can be summarized by the words education and research. Education is the spread of knowledge from one mind to another by means of communication processes between them. The communication may be one way, as when a person reads a book or sees a TV program, or it many be two way as in classroom teaching, conversation and dialogue. Thus education is a process by which what somebody knows or knew is transmitted to others. Research by contrast, is a process by which somebody gets to know something which nobody knew before. The two processes are highly intertwined. In the very act of transmitting knowledge, new knowledge is often created, which is one reason why universities combine the research and education processes. Knowledge is also lost in transmission, which is a kind of negative research, through noise and misunderstanding, which incidentally points up the great importance of dialogue and two-way transmissions if the body of knowledge is not to deteriorate in transmission.

The growth of knowledge in the individual follows a pattern which is closely related to the life pattern itself, and we hopefully suppose that knowledge increases with age. Formal education is an important part of this pattern, though it is not the only source of increase of knowledge. The growth of knowledge even in the individual is not a simple cumulative process by which information is pumped into the head and remains in a reservoir. Knowledge is a structure, and its present form always limits its possibilities of growth. Hence we get the phenomenon of "readiness" for certain kinds of knowledge at different stages of life. We get the phenomenon of wasted information input, which goes in at one ear and out the other, because it cannot latch onto anything in the existing knowledge structure. We get the phenomenon of superstition, or the development of false knowledge, as a result of the acceptance of authoritarian pronouncements and the failure of feedback; and we get the process of mutation through the imagination and testing through experience which is strikingly parallel to the evolutionary process itself, by which true knowledge grows.

The fact that the growth of knowledge has so many parallels to the evolutionary process renders it incapable of exact prediction. We can predict with some confidence that if the present system continues, knowledge will increase, not only bcause it has increased in the past but because we have a very large apparatus for increasing it. On the other hand, we run into a fundamental dilemma in attempting to predict the content of future knowledge, because if we knew the content of future knowledge, we would know it now, not in the future. That is, if we knew what we were going to know in twenty-five years, we would not have to wait twenty-five years for it. Consequently the growth of knowledge must always contain surprises, simply because the process itself represents the growth of improbable structures, and improbability always implies potential surprise. The whole idea of knowledge as a capital stock of information implies, therefore, that in detail its growth cannot be predicted. The difficulty is compounded by the fact that we know very little about the physiological structure which carries human knowledge. This difficulty, however, is less important than it might seem, for the carriers of an information structure are important only insofar as their properties limit the amount and complexity of the information that can be carried. We seem to be so far from the physical limits of the information content of the human nervous system that its physical properties can almost be neglected as a limit on the growth of knowledge.

Even though we cannot predict the specific content of future knowledge, what we know about the pattern of inputs and outputs enables us to venture at least on some probabilities. The distribution of new knowledge among the various fields and disciplines is at least likely to have some relation to the current distribution of research funds among these disciplines. Similarly the spread of knowledge in the world population is going to be related to some extent to the size of the educational industry and the funds allocated to it. I have argued elsewhere[1] that our research resources in particular are poorly allocated in the light of the importance for human welfare of the problems to which they are addressed. I have argued more particularly that the resources devoted to

[1] K. E. Boulding, "The Misallocation of Intellectual Resources," *Proceedings, American Philosophical Society*, 107:2 (April 15, 1963), pp. 117-120.

social systems are absurdly small in the light of the practical importance of these systems, and that whereas a failure of knowledge to advance in the physical and biological sciences for the next twenty-five years would not present mankind with any serious problems, the failure of knowledge to advance in the social sciences could well be fatal. Nevertheless we continue to devote our major effort to the physical, biological, and medical sciences and unless there is a change in this we can expect a continuation of the present imbalance in the growth of knowledge.

Predicting Technology

Many of the considerations which apply to the growth of knowledge also apply to the growth of technology. We can predict with a great deal of confidence that technology will change. In a society like ours, where a good deal of resources are devoted to improving technology, it will be very surprising if technology does not improve in the sense that it increases human productivity. On the other hand, we cannot predict the exact forms which this improvement will take, simply because again, if we could predict it we would have it now. The proposition perhaps is a little less true in regard to the spread of already known technologies to places and societies which do not yet possess them. We have already noted the distinction between education, consisting in the spread of old knowledge to people who did not have it before from people who did have it before, and research, as the development of new knowledge that nobody had before. A similar distinction can be made in regard to technology between the spread of an old technology and the creation of a new one. Strictly speaking, it is only the creation of a new technology which has to contain these elements of fundamental surprise. One might perhaps modify this proposition in the light of the fact that the transfer of technology, like the transfer of knowledge in the educational process, is itself a technology, and this too can be subject to technological change. The great problem of economic development of the poorer countries at the moment seems to be much dependent on an inability to produce an adequate technology for the transfer of technology, and of education for the transfer of knowledge. There may, therefore, be unexpected changes in the technology of transferring technology, and even this, therefore, may be subject to fundamental surprise.

While always preparing to be surprised, however, we can at least make some projections according to the simpler modes of prediction. As in the case of the growth of knowledge, even simple mechanical projections of rates of growth of technology are not meaningless. Perhaps the best general measure of the overall level of technology, in society is the index of output per man-hour. The accompanying chart from *Technology and the American Economy,* (Report of the National Commission on Technology, Automation, and Economic Progress, February 1966), page 3, shows the changes in output per man-hour for the last fifty years or so for agriculture, the private non-farm economy, and the total private economy. It is clear that we have been in a process of rapid technological advance. Output per man-hour has quadrupled in agriculture, tripled in the non-farm eco-

Indexes of Output Per Man-Hour
Total Private, Farm, and Private Non-farm Economy, 1909-65*

Output per Man-hour Index
Ratio Scale

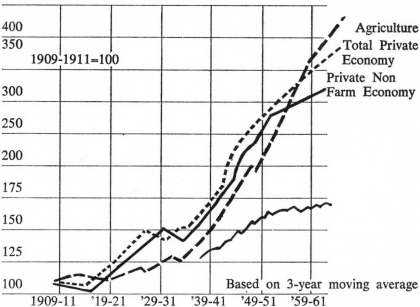

*Compiled from information provided by the U.S. Department of Commerce and Bureau of Labor Statistics, U.S. Department of Labor.

nomy, in little over forty years. If this process continues to 1980, we might expect the output per man-hour in agriculture to be almost eight times what it was around 1920, and in the private non-farm sector to be perhaps four and a half times what it was in 1920. There are no great signs of any acceleration in this process, contrary to some of the pronouncements which have been made by the more excitable writers on automation. In agriculture, indeed, we seem to have something like a system break in the mid-thirties, which could well correspond to the development of large inputs into agriculture, not only for research and development but also in price supports. It is somewhat sobering to project the index of output per man-hour in agriculture as I have done in the wavy line in the figure (which is not in the original). If agricultural productivity had continued to increase from the mid-thirties at the rate which it had followed in the preceeding twenty-five years, in the early 1960s the index would have been barely 135 or 140, by comparison with the nearly 400 which it actually reached. Nothing could illustrate better the dangers of projection, especially projection of trends, even trends which seem to have been established for quite a long period of time. Systems of this kind are always subject to system breaks, and hence the projection of existing trends should be treated with extreme reservations. Just because a boy doubles his height between the age of 8 and 18 does not mean he is going to double it again between 18 and 28, and in growth processes of any kind we have to be on the lookout for exhaustion of the original impetus which gave rise to the growth or the development of new impulses, such as the one we have just noticed in the case of agriculture.

The Qualitative Impact of Technology

We may be somewhat hesitant about the projection of quantitative trends and at the same time we may be more confident about certain qualitative and structural changes which these movements are introducing into the social system and which are likely to continue. We must first notice a phenomenon which is beginning to be of considerable importance in the American and other developed economies. This is that the more progressive sectors of the economy tend to shrink in regard to the proportion of the GNP which they generate or the amount of labor force which they absorb, relative to the technologically unprogressive sectors. This phenomenon is most striking in agriculture, where between 1930 and 1964 the proportion of civilian employment in agriculture fell from 25 percent to 7.6 percent in a little over a generation. We have managed to produce a small increase in agricultural output while reducing the absolute labor force to little more than a third of what it had been in 1929. This is an astonishing technological—and social—achievement. Even if it is repeated, however, and we continue to release people from agriculture, it is clear that the absolute numbers which can now be released are relatively small, and that though agriculture will almost certainly continue to shrink as a fraction of the economy, the resources released from it will not make the very large contribution to the non-agricultural labor force which they have made in the past, simply because there are not very many people left in it.

There is a question in many people's minds as to whether manufacturing is now about to suffer the fate of agriculture, thanks to cybernation. Manufacturing itself, however, is now not much more than 25 percent of the total labor force, so that even if the rate of technological change in manufacturing accelerates in the next fifteen years, and there are no immediate signs that it is doing this, it would be surprising if the proportion in manufacturing dropped to as little as, say, 20 percent of the total labor force. I am inclined to the view, therefore, that the great adjustment has already been made, the great adjustment, that is, out of agriculture. What has been displaced from agriculture has been absorbed largely in government, the professions, the service trades; and those who will continue to be displaced from agriculture and manufacturing will continue to be absorbed on balance in these expanding—because unprogressive—sectors. I will be a little surprised, therefore, if any spectacular change is observed in the structure of the labor force or the industrial structure of the economy in the next fifteen years, though, as I warned earlier, I am always prepared to be surprised.

Some further considerations of a qualitative kind might make the rather optimistic tone of the foregoing paragraphs seem like a very clouded crystal ball indeed by 1980 or still more by 2000. The crucial problem here is whether the development of electronics, automation, cybernation, and the whole complex of control systems does not introduce as it were a new gear into the evolutionary process, the implications of which are as yet only barely apparent. The computer is an extension of the human mind in the way that a tool or even an automobile is an extension of the human body. The automobile left practically no human institution unchanged as a result of the increase in human mobility which it permitted. The impact of the computer is likely to be just as great, and indeed of the whole world electronic network, which represents, as McLuhan has pointed out, an extension of the human nervous system and what is perhaps even more important, a linkage of our different nervous systems. It seems probable that all existing political and economic institutions will suffer some modifications as a result of this new technology; in what directions, however, it is hard to predict. That the ultimate results of this development will be benign can hardly be doubted except by those extreme pessimists who regard original sin as genetic in character and hence regard any extension of man's power as a mere increase in the opportunity to do harm. The faith that an increase in human power will be benign does depend, it is true, on certain assumptions about human teachability in ethics as well as in everything else. The very character of men's nervous system, however, assures us of his teachability, though it does not assure us that we can find ways of teaching him. At least, then, there is no theorem which drives us to a necessity for despair, even though there are plenty of occasions for a very reasonable disquiet.

We see the possible impacts of this new mode of human operation in a number of different fields. It has made the present international system, for instance, enormously threatening and so potentially destructive that it is hard to see how it can survive a generation. The day of national sovereignty and of unilateral national defense seems to be clearly over, though it may take a major catastrophe to convince us of this. As I have put it elsewhere, the world is rapidly becoming a very small crowded space ship in which men on horseback, even cowboys, cannot be tolerated. *The network of electronic communication is inevitably producing a world superculture, and the relations between this superculture and the more traditional national and regional cultures of the past remains the great question mark of the next fifty years.* For regions in which the defense industry is heavily concentrated, this question mark is particularly large, not only because of the economic adjustments which may be necessary, but because they represent prime target areas.

Another possible consequence of the qualitative changes in technology which seem to be under way is what I have sometimes called the "milk and cream" problem. Will the world separate out into two cultures, both within countries and between countries, in which a certain proportion of the people adapt through education to the world of modern technology and hence enjoy its fruits, while another proportion fail to adapt and perhaps become not only relatively worse off but even absolutely so, in the sense that what they have had in the past of traditional culture collapses under the impact of the technical superculture and leaves them disorganized, delinquent, anemic, and poor? In "creamy" societies like the United States, the "cream" may be 70 or 80 percent of the population, and the "skim milk" may be only 20 or 30 percent. The depressed sector, however, may be large enough to be threatening not only to the consciences of the rich sector but even to its security, as frustration and anger lead to violence.

On the world scale, the outlook is even darker. At the moment the separation-out phenomenon is proceeding at an alarming pace. The rich countries are getting richer at an unprecedented pace, many of the poor countries are stagnating or even retrogressing; and the difference between the rich and the poor gets larger every year. This situation can easily create dangerous instability in the international system, though perhaps because of the very poverty and impotence of the poor countries, the threat to the rich is not very great. The greater danger may be that of a stable divided world with perhaps less than 50 percent of the people having made the transition into the modern world and at least half sunk into utter misery and degradation. Such a situation could hardly persist without corrupting the cultures of both the rich and the poor, and the stability of such a system could certainly not continue forever.

Technology is an offshoot of knowledge. Hence we might expect to find something of a stable pattern between the growth of knowledge and the improvement of technology with perhaps a certain lag to account for the application of new knowledge to productive processes and also the spread of these processes throughout the economy. There is some evidence that the diffusion of knowledge into technology is taking place a little more rapidly than it used to.[2] What is difficult to identify, however, is exactly what new knowledge is going to be relevant, for a great deal of new knowledge is created in the progress of the sciences which is not relevant to technology in the immediate future and which may even never become relevant. The plain fact is that if a prediction of future technology were at all easy, there would be no money to be made in growth stocks, for the growth of the right ones would all be anticipated. The fact that fortunes are made as well as lost in new technologies suggests that the uncertainties of prediction here are very great, and that the relation between present knowledge and future technology is not really stable enough to admit of any very secure predictions.

When we add to the general uncertainties of the technological future an attempt to predict the impact on particular regions, the uncertainties become even greater. It would be even more unwise to project, for instance, constant rates of growth for a particular region than it would be for the economy as a whole. A region which is heavily devoted to, say, mining and agriculture, might expect to share in the relative decline of these industries. A region which is heavily involved in government, especially in defense, might be expected to share in the extreme uncertainty of this sector.

---

[2] See, for instance, the report of the National Commission on Technology, Automation, and Economic Progress, *Technology in the American Economy*, February 1966, pages 4 and 5.

THE IMPLICATIONS FOR EDUCATION

Perhaps the most important conclusion which emerges from this discussion for the educational system is that it should plan for surprise. This is not to say, of course, that its policies should not be based on predictions or projections, for all policies have to be directed towards the future and we must have some idea of what the future is going to be like, otherwise all rational decision is impossible. Wherever it is possible to project into the future simple dynamic systems which have had reasonably stable parameters in the past, this, of course, should be done. We do this, for instance, in population projections, which are perhaps one of the most fundamental tools of the educational planner and which are covered in other papers. We should remember even here that the population projections of the mid-1940s turned out to be completely erroneous because of a sudden change in the parameters of the system, particularly in regard to quite unexpectedly large birth rates which have persisted to this day. One would very much like to see a study of the impact of these erroneous projections of the 1940s, particularly in regard to the failure to plan for educational expansion. It would be interesting to see at what moment school systems became aware of the fact that they were going to have to provide for much larger numbers of children than they had previously expected, and how they made adjustments to these new images of the future.

In regard to the more quantitative aspects of technology, a sudden change in the rate of growth of productivity might not be felt appreciably for a few years, but in ten or twenty years the effects might be very noticeable, either in unexpected gains or unexpected declines in the growth of income.

On the qualitative side, it could well be that the most important area of possible technological change is in the field of social inventions, and it is these which might have the greatest impact on the environment of the educational system. The very strains which modern technology puts on society create a demand for social invention which did not perhaps exist before. When material technology is only advancing slowly, social invention may keep pace with it fairly easily. Thus in the course of the last three hundred years we have had such social inventions as banking, insurance, the corporation, the income tax, universal public education, conscription, social security, and even socialist states, all of which represent in a sense a response on the part of the social system to challenges presented by the growth of material technology. With the qualitative changes that seem to be taking place in material technology, new demands are placed on social invention. Certainly at some point, as per capita incomes rise, we may reach something of a watershed after which the traditional values and organizations become rapidly less capable of organizing society, and rapid social invention will be necessary. As suggested earlier, we cannot predict what these inventions will be, we can only suggest a few challenges to which some response will have to be made. We can conclude, therefore, by outlining some suggestions of possible future challenges.

1.   The American educational system in the past has been quite success-ful in preparing people to be middle class, to the point indeed where middle class values permeate perhaps 80 percent of our population. The system has not succeeded in preparing people to live useful and cheerful lives at the lower end of the income scale, mainly because educators are themselves middle class and hence are unsympathetic to the values of a lower-class culture. Maybe a social invention is needed here in the shape of an educational subsystem which will give the culture of the poor a status of its own.

2.   American society up to now has stressed the idea of a "melting pot" and has sought to create through public education a uniform culture. With increased affluence and increased political skill, this ideal can now be called into question. Can we now invent a "mosaic" society, composed of many small subcultures, each of which gives to its participants a sense of com-munity and identity which is so desperately needed in a mass world, and which can at the same time remain at peace with its neighbors and not threaten to pull the society apart? An educational system designed for this purpose would look enormously different from what we have today. Private education would compete on equal terms with public; we might have something like the "voucher" scheme proposed by certain British economists by which each child would be given a voucher which would be exchanged for education in any school, public or private. This would not exclude the possibility of imposing certain legal minimum standards, but it would open up an enormous possibility for experimentation in education, which is something we severely lack under the present system.

3.   It would not surprise me to see the educational system head for a major financial crisis within the next few years. The tax systems by which public education is supported tend to be regressive and inequitable, and they only seem to be tolerable as long as the total tax collections for these purposes are smaller than the needs of this sector of the economy. The contrast in this regard between the public and the private sectors of the economy is very striking, as Galbraith has pointed out so eloquently. A great many studies have indicated that in terms of sheer rate of return on investment, investment in education probably brings a higher rate of re-turn than that of any competitive industry, and when we add the in-tangible benefits, which are considerable, the argument that we are under-investing in education as a whole and grossly underinvesting in certain aspects of the system becomes almost irresistible. We do not need to go as far as Dr. West[3] and propose turning the whole educational system back to private enterprise, for there are good reasons to suppose there would be underinvestment under these circumstances too, even more serious than what we have at present. The fact remains, however, that access to capital is much easier for material technology than it is for human in-vestment, and we need social inventions to correct this. It may well be

[3] E. G. West, *Education and the State: A Study in Political Economy*, London: The Institute of Economic Affairs, 1965.

that a major problem here is that we have not so much supplemented the operations of the price system in this area as destroyed it, and there is a strong case for taking a hard look at the principle that education should be universally free. Public education at all levels can easily result in the subsidization of the rich, and in view of the regressive nature of so many state and local tax systems, the public school system may even result in a redistribution of income from the poor to the rich, or at least from the poor to the middle class. If this is so, it is not surprising that taxpayers become increasingly resistant to any expansion of the educational system, and that the system operates in an atmosphere of increasing financial crisis.

4. The final problem is subtle and hard to put one's finger on; nevertheless it may be the most important problem of all. This is the problem of the role of the educational system in creating what might be called a moral identity. The obsolescence of older moral identities in the face of enormous technological change is a problem which underlies almost all others in the social system. We see this in the so-called sexual revolution; we see it in the inappropriateness of belligerent nationalist emotions in a nuclear world; and we see it also in what may be the most serious social byproduct of automation, a loss of self-respect and "manhood" on the part of those whose skills are being displaced. The greatest human tragedy is to feel useless and not wanted, and with the rise in the intelligence of machines, we may face a period in which the human race divides into two parts, those who feel themselves to be more intelligent than machines and those who feel themselves to be less. This could signalize the beginnings of a widening human tragedy which would require the utmost exercise of our skill and knowledge. I am by no means sure that this is a problem which is really upon us. It is one, however, for which we should be prepared, and in its solution the educational system would play an absolutely crucial role. It would be precisely indeed in the things which our conservatives despise as "frills" that the development of satisfying human identities may have to be found. It must never be forgotten that the ultimate thing which any society is producing is people. All other things are intermediate goods, and all organizations are intermediate organizations. No matter how rich we are or how powerful we are, if we do not produce people who can at least begin to expand into the enormous potential of man, the society must be adjudged a failure. The educational system is peculiarly specialized in the production of people, and it must never lose sight of the fact that it is producing people as ends, not as means. It is producing men, not manpower; people, not biologically generated nonlinear computers. If this principle is stamped firmly in the minds of these who guide and operate our educational system, we can afford to make a great many mistakes, we can afford to be surprised by the future, we can even afford to make some bad educational investments, because we will be protected against the ultimate mistake, which would be to make the educational system a means, not an end, serving purposes other than man himself.

Education And The Problem Of
Capital Investment:
Some Comments On Professor Boulding's Paper
DANIEL R. FUSFELD*

Professor Boulding's paper has called attention to the financial problems of our educational system but has not stressed them sufficiently. One prediction about which we can be reasonably confident is that for an indefinite period in the future education will have inadequate financial support, unless a significant "system break" occurs in attitudes toward the place of education in the political process through which funds are provided to schools, or in the productivity of the educational system itself. At the present time, none of these developments appears to be on the horizon.

We can take it for granted that the growing complexity of our society and the expansion of information will place increased demands upon our educational institutions. This qualitative problem is in many ways more significant than the quantitative one of the larger numbers of students to be served.

There are two great barriers to provision of adequate resources for education. One of these barriers is the prevalent attitude toward private wants and public needs. Money spent by an individual on his own private consumption satisfies both his physical and his psychological needs, and particularly his psychological needs for status and recognition. A new car, a better home, fashionable clothes, and expensive vacations give individual satisfactions and enable one to claim a high status among one's fellows. Taxes paid to support a school system, however, provide a generalized social benefit, not attributable to any one person, and do not enable the individual to satisfy his needs for recognition and status. In an individualistic society we can expect resentment and resistance to payment of taxes requiring that people forego spending on their own personal wants in favor of social needs.

Compounding the problem still further is the fact that the taxpayer pays the cost of education while the direct benefits are received primarily by nontaxpayers—the young go to school while people who already have their education pay the bills. It can be argued persuasively that everyone benefits from a more educated population, and that is undoubtedly true. Education has been one of America's best investments when the full social and economic benefits are calculated. But it is nevertheless true that one group pays while another group obtains the bulk of the immediate and direct benefits. As long as this condition prevails, the attitudes toward education will mitigate against adequate financing.

The second barrier to the financing of education lies in the ways in which capital investments are made. Compare education's access to capital with that of business enterprise. The business firm must only pass

*Professor of Economics, University of Michigan; Director, Manpower Evaluation Staff, U.S. Office of Education 1963-64; Author of *The Age of the Economist* (Scott, Foresman, 1966) and *The Economic Thought of Franklin D. Roosevelt and the Origins of the New Deal* (Columbia University Press, 1956)

the test of the market and show that the potential returns, taking risks into consideration, are greater than the rate of interest. It can then go into money markets, borrow the capital, and pay back the loan out of the profits from the enterprise. It is simple, impersonal, and readily accomplished. This is not true of education. In the first place, the potential gains are not easily measured. Secondly, those who benefit are not expected to repay directly the costs of their education. And finally, educational funds are obtained by a complex political process in which extraneous issues often impinge on a decision made in the emotional heat of politics. In short, the development of education is hampered by institutions which make capital investment difficult and erratic in contrast to the free access to capital enjoyed by business enterprise.

These two factors—attitudes and institutions—would indicate that our supply of educational services will lag behind the growing demand for them.

The only alternative to substantial changes in attitudes and institutions is a significant increase in the productivity of the educational system. Something analagous to the "system break" that occurred around 1935 in agricultural productivity seems to be necessary. But even here an almost insoluble problem appears: "system breaks" in productivity trends usually require massive injections of capital—yet we have already seen that this is unlikely in education, unless there are significant changes in attitudes toward private wants and needs and in the process by which decisions about investment in education are made.

But lest we allow pessimism to overwhelm us, it should be remembered that "system breaks" can occur without warning. I am optimistic enough to believe that the problem of financing education will be solved. One direction that suggests itself is a greater degree of self financing by the individual who gets the education through long term loans from either public or private sources, for example, that will make possible more accurate estimates of costs and benefits and place greater emphasis on individual decision-making. A number of proposals along this line have been made, and they should be carefully evaluated. At any rate, a hard look should be taken at our very heavy reliance on present methods of public financing of the educational effort, even if the educational process continues to take place largely in public schools and colleges.

CHAPTER 13

The New Look In Information Systems

WILLIAM T. KNOX*

"In the beginning was the Word" **John 1:1**

Theologians interpret the opening sentence of St. John's Gospel in a restricted context of religious truth. But to those people developing new methods and equipment for transferring information, the sentence is a strong reminder that the whole of civilization rests on man's invention of language. Language has given man the ability to transfer vast amounts of information to his fellows, either by talking or writing. Information transfer is, in turn, the basic process on which our highly-developed 20th century civilization is built.

For the first time since the invention of writing, man now stands on the threshold of being able to communicate—or to transfer information—while enjoying the best of these two means of communication—writing and talking. He will be able to use the vast store of information traditionally put into printed form, and will use it as easily and flexibly as he now talks to his neighbor. Modern technology will make this possible.

The purpose of this paper is to outline the state-of-the-art and some likely developments in information transfer processes and systems, together with a look at some of the implications of these developments for U.S. society.

EARLY STAGES OF INFORMATION TRANSFER

The characteristics of early societies were markedly different from those of 20th century America. There were relatively few people and relatively little was known about the natural world. Truth or knowledge was directly tied to religion; truth was revealed through religion. Even the small accumulation of knowledge was relatively unavailable; it had to be transferred from person to person by talking or by hand-written manuscripts. There were few people who could spend the time acquiring knowledge; those who did usually became feared and respected and rulers of society.

So it was until about 500 years ago. The first revolutionary change was Gutenberg's invention of mechanical printing. The small store of information accumulated over thousands of years of human thought and activity was made accessible to more people. People also began to write more.

*Office of Science and Technology, Executive Office of the President (on loan from Esso Research and Engineering Co.)

Perhaps it was no coincidence that about 150 years after printing was invented and books were available through most of Western Europe, the scientific Renaissance was in full flower. Simultaneously with the reassertion of more than one revelation of religious truth, people like Sir Francis Bacon and Galileo emphasized again the need for orderly, systematic inquiry into the natural world, as revealed by observation. Explorers ranged the world, adding new information to fuel the fire of man's thirst for more knowledge. The invention of printing made it possible for the new investigators to communicate their findings widely. The flow of new information increased. Equally important, the newly discovered information was put to practical use in raising the material standards of living.

After the lapse of another 200 years, the founders of the United States prescribed the necessity of a basic, publicly-financed education for all. The ideal of democratic education was emphasized by Jefferson, an 18th-century lawyer-scientist-engineer, accustomed to deliberate inquiry into natural phenomena, and to applying the results of his own and his colleagues' experiments to his daily life at Monticello. Jefferson himself had one of the largest libraries in America, and corresponded with friends in many nations. He was an advocate of the power of the written word.

The impact of widespread availability of printed information, the increasing literacy of the United States population, the expanding base of technology, and the ever-intensifying search for new and better communications methods led to the invention of the telegraph, telephone, phonograph, and camera in the late 1800's. A few decades afterwards, the radio was invented. Technology had, in just half a century, added a number of new information transfer processes available for man's choosing, but, with one exception, each new process transmitted either printed or spoken information, but not both. The exception, the moving picture, while transmitting information simultaneously by the printed and spoken modes, was suitable only for information transfer to large groups of people; it was (and still is) too costly for general personal use.

THE NEW LOOK IN INFORMATION SYSTEMS

So matters stood before 1940. Since then another technological revolution in information processes and systems has occurred. Its impact on society, while dramatic in some applications, is still not widely felt and even less widely understood even in this country. Furthermore, the gap between the industrialized and less-developed countries in information systems has been widened by the new technology. There are large areas of the world where information is transferred today by the age-old techniques of person-to-person talking. Even within the United States the oral tradition still predominates in some Indian tribes; the first American Indian alphabet was devised by Sikwayi only 140 years ago.

The new information processing revolution has coincided with an explosive growth in research and development, funded by governments. In the United States, the total Federal Research and Development (R&D) effort cost $78 million in 1940. In 1965, the federally-financed R&D effort had grown to a total of $15 billion, a growth rate of about 20 percent per year over the 1940-1965 interval.

The outpouring of new information about the natural world and the building of new technologies led to an equally rapid increase in published documents. Traditional documentation, typified by the scientific journal, proved unable to handle the increased volume of information, and a new documentary form, the technical report, came into being. About 100,000 such technical reports are published each year in the United States as a result of Federally-sponsored R&D efforts. Journal articles in science and technology (worldwide) increased simultaneously to a level of about 900,000 articles in 1965. The number of new books and monographs in science and technology more than doubled between 1950 and 1965, and the U.S. output now stands at a level of about 7,000 new titles plus 2,500 new editions each year.

The root causes of the large increase in recorded information—the increases in population, increased education of the population, and increases in organized research, development, and application—will continue well into 1980, and probably beyond.

In 1965, U.S. population in the 20-45 age group, a period of high productivity in research and development, was 60.5 million. By 1980 the same age group is estimated to contain 82.4 million, an increase of over 35 percent. The proportion of the 18-21 year age group with a college or university education will also show a marked increase (about 27 percent). In the next 15 years the professional work force will grow from about 10.4 percent to 17.7 percent of the total labor force.

Organized research and development will continue to grow at a rapid rate, not as rapid as during the past decade, but still well above the average growth rate for the U.S. economy as a whole. One measure of its growth rate may be the long-term trend which has been about 7 percent per year increase in Ph.D.'s in science and engineering. The current growth rate is about 10 percent per year.

Not only has the volume of new information increased dramatically, but equally dramatic is the increased speed with which U.S. society in 1966 applies information to serve useful social ends. New drugs, once introduced over a period of decades as the general practicing physician adopted them in one sector of the U.S. after another, now are made available after testing to the total U.S. population simultaneously in a mass-marketing program. The jet-powered airplane displaced the piston-powered airplane almost completely on long-distance and middle-distance hauls within 10 years after the introduction of the first commercial jet.

Such events will also happen in the future. Their effects on the structure of U.S. society, and the character of people's lives are profound and lasting. Whereas a century ago there was time for reflection, time for the traditional information system to bring new information to the decision-makers before undesirable applications took place, the traditional information system is no longer adequate.

One of the glories of the new revolution in information transfer technologies is its promise that the vast body of knowledge, growing vaster by the day, can also be more effectively used by more people. Hopefully, wiser decisions will be made, and the body of knowledge built by millions of people in past years will be used more completely for the benefit of the present and future generations.

THE COMPUTER REVOLUTION

The digital computer is the heart and muscles of the new information system. The mathematical languages and programs used to control computer operations, together with output devices, such as the teleprinter and the cathode-ray display tube (as in TV) correspond to the control and recognition functions of the nervous system. Together these items of hardware and "software" make possible the processing of huge amounts of information under urgent pressures for rapid correlation and recall.

The digital computer must be thought of today as an information processor, not as a device to do arithmetic. It can be used to process all kinds of information which can be represented by symbols. Although the computer first was and still is widely used for accounting purposes, *its future major impact will be as an information processor* handling the total diversity of problems encountered in the course of daily living.

The size and shape of the computer impact on U.S. society can be gauged by the growth in numbers of digital computers from about 1,000 in 1955 to an estimated 80,000 or more in 1975. The federal government spent over $840 million for computing in the year ending June 30, 1966, employing about 1,800 computers, mostly for business and accounting purposes.

Part cause, and part effect of the tremendous growth rate shown above are the improvements (past and future) in computers. The size of computers will probably decrease by a factor of about 1,000 by 1980. Computer speeds will increase to a level of about one billion operations per second by 1980, and the cost per operation will have decreased by a factor of about 200 from present levels.

Well before 1980, computers will be small, powerful, and inexpensive. Computing power will be available to anyone who needs it, or wants it, or can use it. The new situation will accent personal rather than organizational use. In many cases the user will have a small personal console connected to a large, central computing facility; in other cases he may have a small personal computer. Corresponding developments in man-machine interaction, such as in programming language and in display equipment, will make it as easy to learn to use the new computers as to learn to drive a car.

THE COMPUTER AND INFORMATION SYSTEMS

For information systems involving large amounts of stored data, it is necessary to consider the computer "memory" or store of information. Most computer applications today rely on large stores of information contained on reels of magnetic tape or in decks of punched cards. An estimated 50 percent of computers installed today operate on routine business data in these forms.

However, the more exciting developments in information processing are based on "real-time" computer use. In these uses, the computer memory and processor are large enough to handle within seconds a variety of jobs, without needing to call for additional information from a non-computer store, such as punched cards. There is in these cases potential opportunity for the human operator to interact with the computer at a speed not too different from person-to-person conversation.

It is estimated that the entire store of non-redundant information in the world's libraries amounts to 10^{15} (one quadrillion) bits, or 10^{14} characters.[1] At present this information is, of course, stored in printed form. Since the size of the store is doubling every 15 to 20 years, by 1980 the total amount of information will amount to 2×10^{15} bits.

A leading computer manufacturer has recently announced the commercial availability of a new type of direct access computer memory. The memory will hold 10^{12} bits, equal to one-thousandth of the world's recorded information. Further increases in computer memory size and speed of access will undoubtedly occur by 1980.

There appears, then, the possibility that a reasonable number of direct access computers will suffice to store and process in "real-time" all the significant information now in the world's libraries.

NEW COMMUNICATIONS TECHNOLOGY

While these changes have occurred and are predicted for the computer itself, equally significant changes have taken place in the technologies of communications. The satellite is the most dramatic addition to man's alternatives for communicating with his fellow. Already experience with the first commercial satellite has shown the potentialities for significant lowering of today's costs of communication via wire or wireless. A worldwide network of communications satellites will make it possible to transfer information across oceans with clarity and ease. Further developments in boosters and relays may also make satellite communication the preferred mode for intracontinental communications, such as from the East Coast to the West Coast of the United States. The United States is now relatively well-served by existing wire and wireless circuits, but as new demands for circuits arise, there will be marked changes in the technology (perhaps arising out of lasers) leading to lower communications costs, faster speed of information transfer, and greater flexibility to meet consumer preferences.

Paralleling the development of new communications technologies has been the development of image transmission over the communications channels. First popularized by the familiar newspaper telephoto, very recent developments include image transmission using xerography to make printed copies, and the coupling of telephone and images of the people

[1] J. C. R. Lickider, *Libraries of the Future*, M.I.T. Press 1965—p. 14-16.

talking. These developments, now limited because of expense, will be commonplace by 1980.

The last-to-be-mentioned new technology is rapid copying of printed matter. No estimates can be made for the growth of this exploding phenomenon beyond the next year or two. Rapid copying has already changed office routines, and its continued growth poses problems for publishers and authors. Its impact on information processing systems of 1980 is impossible to predict; its effect on journal publication may be large. The only safe prediction is that rapid copying will thrive in the period 1966-1980.

DIRECT ACCESS COMPUTER SYSTEMS WITH REMOTE TERMINALS

The development of computer-remote terminals systems has opened the door to the best use of both the new computers and the new communications methods. In addition, computer programs have become more efficient so that the full power of the computer is used as much as possible. The latest development is called "time-sharing." The time-shared computer system makes use of the time spent by a person between receipt of information and reaching a decision on his next step. This time, necessary to the human user, is wasted time to the computer. Clever instructions or programs have been developed for the ultra-large, ultra-fast computers which switch the computer from one user to another in fractions of a second, thus keeping the computer busy nearly all the time. A number of users can use the computer without interfering with one another. Plans are being laid for systems serving 250 users simultaneously.

Several time-shared computer systems were operating routinely in 1965. Their uses vary from police department criminal records to airline reservations to university research.

The development of the direct access, time-shared computer system, with remote terminals (such as teletypewriters, dial telephones, or light beam "pencils" projected onto a cathode-ray tube) is *the* revolutionary development.

Man has nearly always preferred to get his information directly from another man. This does not mean that wise men suffer fools gladly, but only that when the volume and quality of information transfer are equal, a direct human channel will nearly always be preferred to an indirect, impersonal channel, such as documents. Impersonal means of information transfer are used only where the personal channels are of lower quality (greater noise, incompleteness, redundancy, lower speed, etc.) or are clearly impossible to use (the author is dead).

The reasons for this behavior may lie partly in the psychological-sociological realm, man being a gregarious creature. There are also some sound engineering reasons for it. A message is best communicated when the physical characteristics of the equipment used to send the message match those of the receiver most closely, other things being equal. Messages are also communicated most quickly and accurately if there is immediate opportunity for the receiver to ask the sender to clarify uncertain items. Both of these conditions have been better met by direct human channels for information transfer rather than by conventional indirect, impersonal channels.

The inspiring potential of the remote terminal, direct access, time-shared computer system is simply that it allows many users to have immediate access—in their own language— to the total store of information contained in the computer memory. Computer programs have been developed by which an almost human-to-human dialogue can be conducted, although one of the "conversationalists" is the computer. A sample of dialogue on Project Mac's time-shared computer is given below:

User: Men are all alike.

Computer: IN WHAT WAY?

User: They're always bugging us about something or other.

Computer: CAN YOU THINK OF A SPECIFIC EXAMPLE?

User: Well, my boyfriend made me come here.

Computer: YOUR BOYFRIEND MADE YOU COME HERE?

User: He says I'm depressed much of the time.

Computer: I AM SORRY TO HEAR YOU ARE DEPRESSED.

In addition to typed messages between the user and the computer such as illustrated above, the computer can respond in a human voice over a conventional telephone. Such a system is in commercial use in the U.S., giving stock quotations in response to inquiries made by simply dialing the appropriate alphabetical symbols. People seem to like the immediate, human voice response more than reading the slower stock quotations on the conventional ticker tape.

Finally, the user and computer can interact through visual display equipment, such as cathode-ray tubes. Already a university civil engineering department employs a time-shared computer coupled to a cathode-ray display tube and a light-beam pencil operated by the user to help its student engineers solve structural design problems.

The examples cited above share an important characteristic: the human user has, in effect, coupled the computer's fantastic memory and calculating speed to his immediate requirements for information. Words alone cannot convey this messege to the reader of this article. The ease and flexibility with which problems can be solved in such a man-machine system can be understood fully only after one has personally operated the system.

One may conclude then, as stated at the beginning, that the invention of these new technologies has made it possible, for the first time since the inventon of writing, for man to enjoy the best of two modes of communication—the written and the oral modes. He can now almost "talk" with a substantial amount of recorded information, manipulate and organize it to serve his purposes, and leave the newly-organized information in the memory for others to use. *The impact on U.S. society of this development will exceed the impact of the automobile.*

U.S. ORGANIZATIONAL AND STRUCTURAL DEVELOPMENTS

Although the shape of things to come can only be seen with some certainty for a year or two ahead, between 1966 and 1980 the further development of the computer and of remote access, time-shared, computer systems will undoubtedly have a profound effect on parts of the U.S. economy. The publishing industry, library services, the educational establishment, and federal, state, and local governments, are all deeply involved in transferring and using information. The highly-organized professional societies in science and engineering are primarily information-transfer organizations, and several of the largest societies have large publishing activities. There are also, of course, two sectors of business which supply the mechanical hardware and necessary technical services—the computer industry and the communications industry.

These sectors of the U.S. economy vary in their method of management and financial support from a fiercely-competitive traditional free enterprise sector such as commercial publishing, to a government-owned and operated sector such as public education. There are numerous variations between these extremes. The communications industry is privately-owned, in general, but regulated by the state and federal governments. The newest form of communication—by satellite—is half federal government-owned and half privately owned. Professional societies are not-for-profit, but their use of commercial advertising to support publications is currently being studied as a profit making element by the Internal Revenue Service. Library services cover a wide spectrum of user groups and operations; there are elementary and secondary school libraries, college and university libraries, libraries for the general public, special libraries such as in medicine and agriculture, and thousands of privately-owned libraries serving business and industrial firms. The computer industry, although it has a large and growing civilian market, still carries out its advanced research and development almost exclusively for federal government purposes.

With this mixture of markets, management motivations, policy and operational controls, and financial support, it is small wonder that there is no single, definite plan for the logical exploitation of the new information storage, retrieval, and transfer technologies. The problems and opportunities presented by these technologies have, however, been recognized by the Congress and the Executive Branch to be of national importance, warranting considerable planning effort.

FEDERAL GOVERNMENT ACTIVITIES

Several far-reaching steps have recently been taken by the federal government. A coordinated federal mechanism for management of the almost 2,000 computers operated by the federal departments and agencies was initiated by a report to the President by the Bureau of the Budget entitled, "The Management of Automatic Data Processing in the Federal Government."[2] "Recommendations for National Document Handling Sys-

---

[2] Bureau of the Budget, Report to the President on the Management of Automatic Data Processing in the Federal Government, G.P.O. 1965.

tems in Science and Technology"[3] was also issued by the Committee on Scientific and Technical Information of the Federal Council for Science and Technology. The basic recommendation of the report was that the federal government should assume a responsibility to insure that there exists within the United States at least one copy of every significant document in the world-wide scientific and technical literature, and that this copy be readily accessible to any qualified individual. The report also recommended the establishment of a top level federal organization to guide and oversee the development of an integrated *national* network of document-handling systems in science and technology.

Some federal agencies have moved rapidly in the past three to five years to establish computer-based information services. Most of these supply computer records of titles, abstracts, etc. of literature articles and technical reports in fields of technology related to the agency mission. The Atomic Energy Commission, National Aeronautics and Space Administration, National Library of Medicine, Department of Defense, and Department of Commerce, all have computer-based systems of this type, and NASA is installing remote terminals connected to the central time-shared computer.

The first national information system in *science* based on computer storage and retrieval of information is now under development by the American Chemical Society, a not-for-profit professional society operating under a Congressional charter. The system development costs are being largely underwritten by federal agencies operating together in a coordinated program, although a large amount of related research and development is being supported by chemical industry and individual chemists. Whether other national information systems in other fields of science will follow this pattern has yet to be determined. Since, however, it makes little economic sense for more than one organization to acquire, index, and otherwise organize the world's published literature in a given subject field, it is fairly certain that by the year 1980 there will be a series of such computer based systems.

INFORMATION SYSTEMS OUTSIDE SCIENCE AND TECHNOLOGY

Where do the non-science activities of the U.S. stand? And how will they relate to the strong thrust forward into the computer-based era that is now characteristic of the physical and life sciences and technology? These questions are of great importance—not only to the non-scientist professionals and the general public, but also to those providing library services.

The legal profession has for some years sponsored development of computer-based legal information systems. An unusual form of indexing—the citation index—was, in fact, first developed by the legal profession and is the foundation for a successful, privately owned system. One may

---

[3] COSATI/FCST, Recommendations for National Document Handling Systems in Science and Technology, November 1965, (PB-168, 267/AD-624,560) Clearinghouse for Federal Scientific and Technical Information, Springfield, Virginia 22151.

safely predict increasing use of this, or similar systems by legal practitioners.

But in most other less advanced or non-scientific fields, the traditional use of documents reigns supreme. Libraries are generally staffed by people trained in the humanities. The existence of large collections of books predisposes people to think first of books for locating information, and their use of libraries gives librarians the sense that they are adequately satisfying the public's need for information. In science and technology the development of new information has been too rapid in the last two decades for books to play their once predominant role. The journal, technical report, preprint, technical meeting, and tip sheet have taken over the primary information-transfer function. This situation does not yet exist in the humanities. However, the social sciences and history are beginning to feel the same need for rapid access to the massive store of recorded information that has characterized the physical scientists and engineers in recent years. As Arnold Toynbee said, "We have to grapple with the stark difficulty of overcoming the disparity between the overwhelming mass of the data and the limited capacity of a single human mind."[4]

The increasing pressures of U.S. society on all learned professions and disciplines to apply existing knowledge to enrich the quality of individual and group human existence will, by 1980, have shattered the almost exclusive reliance of the humanists and social scientists on the printed word. This, in turn, will bring great changes in libraries serving the adult working force. The computer will be the primary method by which working adults gain access to stored information of utility to them in solving day-to-day problems.

Several states in the U.S. have begun to plan statewide library networks, based in part on the new technologies. The State University of New York, for example, planning an interconnected, computer-based system linking several of its major libraries. Rapid exchange of bibliographic and textual information between libraries is certain to make it less necessary for each library to build a self-sufficient collection. The balance between self-sufficiency and interdependence of libraries will progressively change over the next 10-15 years in favor of interdependence, with the development and application of the new communications and computer technologies.

APPLICATIONS OF THE NEW INFORMATION PROCESSING TECHNOLOGIES

In preceding paragraphs, a number of examples of new information storage and retrieval systems have been given. These examples were mainly those cases where the new technologies will make it possible to do present jobs more quickly, more easily, or more accurately and completely. More importantly, the new technologies will make it possible by 1980 to do many things not now being done.

Some have spoken of "computer utilities" of the future, when computing facilities will be so readily available in an interconnected grid and

---

4 Toynbee, Arnold. *A Study of History*, Vol. XII, Reconsiderations, p. 132, Oxford Univ. Press, 1961.

at such low cost that a "computer utility" will be as common-place as electricity and water utilities. This is no futuristic dream; already two large computer manufacturers have announced commercial computer services employing remote access, time-shared computers in metropolitan districts across the United States. A national communications firm has also announced similar plans, coupled with a statement of its objective as: "to establish a national information utility that will make it possible for large and small users of every kind, everywhere, to fill their total needs for information systems and services."

Library Services

The most marked change in libraries by 1980 will be their change into complete information services. Beginning with the use of computers for library housekeeping chores, the exploitation of the computer will spread to cover on-the-spot searches of computer files containing a major fraction of the information needs of its users. Less-used material will be housed in regional centers. Libraries will be integral parts of informational and educational service networks.

Librarians will need to re-think their concept of library service, and to re-define their role in the continuing education process.

Health Care

Two of the most important applications of the new computer and communications technologies are in health care and education. The achievement of the national goal of good health for every citizen will require an efficient, effective, information transfer network, built by vigorous, coordinated actions by private enterprise, the medical and educational establishments, and local, state, and federal governments.

By 1980 there will exist in the U.S. a complex of interconnected hospital-based information systems containing complete medical records for an increasingly large number of patients. This system will allow rapid retrieval of medical histories as people move from one location to another. The massive collection of patient treatment data, using new drugs and other healing techniques, will also allow much better determination of the effectiveness and safety of the new techniques and at an earlier stage. These data will also permit the establishment for the first time, of the "normal" health of the population—a value which is greatly needed in order to determine whether new drugs, changes in living conditions, and other changes in man's environment affect the "normal" population.

Computer techniques, as already demonstrated at the Massachusetts General Hospital, can greatly reduce the clerical work now done by doctors, nurses, and pharmacists, and in addition can increase the accuracy of hospital patient therapy. The automation of medical testing and the use of computers to screen out those individual records which should have the attention of a physician, are two developments which, over the next 15 years, will make possible a preventive medical program for the entire U.S. population. Since the U.S. faces a severe shortage of professionally trained medical practitioners when an increased commitment has been made for improved health care, these pressures will speed the application of computer based information processing.

Education

The application of new information processing technologies to education is lagging, although education has most of the management and operating problems faced by industry. Part of the reason is undoubtedly the expense associated with using computers today, and the traditional impoverished state of schools and colleges. Concern about this problem is increasing rapidly, and it appears likely that by 1980 the combination of cheaper computers and various types of financial support will provide computer service for all college and university students having a need for it in their course of study.

Perhaps an equally important factor in the educational lag is the traditional humanities orientation of educational administrators, and an unawareness of the power the new technologies can give both in administration and in instruction. These problems can only be overcome slowly, but by 1980 perhaps half the public school districts and all of the colleges and universities in the U.S. will be employing remote terminal, direct access computers. Small steps into the new universal technology will be taken first, such as teaching all children the use of the typewriter, as the New York City school system has recently decided to do. School business office use of computers has already begun and will be essentially routine by 1980. Scheduling pupils and classes, now requiring much intellectual effort by school administrators, will be routinely done by computer as is already the practice in some school districts.

The use of computer technology for instruction has barely begun in a few experimental situations. A great deal of the benefit derived by the student by operating on a large computer appears to be duplicable by printed programmed texts which are analogous to the computer program. The increasing availability of the computer, however, coupled with the heightened interest the student brings to an instructional session involving "glamour" hardware, foreshadows a decade of progressively greater use of the computer for instruction.

Employment

The National Commission on Technology, Automation, and Economic Progress has recently[5] called for the establishment of a computerized, nation-wide service for matching men to jobs. The Commission concluded that "the technological knowledge is available for the development of the equipment, and the costs are within reason" for a system in which local centers feed information to regional centers which, in turn, feed a nation-wide job and manpower bank. The organization and placement of such a system within the part private enterprise-part governmental economy characterizing America in the late 20th century, will require much study.

---

[5] National Commission on Technology, Automation and Economic Progress, *Technology and the American Economy,* Vol. I, p. 50, February 1966.

Urban Government

The rapid growth and changing environments of U.S. urban areas, in which it is estimated over 75 percent of the nation will be living by 1980 have placed a heavy burden on public policy makers and administrators for better decisions. Better policy making depends on better planning, which depends in turn on better data. Urban data centers will be common in the 1980s in the U.S., using the new information processing technologies. Information will be stored, correlated, analyzed, and retrieved on demand on such subjects as land use, housing conditions, housing occupancy, school requirements and facilities, and business district operations. Already the feasibility of such an information system has been proved by the Metropolitan Data Center Project of the Urban Renewal Administration. Collection and analysis of information on such a large scale would have been prohibitively expensive without computer technology.

The Graphic Arts Industry

By 1980, all significant commercial printing will employ computer-processable tape, either to set type or to drive photocomposition devices for offset printing. These tapes will be the information base for subsequent abstracting and indexing, and will be used directly for input to the ultra large computer memories foreseen for the large central libraries in the U.S. Remote access computers will also be used by an increasing number of authors, who will prepare, revise, and finally okay a manuscript without ever having had a printed version; the final computer tape will be used directly to prepare offset masters via photocompositors, and then will be ready for the other uses mentioned above.

SOME PROBLEMS AND IMPLICATIONS

Perhaps the largest barrier to achieving the potential benefits of the new information processing technologies will prove to be a lack of understanding about its possibilities. The changes in information transfer processes are too radical for the present generation in management to feel comfortable with them and to push for their adoption. But within the time span of this forecast, a new generation of management will have taken over, and rapid exploitation of the new technologies will take place.

The need for education and retraining in the new technologies is obvious. Since the new technologies are themselves in a state of rapid change, there will need to be corresponding retraining opportunities available for as far ahead as one may guess. Many thousands of computer programmers and technical specialists will be required. Here, however, the new information transfer technologies themselves will provide more effective and economical education.

Another large problem directly affecting the health of a major U.S. industry—the commercial publishing industry—concerns copyright in a computer based information system. Not only is there a question about whether a computer-produced work, such as a data compilation, is entitled to the traditional copyright of an "author." There is a larger question concerning protection against unauthorized use of copyrighted material stored in a computer memory. A new copyright bill pending before the Congress endeavors to deal with these issues, but it can safely be predicted that they will not be completely resolved in actual application for a decade or more.

The copyright problem is related to the diversity of ownerships, management, and financial support found in the U.S. information transfer industry. The new technologies will be handled (financially) most easily by a private organization owning and operating its own information system and getting its information in machineable form through purchase or other distinguishable methods. When, however, an organization's information system (i.e., computer) is tied on-line to a network, with multiple remote access users adding to and drawing from the network memory, the fiscal accounting becomes more difficult. The problem would be compounded in cases where the network memory contains privately-owned and public domain information. The computer's own magical powers of arithmetic can, of course, provide the solution, but only after suitable policies and regulations have been established.

Not a problem, but an area for further research which the new information technologies will stimulate, are the processes by which man actually uses information. At present we are still dependent on information being received by a man's eyes, or ears, being converted into electrical impulses and then assimilated by unknown mechanisms into the neural network that is the brain. The process is not understood, but there is evidence it is very inefficient. Research into this process—which is at the heart of learning and education—will steadily increase during the next two decades.

The advent of large information files in local, state, and national government agencies brings with it the problem of controlling the use of these files. It has been said that "the ultimate safeguard of the citizen is the fallibility of the government." Everyone (except those caught) applauds the national information file used to intercept drivers who have had their licenses revoked for serious offenses. Would people be happy if this were extended to cover parking violations? Such is the power of modern information technology that a vast store of information can be easily and cheaply built regarding each citizen. Some of the elements already exist, generally safeguarded from misuse by statute, regulation, and the ethical sense of the operators, but potentially exploitable. A major problem for our society is to use such files for beneficial purposes to the fullest extent, but to preserve equally completely the civil rights of the individual citizen.

The problems mentioned above are real; their solution will take time and effort on the part of all segments of U.S. society. It is essential that they be faced early; the spread of the new information system technologies is growing wider and faster.

Nonetheless, these same technologies offer man a revolutionary opportunity to expand his control over himself and his environment.

CHAPTER 14

The Future Of The Humanities

RICHARD F. KUHNS, JR.*

Biologists have observed the persistence and ingenuity with which organisms threatened with extinction defend themselves. Mutations appear at times to be far from accidental, but rather a genetic response to need. The poisons of industrial technology have, to be sure, extinguished some species; but others survive in forms that make living in a transformed environment not only possible but occasionally simpler. If natural enemies are destroyed, the survivors may flourish and indeed perhaps multiply in ways heretofore inconceivable. Coupled with these observations, the biologist's fancy might lead him to picture a world in which the few hardy survivors, having made genetic compacts with their altered surroundings, riotously reproduce in fantastical forms terrifying the natural scientist of the future.

The condition of the humanities which we now confront is analogous to that just described, for a technologically revolutionized environment has stamped out some traditional species of art, altered others beyond all recognition, offered the survivors an opportunity for explosive reproduction, and challenged the cultural historian with questions that have never before been posed. The humanities—which I shall interpret to mean primarily the fine arts and the occupations connected with them, such as criticism, scholarship, humane letters, art history, and the history of ideas—have survived, one would think, the worst that the machine age and the electronic age can do, for they everywhere burgeon, yet in mutant forms which puzzle and frighten us. Where the traditional forms persist, specimens in our university museums, they may be considered by artists working today as antiquarian curiosities; or, by a large part of the puzzled regarding public, as aesthetic consolation.

The chasm between what we see produced by artists today and the preservation of our artistic past in our institutions is part of what we refer to when we speak of the "Crisis in the Humanities." The other aspect of the crisis is the widening gap between science and the humanities. So far the crisis has provoked defensive action of two sorts: (1) Some of the humanities have tried to take over methods of inquiry and modes of evidential statement which ape the sciences. Computerized style studies, cybernetics research in behavior, the uses of machines as models, are put forward as "the new sciences of the humanities." (2) Traditional humanities

*Associate Professor, Department of Philosophy, Columbia University; Chairman, Humanities Staff, Columbia College; Author of *The House, The City and The Judge: The Growth of Moral Awareness in the Oresteia; Philosophies of Art and Beauty* (with Albert Hofstadter); articles on art and criticism.

231

are protected and insulated by academic programs in the arts and by foundational support of a select group of artists and scholars whose concern is to have the comfort of the past rather than fight with the direction of current creative work. But then we must ask if we can give orthogenic and constructive direction to the art movements of our time and the near future. Though we are, I believe, incapable of making art take a specific direction—a fact sadly ignored by rigidly controlled societies—we can think about the future in a realistic way to see what, under present conditions of mutation, might be produced through selective breeding. There might be a possibility of controlling some characteristics of future artistic births even though the forms themselves, as with animal life, are unpredictable.

HISTORICAL CHANGE IN THE HUMANITIES

Even though the condition of the arts now and in the future is largely influenced (perhaps even controlled) by the technological mass society we have created, the development of the arts is far different from the development of the sciences and the application of science to technology. The academic humanities have always been conservational and therefore conservative in nature, while the sciences and the inventions of technology have always been more progressive. That is to say, historical change in science and technology is logical, cumulative, transitive in that each discovery or invention, each progressive step tends to leave the previous ones behind. We need not know the history of science or technology to be good scientists or engineers; the job of work is always to take the next step, and the next step is in certain predictive ways recognized even before it has been taken.

But this is not the case with the humanities which have always depended for their evolution upon a knowledge of and intimate acquaintance with the past, and in which stylistic as well as contentual changes have always been traditional in a specific sense. Certain dominant themes and ideas and forms appear and reappear, slowly mutate, take on new life, run through stages of initiation, development and decline, only to be followed by yet further transformations. But the continuity is not only apparent to the historian: it exists within the works themselves as part of their content. Thus modern drama employs situations and themes first worked out by the Athenians two millenia past; painting explores subjects treated again and again in the past often with self-conscious elaboration; sculpture imitates primitive and archaeological forms in its modern restatement; music not only departs from tonality but in departing presupposes knowledge of and surfeit with its classical heritage. When we introduce the young to humanities as we do in most of our secondary school and college courses in the arts, philosophy, languages, and history, we emphasize the great works of the past and demand they be known both for their intrinsic goodness and their contribution to the humanistic values we hope to preserve.

We therefore impress upon the young the conservational and conservative intentions of the humanities. If spontaneity is encouraged, it is within the boundaries of tradition. You must develop your own style, the academy says, but let it be reminiscent of the great past.

Style, in fact, is the key to change in the humanities, for we are now going through what may be the end of an ever-intensifying style experimentation. It appears to be historically true that style change has evolved more and more rapidly as we have moved toward the present day, so that at least in the West (and this may now be true in the East also) style innovations have become a part of humanistic experimentation, as much a part of artistic evolution as gene mutation under the influence of X-ray is for organismic evolution. The fact of style innovation overwhelms us today because we have seen in painting the movements of impressionism, cubism, abstract impressionism, Pop art, Op art, constructional art, and several other styles all treading fast on the heels of their predecessors; in theatre the drama of the absurd follows hard upon varieties of realism; in music the shift away from tonality to the atonal, new scale structures, the use of electronic instruments; in literature a radical experimentalism going back to the early days of this century, bursting into the vulgarities of the comic strip, the comic book, fantasy journalism; and finally the still unexplored art of the cinema.

It is the last mentioned, the cinema, which gives us a clue about what has happened that can be of immeasurable help to us in thinking about the future, for the cinema is for us today the popular art which more than any other competes with the traditional and more conservational arts of concern to the schools. The cinema provides for us what other forms of popular art provided in the past, a sensational, easily assimilated, exciting, and relevant statement about what is happening both within ourselves and without ourselves in the social and political events that seem hidden and mysterious in the confusion of daily routine. The cinema structures life for us in somewhat the way popular New Testament stories structured life for persons living in late Hellenistic times. Caught as they were between the "great works" of the classical age, and the moral and religious aspirations of their own time, they then, as we now are doing, developed a new and more immediately satisfying form of story. Of course the learned retained knowledge of the ancient story forms, but what they were good for, and why they ought to be preserved was a recurrent question. So today, we find difficulty in adjusting the traditional subjects of the humanities to the needs so much more obviously met by the products of the movie studio.

With the wide-spread dissemination of the movie, the urban center ceased to be the place where, necessarily, art had its home. The artistic diffusion started by the cinema has now spread to the other arts with the rapid development of reproducing mechanisms. And this in turn has worked a radical revision of our concept of art, for it has attentuated the power of the art monument.

Just remember, there was a time not long ago when the well-educated man could know a few monumental art works and consider himslef well-versed in the arts. A Greek temple, a Gothic cathedral, a few important books, paintings, sculphures, and musical works were all that he needed to be aware of the humanistic achievements of his civilization. Perhaps more significant, these were all he needed for thought about the humanities. Not long ago thought about the arts could concentrate on "great works," analyze them, draw stylistic conclusions from them, relate and contrast them, and use them as prime examples for distinguishing classes. How plausible it seemed for the discussion of art to find sufficient examples in Sophocles, Raphael, Beethoven. How limiting these examples would be for many critics today, not because they are unimportant but because they are no longer monumental and exemplary. If we look at the intelligent writing about art which increases as we move into the late 18th and through the 19th centuries, we will become aware of the fact that there is an increasingly uninhibited interest in the new, the experimental, the transformation of the traditional into the modern. The concept of the art monument slowly disappears. Yet, despite this historical development, the art monument persists in great books courses, in art history courses, and in music appreciation courses. We ought not wonder then why it is that to students required to attend to masterpieces as a condition of their training in the humanities, the monuments of the past appear irrelevant and archaic, anachronistic and arcane.

Our situation today in the teaching of the humanities is curious: on the one hand we have highly organized educational conservatism concentrating on the humanistic products of the past and on the other hand a popular experimentalism which makes the conservatism of humanistic instruction increasingly out of joint with the rapid artistic change, the proliferation of new artistic forms which surround us. We suffer, therefore, not to much from a split between science and the humanities as we suffer from a split within the humanities themselves.

Thinking about this division is far more constructive, it seems to me, than thinking about the division between science and the humanities. For if we consider carefully the implications of our conservational stance in the teaching of the humanities, and contrast it with the revolutionary outbursts in the direction of the ingenious, the shocking, the experimental in contemporary art, we see that we are suffering from a destructive ambivalence towards the humanities. On the one side we favor a canonical set of "great works" as the condition for becoming educated; on the other we want the humanities to include the novelties—however trivial—of contemporary creativity. The conflict between the two sorts of cultural achievement enters into our evaluations of the creative work we hope to encourage in the future.

MEANS OF COPING WITH THE MODERN

The defense of tradition, it has been pointed out, is realized in the universities where scholarship proceeds pretty much on the basis of monumental surveys, a procedure acceded to by most graduate students because conservation is the condition of employment.

But there are young college undergraduates too, and they bring with them a Bohemian counter-offensive, a desire to be artistically creative themselves, intellectually "up" on what is going on in the experimental art around them. The universities have developed compensatory techniques for the young who would be impatient with more humanistic travelogues devoted to the great works of the past, by making room in the curriculum for the experimental, the outlandish, the very recent. Courses in "Theatre of the Absurd," "Music from 1918 to the Present," "Modern American Poets," are common in college catalogues. Under the pressure of these demands we find it more difficult now to honor, and little longer will be able to sustain, the distinction between the classic and the popular. Within the universities the distinction is rapidly disappearing even though fundamentally many universities exist on the pretense that they are conservational.

They have come to express their conservationalism by taking up the "adversary culture," as Lionel Trilling has aptly named it, into the college curriculum, combining the traditional with the new in strange, and possibly destructive ways. For the fresh impulses and experimentalism of artistic creativity are finding sanction within essentially conservative establishments. This means that those who would a short while ago have lived and worked outside the academy, perhaps living in opposition to all the academy artistically supported, now do their artistic work within the academy as students under the guidance of the "poet in residence," "painter in residence," "composer in residence," while they study in class the most recent artistic innovations as if they were established members of a tradition.

Along with this, naturally and inevitably, arts programs have grown up as adjuncts to the college curriculum. It is now possible to take a Fine Arts Degree, spending one's college and postgraduate years learning to be an artist. This is a strange phenomenon in a society which but a few years ago saw an artistic revolt against the academy. But perhaps there is a reason why social constraints have been put upon the arts in this way: if the adversary culture becomes too dangerous it must be institutionalized. Is it possible (and this is simply speculation) that just as the city elders in Athens made the drama festival a restraining response to the Dionysiac celebrations imported from abroad, so we, finding a humanistic indictment of ourselves in the arts of recent years, have moved to make it harmless, domesticated, assimilable, by capturing it in the curriculum?

However, another explanation is more likely: the development of the arts program in the colleges—one of the most significant developments for our consideration of the humanities in 1980—is an extension of an evolution that has been going on for a long time: namely, the growth of the "service schools" such as schools of journalism, business, engineering, and the teachers' college where students are trained to teach almost every kind of subject, the humanities included. Why not then be taught to be creative in the arts? In this development I think we can see the arts program as a reflection of a changing notion of community, one in which the arts as such are overseen by "responsibly" trained and "knowing" persons.

Our way of coping with the modern then has been to ingest all that goes on humanistically into the huge organism of the university. This leaves little outside as adversary culture, and has important implications for us in our planning for the future.

SOCIAL IMPLICATIONS OF THE NEW ATTITUDES TOWARD THE ARTS

Institutions of higher learning are not simply expressing their wider cultural concerns by including the contemporary arts in their curricula, but are also responding to a profound change wrought by technology. Not only has the cinema become the available popular art, but those art forms traditionally reserved for the rich, are now everywhere available, for factories flood homes with pictures, music, decorative objects. The city itself has become self-consciously "aesthetic," that is, in our thought at least, artistically ordered and controlled even though the actual urban environment is still aesthetically repulsive. But recent art movements seem to be solving the problem by transforming the repellent into the aesthetically acceptable. Hence we are beginning to see a period in which *all* the arts are popular arts. Not only is a machine fit for a museum, but even the monumental works of the past to which one might journey over vast distances and towards which one might sustain an attitude of veneration, are now in almost every dwelling, every classroom, every small-town museum. Photography, television, electronic recording have made all human products available, common, familiar, perhaps even commonplace. With greater familiarity goes, naturally, an increasing interest and demand for novelty, the stimulating, the radical in experience. Indeed, experimentation, novelty, stylistic change and development are necessary functions of the technological culture in which we find ourselves. But this has a further implication, for it drives us to transcend cultural boundaries as they were traditionally defended, to absorb all of the art of East and West, of past and present, into a new art synthesis.

Further extensions of artistic boundaries are pressed to embrace the products of technological engineering so that we confront today the possibility of everything becoming art because we are confused about what the artistic could reasonably exclude. In letting impulse guide us here, we are realizing the fantasy David Hume entertained of the natural order in which, rationally considered, anything could follow from anything, any event might be joined to any other event. We, in our stylistic experimentation, feel ourselves to be helplessly floundering when we look to the seemingly ordered, controlled sciences. And it is this sense of loss of control which lies behind C. P. Snow's distress when he surveys the sciences and the humanities. He is recalling the centuries past when literature and the arts had a controlling sense of tradition.

But new art forms have the impact they do precisely because they are in part at least expressing criticism of and dissatisfaction with some of the scientific and technological developments of our time. I do not think it is far off to say artists by and large are critical of and dissatisfied with the pressures of our age of engineering partly because it has confused us about what is art, and partly because it has allowed the factory to compete with the artist. Whatever the cause—and I cannot go into it here—the recent arts such as the theatre of the absurd, Pop art, electronic music, and other forms are understood by many critics to be expressions of a problem which Durkheim described by using the term "anomie." That is, many people today feel alienated from themselves and from their society, from their work and from their community. They are led to ask, as people in times other than ours also have asked, but perhaps with less insistency, what are the purposes of human life, and what is it in human-ness itself that counts for most. Certainly the humanities ought to have something to say about this, and they do, especially in those forms which we properly call "humanistic." The art and philosophy of our time ought to be instrumental in helping us to think about ourselves and our social commitments, and certainly ought to be important for the future shape of our society. What we do now in the humanities does, I believe, have a large influence on the quality and scope of our humanities in 1980.

The humanities as we used to respect them, and as we try now to sustain them, had two things of fundamental import to say, it seems to me. The first is that art itself is an ultimate human value with an ultimate good in its intrinsic nature which makes it worthwhile as a human pursuit. The second is that art is a means we have of coming to know truths about ourselves which no other process or product of human agency can show us. Whatever the specific content of recent art—and I will comment briefly about some of its more unpleasant themes in a moment—it is the best and only means we have to explore the question: What is it to be human? It remains, along with the other humanistic pursuits, the way of answering questions such as: What are the modes of conduct and the creative visions in which human-ness is best realized?

The social potencies of the arts are tied, therefore, to our thoughts, beliefs, and hopes about ourselves as individuals and as members of a community, because the arts are ways we have of coming to shape those beliefs, to arouse and alter those attitudes, to stimulate hopes, and to characterize fears. But this instrumentality of the arts (and I am not discussing it because I think it is the only or even the most important function of the arts) is apt not to be efficacious under the present conditions in which the critical and heretical functions of the humanities are, to some extent at least, blunted or diluted in their having a secure place within the university world, or, more relevant for our discussion here, within the world of government subsidy, federal help, national tendance and conservation. There is, I believe, a double problem which confronts us: (1) The first is the problem of the split between the sciences and the humanities which we happily believe will be overcome by the subsidy of the arts on a plan analogous to the subsidy of the sciences. We rejoice, we humanists, because we now, like our more powerful brethern the scientists, towards whom we for so long have felt envy, can share in the national liberality. (2) The other is the split between the conservational, tradition-regarding, uses of the humanities in our universities and the need of our society to benefit from the critical, untraditional, perhaps violently original and therefore shocking and unconsoling creativity in the humanities. We can use the past; we must create the future; genuine creativity implies non-conformity and insistence on seeing the truth.

THE FUTURE OF THE HUMANITIES

To think ahead to 1980 is really a very short time in the humanities —at least it would have seemed a short time one hundred years ago. Perhaps now, as I have pointed out, it is not a short time because there is such radical change going on in the arts. The arts are changing not only as a response to rapid change in our technological and social accomplishments, but they contribute to it themselves. Within the next twenty years there will be, I believe, forces at work which will alter the pattern of the arts in their social and political involvements. These must be honestly faced.

Two powerful forces for change will in the next few years work upon the humanistic preoccupations of our artists and scholars. The first is the federal money now and in the future ready to be used on behalf of the arts and humanistic scholarship. The second is the active sponsoring of the arts by institutions of higher learning and by exurban art centers. Of course the two are related since it is from the government that the universities and the towns are already getting and in the future plan to get large sums of money for active arts programs. For the first time since the arts works projects of the 1930's an agency of the federal government is ready to sponsor and therefore to encourage the arts. What does this mean for our future,

The first wide-spread effect will be the proliferation of arts centers in urban and exurban regions supported by federal funds and overseen by local arts groups. For the first time in many years the local painter, writer, movie maker, dancer may have a chance to do something in his own community rather than travel to the city for employment. Something akin to the local opera house, which for the last two hundred years has animated much of European art, will grow up in middle-sized communities across the nation. But the concept of the arts sponsored therein will be much wider than anything we have seen in Europe. The American art center, as I imagine it, will most likely be patterned on the adult education programs of study already a significant part of our high school evening education work. Now, however, instead of learning enameling or bookbinding, or listening to a series of lectures on the origins of World War I, there will be an ambitious arts program encouraging writing, the plastic and dramatic arts, overseen by people of far greater training and competence than we have had available heretofore.

The arts programs will be guided by teachers and artists whose ideas about the arts will be quite different from those of the traditional high school instructor. The arts are bound to become part of a polemical situation that has many interesting aspects about which we ought to speculate.

By a polemical situation I mean that the arts, when they become the object of national interest because supported by federal money, will be shaped and defended by a variety of ideologies, including, of course, the position that ideologies have *no* rightful place where the arts are concerned. The arts programs will be carried out under the aegis of various guiding ideas, and I think we ought to consider carefully what ideas may be taken as establishing the values in terms of which our future artistic and humanistic studies will be guided. I think it most likely that there will be a radical difference between the ideas about art in the academy and the ideas about art in the arts centers outside the academies. The academy will in most likelihood maintain standards of artistic excellence derived from the past, while the arts center might well be the testing ground for radically new conceptions of art. Yet as soon as this is said, we see the possibility that the art center will become the stronghold of the most superficially folksy kind of art, and therefore conservational of the trite and the trivial, cut off from the past and prevented by its communal involvement from innovation and experimentation. But whatever the next few years may bring in the balance of power between the universities and the communal arts center, I think there are some interesting ideas that will be much discussed as the arts programs come into being. I would like to mention these ideas under the following headings: (1). Art must be close to, a part of, daily life. (2). Art must define the "human condition." (3). Art must be a liberating opportunity for industrial man.

Relation of Humanities Programs to Life

The first statement is exemplified in social reality by the arts programs I envision. Soon there will be artistic participation on a far wider base than anything we have known before: more people will take a shot at practicing an art, more will be observers of artistic performances. The connection with daily life will be obvious for it will no longer be necessary to travel to urban centers for theatre, music, painting, but there will be artistic work done and seen in one's own small community. Leisure will be considered well-spent in the pursuit of the arts.

But there are obvious dangers in the intimacy thus encouraged: one is in the direction of the homey, corny, familiar, low-standard art that we know from television and the evening high school program. This amounts to art as a pastime. The other which falls under a distinct ideology, will be far more refined, and although possibly repetitive and unoriginal, yet regarded as liberating. This is the art which, in claiming to address itself to defining the "human condition," follows in the mode of the experimental drama, novel, and plastic art of the past twenty-five years. It is the art sometimes referred to as "existential."

The Humanities and the Human Condition

There will be a conflict between these two directions of artistic work which will result in a wider and wider separation between pastime art and ideological art, and which will generate an interesting internal criticism. Ideological art, addressing itself to the separation many persons feel today between themselves and their natural environment, will see human beings as finding themselves through a denial of the more conventional, homey, and socially cooperative activities. The prototype here is the man represented by Dostoyevsky in *Notes From Underground:* the man who observes life through the mousehole, who has found no possibility for a center of meaning in life because his self-awareness is so developed that he is always acting out a part. There is no center because all behavior is role taking, and all expression of feeling suspect because he never knows what is genuine. Every experience can be undercut by a suspicion of deceit, of bad faith. Selfhood, this view goes on to assert, is realized in the separation from, denial of, and antagonism toward conventional social restraints. Liberation from the communal confinements on personal freedom are to be found in those experiences in which total degradation or total moral alienation frees the individual from his obligation to respond to social demands, from the need to conform to socially approved goals. It is this point of view which has exerted a strong claim upon the moral thought of our time; it is the theme much contemporary art explicitly articulates, or alludes to in a variety of subtle ways. It is a recurrent theme in contemporary art because it is a real problem for us, especially when we find ourselves pushed towards conformity and group participation in planned exercises for cultural betterment. It is then, not unrelated to what we here are talking about.

The arts programs of the future, supported by enlightened, humane individuals acting under federal sponsorship with federal funds will want to set up the sorts of programs which the artistic expressions I have just discussed, will be aimed at negating. The arts programs are apt to make the arts either trivial pastimes, or, if they encourage something more, to encounter ideas about art which will challenge the purposes and values of the programs themselves. An intolerance of this second consequence could stifle the vigor and the creative experimentation to which we, in our planning for the future, ought to be dedicated. If we do not recognize this obligation, then we are in danger of losing a great good which the humanities can bestow. One aspect of humanistic concern is the critical opposition which the arts, standing outside the common assumptions about behavior, norms, goals, and judgments permeating a large society, clearly and shockingly enunciate. I can envisage a society in which many write poetry but there are no poets; painting flourishes but there is no art worthy of serious attention; drama fills local theatres but no depth of insight makes it worth recalling.

While the arts, to be important, must sink into the mind and there slowly give birth to statements in contemporary styles and with historical self-consciousness, they can also be mere entertainment, the passing show of expressive gesture to hide reality rather than reveal. I fear the arts, pruned and watered, directed and sustained by large communal projects may bring the benefits of an aesthetic which is anaesthetic: the deadening of sense, the insistence on the *á la mode,* the repetition of accepted forms.

But let us suppose the programs further not simply a trivializing of the arts, but the bitter, self-critical, nihilistic point of view I mentioned earlier as the substance of Dostoyevsky's Underground Man. This is a likely adversary to the anaesthetic: an aesthetic of the absurd. I find the prospect of this development, were it to become popular, obnoxious and dangerous, for I think it a perversion, a denial of the best possibilities for human beings and for the arts themselves. I do not think human beings are best realized in their morally nihilistic aloneness, nor do I think the growth of self-consciousness, through art, is necessarily a step to the incapability of having genuine feelings and taking a moral stand. Yet I assert this as a faith based on the arts of an earlier and in some ways socially more indefensible period in our history. We all deplore the arts as the private consolation of the aristocratic or the rich; we all would have the arts meaningful to the whole society, speaking to the well-educated and to the "disadvantaged." We urge ourselves to simple, socially inspiring distribution of aesthetic benefits; aesthetic security belongs to the good society too. And yet, what we are setting ourselves to do will realize, I believe, only a few of the benefits the arts can confer and deny to ourselves and our descendents the very great things of which the arts are capable. How can it be that socially sponsored, federally supported, university nurtured humanities programs can be a liberating opportunity for industrial man?

The Humanities as a Liberating Opportunity for Man

This is my final question, and I must leave it as a question because I do not know the answer. But I fear it is a question the answer to which will be repugnant to us. The answer may be that if the humanities are to be liberating, they must be to some degree private, eccentric, adversary to our own accepted modes of conduct; questioning, critical, experimental, and wildly subversive, just as in the past the arts and the humane scholarship which has brought us the most good (that is, the most wisdom) has been the hardest to bear, the most painful to accept, yet in part for that reason the most moving, the most instructive, and the most truthful. But then, we ask, why not devote our federal mechanism to the promotion of the great art and humanistic study of the past: Shakespeare in every theatre, classical philosophy in every classroom? I would like to urge that there be proper regard for the conservational nature of the humanities; that they continue as they have in the past as preservers and conservers. Yet they cannot be that alone if they are to enrich our lives, for it is in creative originality and in critical stands that we develop as self-consciously controlling agents who direct our destinies in our social progress. One can all too easily imagine a Swiftian Laputa of the arts for they too, like the sciences, and most especially in our time when the sciences are of overriding power, can be perverted.

If the humanistic pursuits are to be liberating for our highly developed technological society they must have the opportunity to be openly subversive of the very processes which make possible a widespread flourishing in the humanities under federal sponsorship. We are caught in an ironic dilemma of a richness which will make the humanistic endeavors more available to all; yet which for its encouragement can expect—perhaps from the most amply gifted—a lack of appreciation, even bitter critical opposition. Its success depends on its failure. I wonder if that is an outcome we can tolerate.

CONCLUSION

The history of the arts has been marked by successive revolutions in art production and consumption, as well as by radical changes in the methods of teaching the arts and training artists. In a consideration of the future of the humanities from our vantage point, the most pressing question is what will happen to the arts when legislative sanction as well as governmental interest directly works upon the production of and consumption of art. I have tried to describe in this essay some of the problems this new situation will present to us, and to warn that a sensitivity to change is necessary if we are to derive from the arts their most instructive and liberating benefits.

I first distinguished two tendencies in the contemporary teaching and use of the arts: one, a conservatism which tends to perpetuate the past as the representative of humanistic values always relevant to a society which wishes to defend a tradition; the other, a radical experimentalism which, working against tradition, raises serious pedagogical problems for our institutions where the arts are perpetuated. I pointed out that many of our institutions of higher learning have tried to digest the contemporary innovating arts and place them alongside the traditional, with results that are confusing for both the older and younger generations. These confusions come out of the naturally critical and visionary aspects of the new art forms which, in their objections and innovations, open the way to important creative achievements. This very openness and experimentalism poses a problem to federal sponsorship of the arts and creative activity since the work supported will be deeply critical of just those values which animate the national interest in the arts.

A puzzling conflict is therefore generated for those who teach the arts and for those who have the responsibility of supporting art centers and individual artists. To cope with this conflict successfully, the critical and visionary character of the arts must be recognized and tolerated, for what may appear at first to be the failure of a new way of treating the arts may in reality be the realization of values for which we conserve the past, and for which, if we understand the arts, we encourage creative spontaneity in the present.

CHAPTER 15

Human Responsibility
In the Emerging Society

ROGER L. SHINN*

In human affairs prediction at best is a risky though necessary enterprise. Obviously forecasts are not equally reliable in all areas of culture. In some spheres a projection of present movements is a fairly reliable clue to the future. But wherever human creativity is decisive, man may reverse current tendencies or strike out in new directions.

The vast area of my assignment includes several human activities and intellectual disciplines: ethics and moral values, philosophy, and religion. All of these are concerned with the human element in social change, with the movement of the human mind and spirit. Clearly mankind will have to respond to certain discernible and measurable movements of our time; hence prediction is possible. But the character of the response of the poet, the prophet, and the political leader is not equally predictable.

For example, during World War II the evidence was available for a prediction of racial unrest in the years to come. But no projection of trends could then show the future emergence of the non-violent movement and of the style of moral protest symbolized by Martin Luther King, Jr. Similarly, in the age of McCarthyism and of conformism, astute social analysts might predict—although few of them did—that a new uneasiness and social protest would soon emerge. But the best of them did not foresee the shape and the dynamics of "the new left."

My procedure, therefore, in this venture of prediction will be to move from the known to the more conjectural. This means a movement from identification of social processes that set the issues for human decision to the analysis of the styles of decision that may now be emerging.

ASSUMPTIONS

Of the many movements that are radically reshaping society, I shall mention five that have major impact upon ethics, philosophy, and religion.

Population Increase

Barring nuclear holocaust, the population explosion can be expected to continue. The present rate of growth—a rate that doubles the earth's population in 35-40 years—faces many families and societies with crises.

*Dean of Instruction and Professor of Applied Christianity, Union Theological Seminary, New York City, and Adjunct-Professor of Religion, Columbia University; Author of numerous books, including *Christianity and the Problem of History*, *The Existentialist Posture*, and *Tangled World*; Editor of the symposium, *The Search for Identity: Essays on the American Character*; Member of the editorial board of *Christianity and Crisis*.

243

Mankind can exploit new possibilities for production of food and the use of living space. But the combination of the threat of population growth to the quality of life and the availability of improved contraceptives is leading to increased efforts in planned limitations of population.

The changes will come through both personal and governmental decisions. In the most technologically advanced societies a majority of families have made their decision for deliberate family planning; in other societies the same movement is on the way. In governmental policy the pace of change is evident in a comparison: under the Eisenhower administration the President stated that birth control was not a proper realm of governmental activity; under the Kennedy administration modest governmental activity in this area began; under the Johnson administration national and state governments are actively providing contraceptive information and devices, both internationally and domestically.

One obvious result has been the rethinking of many ethical and religious traditions throughout the world. Some of the religious and social groups most resistant to acceptance of contraceptives have now revised or are in the process of rethinking their ethic of sex and family.

Technology

As spectacular as the explosion in population is the explosion of knowledge, especially technological knowledge. The new knowledge brings increased power, control of environment, and productive capacity. It also means highly organized forms of political, economic, educational, and other social institutions. It produces mass communications with worldwide potential.

The reverberations in man's self-understanding and his ethics are immense. Three are worth special mention. (1) Provincialism becomes increasingly obsolete. Every culture and every religion must take seriously the significance of differing cultures and religions, just as mankind must take seriously the possibility (or probability) of life on many planets in many galaxies. (2) Ethics, which has sometimes limited its domain to personal acts and attitudes, must increasingly give attention to the organizational structures that shape human life. (3) Cybernetics, facing man with the powers of the computer, requires him to ask in new ways the old question concerning what it is to be human.

Urbanization

A combination of technological and population growth is urbanization. The United States, 40 percent urban in 1900, was 70 percent urban in 1960. The rate of urbanization is even faster in some other parts of the world.[1] In some respects the impact of urbanization is less obvious in the Rocky Mountain area than elsewhere in the United States, but the urban style of life is not limited to regions of high population density.

---

[1] E.g., Japan, the Soviet Union, Puerto Rico, and much of Africa. See Julia J. Henderson, "Urbanization and World Community," *Annals of the American Academy of Political and Social Science*, Vol. 314 (Nov., 1957), pp. 147-148.

Urbanization faces society with profound ethical decisions. In the United States, for example, urbanization has—in fact, if not by necessity— produced desperate and frustrated racial ghettoes. It has raised unsolved problems of social responsibility, as cities seek to finance necessary serv- ices by taxation, while those most able to pay frequently escape to suburbs. At the same time the city maintains something of its traditional role as the center of culture, so that urbanization means increased cultural oppor- tunity for many citizens.

The Military Situation

The number of nuclear powers in the world (one in 1945, five in 1966) is on the increase. One informed estimate is that there may be as many as thirty in 1980.[2] China, recently one-fifth and soon perhaps to be one-fourth of the human race, is increasing its nuclear capacity. As the conflict between the United States and the Soviet Union relaxes (as shown by the loss of cohesion in both NATO and Warsaw Pact powers), rela- tions between the prosperous nations and the impoverished, revolutionary nations become more difficult. Even small nations (e.g., Viet Nam) can precipitate major conflicts, and the number of potential Viet Nams in Asia, Africa, and South America is incalculable.

The restlessness of the world combined with the increased chances for military disaster mean unprecedented possibilities of chaos and de- struction. These in turn produce unprecedented impulses for some kind of international controls. What this will mean for future world organiza- tion remain unclear.

Bertrand Russell has written, "The human race has survived hitherto owing to ignorance and incompetence; but, given knowledge and com- petence combined with folly, there can be no certainty of survival. Knowl- edge is power, but it is power for evil just as much as for good."[3] In the new historical situation the demands upon man's intelligence and ethical insight are obvious.

Human Rights

The revolution in human rights, a world wide demand in the 1960's, will probably continue and increase. The United States, as a large, ethnically diverse society, is involved in this revolution to the hilt.

The struggle over human rights has many specific regional mani- festations. The Negro, once concentrated in the agricultural South, con- tinues his move to the urban North: now New York, Chicago, Oakland, and Los Angeles are as haunted by the race problem as is the black belt of Alabama and Mississippi. Spanish Americans are an important ethnic group in Eastern cities and in the Southwest. The long abused American Indian asks for human rights across the country, especially in the West.

The United States, with its long traditions of freedom and justice, faces new ethical issues in seeking to make good its traditional values in his-

---

[2] Harrison Brown and James Real, *Community of Fear* (Santa Barbara: Center for the Study of Democratic Institutions, 1960), p. 24.

[3] Bertrand Russell, *The Impact of Science on Society* (New York: Simon and Schuster, 1953), p. 97.

tory's vastest experiment in devising a large-scale, industrialized, pluralistic society. Not many precedents are helpful in a situation that calls for innovation.

THE HUMAN EFFECTS OF CHANGE

This preliminary identification of social movements in our time has already made evident a considerable agenda for ethical and religious concern. The agenda will increase as we move from the consideration of these easily-definable historical tendencies to a probing of some equally real but less tangible issues in the value-structure of our culture.

In each of the current changes that I shall mention, the years ahead appear as both opportunity and threat. For some persons the opportunity is more obvious; for others the threat looms larger.

The Undermining of Authority

In a time of major social change, established authorities lose their persuasiveness and perhaps even their relevance. The questioning of authority is widespread today, most noticeably among the "new left," with its attacks upon "the establishment" and its frequent question, "Can we trust anybody over thirty?"

If some assaults upon authority are merely petulant, others rest on substantial reasons. We have discovered that many seemingly immutable moral laws are simply the *mores* of a particular culture, that some "eternal values" are merely customs, that "self-evident truths" may be only the preferences of some societies. Furthermore, even those who are temperamentally inclined to trust traditional authorities find that those authorities —especially when they take the form of legalisms—say nothing about the ethical issues arising in new social situations.

The American society, therefore, is moving to an increasingly experimental ethic. As the role of tradition declines, the importance of inquiry increases. Even when authority remains powerful, the reason it does so, is less because it is authority than because it vindicates itself in practice.

The threat and opportunity in such a situation are both real. The threat is of a loss of standards, a tyranny of the peer group in the place of other authority, the subservience of human values to the expediencies of a nationalistic (perhaps militaristic) and technological society. The opportunity is for increasing sensitivity to human needs as formal codes yield to a more imaginative ethic. The same groups in our society may show both impulses: a cavalier disregard for disciplines and procedures established over a long history, together with a remarkable courage and vision in struggles for human rights.

Affluence and Poverty

The twentieth century has seen the emergence of a new kind of human society in the United States and a few other parts of the world— the affluent society. This is a society that has learned the skills of production and has distributed its economic benefits to most of its people. In the affluent society nobody need go hungry or ill-clad because of scarcity of food and clothing. When people suffer deprivation, the reason is not a lack of economic goods. (Housing presents a more difficult issue, but it is certainly soluble, although not yet solved.) The affluent society does not persuade its members to restrain their consumption for the common good; it persuades them to consume more so that the economy will thrive.

Thus far the affluent societies are islands of wealth in a world of poverty, and they face great ethical and political difficulties in relating themselves creatively to a world of want. One of the urgent ethical issues of the years ahead will concern the responsibility of the rich nations toward the poor nations.

Furthermore, poverty persists within the affluent society, where it both disturbs the conscience and threatens the well-being of the society. The current debates about social security, medical care for the aged and for others, subsidized housing, and the guaranteed annual wage may be prototypes of the ethical debates of the future. They are discomforting debates to many within our culture, both because they do not permit the neat isolation of ethical from political decisions and because no traditional ethical authorities provide pre-packaged answers.

If poverty within the affluent society raises disturbing ethical issues, affluence itself raises others. Even if the American society succeeds in eliminating severe poverty, the ethical issues of affluence will remain. Affluence means the obsolescence of the so-called "Protestant ethic"— the ethic of hard work, saving, no borrowing, cultivation of deferred enjoyment, economic sanctions against the lazy and unlucky. To the extent that the disciplines of a society are built upon an obsolescent ethic, the passing of the ethic disturbs the society. Some see the loss of all discipline. Others see the invitation to develop a discipline more appropriate to a technological world.

The affluent society offers the opportunity for an ethic that knows how to enjoy leisure and to provide opportunity for all its citizens. Its threat is the situation of satiety-starvation—where a people satiated with consumer goods become starved for satisfactions, to the extent sometimes that even sex becomes a commodity for the acquisitive consumer, totally unrelated to traditional virtues of fidelity and shared experience. One of the curious phenomena of our society is the interaction of the "Playboy ethic" of affluent hedonism with the calls for sacrifice in war, the Peace Corps, and the struggle for civil rights.

Shifts of Power

In any society the dominant ethic is—in part—a reflection of the power structure of the society. The established authorities are likely to sense any attack upon their authority as a threat both to their values and their power. The far-reaching social changes of our time are bringing shifts in both the values and the power-structures of society.

Theoretically the American democracy allows all its citizens the right of particpation in public processes and access to power. In actual fact, some citizens have been excluded from meaningful power, either by overt racial discrimination or by a more subtle process of rejection from the mainstream of the culture. Hence some of the major ethical debates of the present and the emerging future center on issues of power.

A conscience-stricken society may be moved by persuasion to grant certain privileges to the groups who have suffered its injustices. But the victims may not be content to accept gifts; they may want to claim rights. *It is easier for the powerful to extend largess than to share power.* The American ethical consciousness has been negligent on this issue because of a tendency in our culture to regard power as evil. Ethics has then operated through persuasion and neglected the urgent issues of power.

This issue will be settled neither by rebels who ritualistically declaim against "the power structure" nor by highly moral people who neglect the importance of power. The debates about power in the 1960's have taken concrete form in questions of the participation of the poor in the war against poverty and of the organization of the poor for community action, sometimes in the manner of the controversial Saul Alinsky. Those issues will continue to concern this society.

The American society will also have to face the issue of power in the world of nations. This six percent of the people of the world are the dominant power in the world. Nobody expects that the United States will in this generation reduce its power to the six percent that a strictly proportional system might require. But it is also unlikely that this one country will maintain the vast dominance of power that it has so briefly exercised. The response to shifts of power, both internationally and domestically, will constitute one of the major ethical issues before the American people in the years ahead.

Questions of Identity

In a stable society personal identity is conferred upon the individual. Society recognizes the person and he recognizes himself as the son of a family, often living in the same homestead and pursuing the same vocation as his father. He need not constantly identify himself—to strangers or to himself. He knows who he is.

In the mobile American society identity is no longer conferred; it must be discovered or created. The question, "Who am I?" is constantly asked, especially among youth. Deans of educational institutions report that one of the most common reasons given by students, both for entering schools and for dropping out, is to discover their identity.

Personal identity in the American society is often "up for grabs." The abandonment of traditional male and female roles produces a confusion in sexual identity, which is one reason for the impulse to sexual experimentation. Ethnic identity is a perplexing issue; many a Negro is unsure whether he wants to escape or to acclaim his racial heritage, and many a WASP (white Anglo-Saxon Protestant) who has taken his identity for granted is now uneasy in it. The youth culture, which once sought to submerge its identity in an eagerness to become adult, now asserts its identity in protest against adult culture.

The opportunity in the current situation is freedom; a person may choose his identity. The threat is a confusion of values and self-identification that drives some to the edge of, or over the edge of, pathology. We can expect the struggle for identity to persist and probably increase in the years ahead.

Alienation

Closely related to identity is the issue of alienation, one of the most persistent words in the vocabulary of youth. Alienation is a concept with a profound philosophical and theological heritage (e.g., the young Karl Marx and Paul Tillich) that has rather suddenly become one of the "O.K.-words" of popular culture.

Only recently the observers of American culture were noting the compulsion toward conformity in David Riesman's "other-directed" man and W. H. Whyte's "organization man."[4] Only ten years ago a sociologist's study of American college students described them as "gloriously contented" and "dutifully responsive toward government."[5] That era is not *totally* gone. Riesman's title, *The Lonely Crowd,* is still a marvellously apt one. But the campus rebellions, most notably at Berkeley and in less explosive ways at many other colleges, have established alienation rather than conformity as the great moral problem of the current campus generation.

Alienation takes many forms. It is evident in the ethical passion of students in the civil rights movement, alienated often from parents and the values of a "materialistic" society. It appears in the impatience—sometimes sublime and sometimes immature—with the normal social processes and the resort to "direct action." It appears in the juvenile delinquency, once ascribed chiefly to slums but now growing most rapidly in suburbs.

A major ethical problem of the American society in the decade ahead will be to appreciate the valid protests within this alienation and to correct its destructive impulses.

THE NATURE OF RESPONSIBLE DECISION

In a historical period like our own the most penetrating and profound issues of ethics shift from the maintenance of an inherited code to the more difficult and dynamic task of making responsible decisions. This does not mean that we can look condescendingly at the past. A succession of prophets, priests, artists, and philosophers offer us an inheritance of insights won in their experiences of struggle, suffering, and joy. *Humanity always lives close enough to its own destructive powers of hostility and frustration that it cannot afford to ignore any wisdom from the past.*

---

[4] David Riesman with Nathan Glazer and Reuel Denney, *The Lonely Crowd* (New Haven: Yale University Press, 1950). William H. Whyte, Jr., *The Organization Man* (New York: Simon and Schuster, 1956).

[5] Philip Jacob, *Changing Values in College* (New York: Harper and Row, 1957), pp. 1, 2.

The transmission and renewal of the religious and humanistic inheritances of the past remains one task and opportunity of each generation. But the insights of the past can never simply be transmitted in documents, works of art, or institutions. Each age must reappropriate its heritage—and in the reappropriation somehow modify it. Furthermore, the present must ask anew the meaning of its most treasured values—its awareness of the nature of commitment, generosity, tragedy, love, justice, and forgiveness —for its own time.

We can recognize the nature of responsible decision by looking at two examples of the kind of ethical decision that faces this generation.

Personal Integrity in Mass Society

The urbanized, mechanized, computerized society with its mass communications and its mass treatment of individuals is a momentous achievement. Its efficiencies offer amazing new possibilities for the liberation of the human spirit. But it is altogether possible that man may become the mechanized slave of the system. As economist Robert Heilbroner puts it, "It is not mere rhetoric to ask if Things are not already in the saddle riding Man."[6]

In such a situation the ethical problem requires attention to both the organizational structures of life and the most personal qualities of living. I shall comment on each in turn.

In organizational structures. The structures of a society have their own ethical impact upon persons, regardless of the moral qualities of the human beings who work within the structures. For example, a despotism has a different quality from a democracy, even though the despot be benevolent. A segregated society works its damage upon people, even though individuals may have real affection for each other across the walls of segregation. War, especially modern war with its new potencies, destroys lives and values even though individuals may perform acts of gallantry in it.

Contemporary society with its high pitch of organization requires ethical attention to its social structures. A long tradition of pietistic and individualistic religion in America has schooled many people to see ethical decision only in their personal lives—a limitation that becomes increasingly harmful as social institutions grow more complex and pervasive in their impact upon persons.

Hence our world needs "social inventions," to use the phrase of Harold Laswell. It needs to discover ways by which people can participate in major decisions of government and the corporation. It needs devices to keep vast institutions responsive to human needs rather than to the will of elites or the impersonal mechanisms of machine-efficiency.

In personal qualities of living. Entirely consistent with this ethical attention to institutions is the concern for persons. In many cases the efficiency of the system is the best way to serve the interests of individuals. For example, an effectively functioning social security system can serve

---

[6] Robert L. Heilbroner, "The Impact of Technology: The Historic Debate," in *Automation and Technological Change,* edited by John T. Dunlop (Englewood Cliffs, N. J.: Prentice-Hall, 1962), p. 7.

personal dignity far better than a "personalized charity" in which the rich give gifts to the unfortunate poor. Yet the best social machinery is no substitute for personal awareness and concern.

In 1932 Aldous Huxley first published his *Brave New World*— a fictional description of the efficient, stable utopia where morality and freedom have disappeared in a society that standardizes human beings and answers every human need according to its own plan. At that time he suggested that the utopia might be realized in A.F. (After Ford) 600. In 1946 he wrote a new Foreword, suggesting that the foreboding future might be upon us within a single century.[7] In 1958 he wrote a book of essays in which he found his gloomy expectations still closer to achievement.[8]

If Huxley were available for comment today, he might point to the latest confirmation of his fictional prediction. He had described a world in which *soma* provided people "Christianity without tears," and other drugs offered a Pregnancy Substitute and a Violent Passion Surrogate to people for whom sex had lost all mystery and devotion. Now he could note that LSD "trips" provide excitement for a people who have separated casual sex from passion and fidelity.

It is not surprising that our culture has produced an ethic of revolt that glories in alienation. The problem will be to maintain the validity of the revolt within a setting of social responsibility.

Frontier Issues in Ethics

In addition to reshaping the structure of society modern knowledge has confronted man with new powers that require quite specific and unprecedented decisions. Biological and medical knowledge, in particular, create new situations.

The most obvious of these is the result of convenient, effective contraceptives. To the extent that fear of pregnancy has been a discipline upon sexual activity in the past, the scope of sexual freedom has been widened. Obviously contraceptives are not the sole cause for the much publicized "revolution in sexual morals." If such were the case, we would not see the striking rise in illegitimate births.[9] But there is no doubt that some persons, who in the past might have been inhibited from pre-marital or extramarital sexual relations, now feel free to indulge.

This does not necessarily mean a decline in moral standards. It may mean an actual heightening of standards, as persons decide what meaning they wish to find in sex rather than restrain themselves out of fear. But it faces society with some puzzling choices. Shall college health services issue contraceptive pills to feminine students?[10] What about high schools—

---

[7] Aldous Huxley, *Brave New World* (New York: Bantam Books, copyright 1946).

[8] *Brave New World Revisited* (New York: Harper and Row, 1958).

[9] Recorded rates of illegitimacy, measured in number of live births per thousand unmarried women, are as follows: 1940—89.5. 1945—117.4. 1950—141.6. 1955—183.3. 1960—224.3. 1961—240.2. 1962—245.1. 1963—259.4. *Statistical Abstract of the United States,* Bureau of the Census, 1965, Table 53. It is possible that more accurate methods of reporting account for part of the rise.

[10] One recent judgment is that colleges might well provide contraceptive information but not contraceptive devices. See *Sex and the College Student* by The Committee on the College Student, Group for the Advancement of Psychiatry (New York: Atheneum, 1966), p. 135.

in particular junior high schools, where increasingly boys and girls are making their decisions? Should parents advocate chastity for their children, or should they, assuming that the children will take their signals from their peers, provide children with contraceptives as a matter of expediency? These are the decisions perplexing many families today.

It may be expected that some persons will continue to practice chastity and fidelity by choice, that others will indulge in promiscuity by choice—as has always been the case. In the future the opportunity for a choice, uninhibited by external factors, will increase. The locating of the moral choice in a deliberate and informed decision is to be welcomed—except that this highly significant choice is often made in a stage of immaturity under the pressure of a peer group.

Other medical developments are creating a new set of moral questions for which mankind has little preparation. The development of drugs that control personality raises issues of the right of the expert to manipulate the personality of his patient. The expected cracking of the genetic code will raise the same issue to a new height and significance.

Recent experiments in the transplanting of organs and the development of artificial organs are leading to perplexing questions in medical ethics. The success of research on degenerative diseases has led the British physician, Sir George Pickering of Oxford University, to fear that people "with senile brains and senile behavior will form an ever-increasing fraction of the inhabitants of the earth."[11] Norbert Wiener, the specialist in cybernetics, viewed with some alarm the possibility that medical science might learn to prolong life indefinitely. Humanity, he wrote, "could not long survive the indefinite prolongation of all lives which come into being." Someone, then, would have to make the difficult "moral decision" about the prolongation or termination of life.[12]

Of such disconcerting decisions the ethics of the future may be constituted.

THE ROLE OF PHILOSOPHY

Traditionally philosophy has been the intellectual enterprise in which men articulate and think with some precision about the major issues of life (apart from those specific issues that can be resolved by the methods of a particular discipline). But philosophy, in the modern United States, has been quite unsure of its role.

The major philosophical tradition in the first half of the twentieth century in this country was the pragmatism represented by William James and John Dewey. It was empirical in temper, experimental in outlook, interested in science, and future-oriented. Dewey liked to say that he was less interested in thinking about the problems of philosophy than in thinking philosophically about the problems of men. Interestingly both James and Dewey exercised their influence in part through disciplines other than

---

[11] From a statement at a Columbia University symposium, "Reflections on Research and the Future of Medicine," New York *Times*, May 27, 1966.

[12] Norbert Wiener, *God and Golem, Inc.* (Cambridge, Mass.: M.I.T. Press, 1964), p. 67.

philosophy—James through medicine and psychology, Dewey through education.

Following the death of Dewey in 1952, the field was left for the most part to a new breed of philosophers, who wished to make philosophy a specific science. Reversing Dewey's choice, they sought to work on the problems of philosophy rather than on the problems of men. In the face of the explosion of knowledge, they had no desire to dabble as amateurs in all realms of knowledge, but reduced philosophy to logic and semantics. This led to an abdication of the historic role of philosophy, which went instead to courses in intellectual history in the history department of the university. Thus Crane Brinton, the Harvard historian, wrote his book about history of the "Big Questions"—the questions man asks of the universe and of himself.[13] Many philosophers, especially the brasher of the logical positivists, avoided these questions by designating them as pseudo-questions. Some declared that all ethical, metaphysical and theological questions were meaningless; and answers to them were neither true nor false but also meaningless.

Now once again philosophy is returning to the temporarily neglected domains. The vogue of linguistic analysis has largely replaced the more dogmatic positivism. Linguistic analysis is sophisticated; it is determined not to be pretentious and not to be muddled. It avoids grandiose speculation and system building. But it has once again extended the concept of meaning to recognize all the "Bib Questions" in the whole tradition from Socrates until modern times. Perhaps this return was inevitable. Even the most abstemious philosopher could hardly declare that the controversies over civil rights or the American position in Viet Nam are "meaningless." He could distinguish the type of meaning from that of the physical sciences, where verificational procedures are highly elaborated and widely accepted. But he could not deny that moral discussions are worthy of human attention.

One accomplishment in this withdrawal and return of philosophy has been a more clear recognition of the factual and the valuational elements in human discourse. If Dewey was a little too glib in claiming that scientific method could resolve ethical questions, and if the logical positivists were too condescending in denying meaning to ethics, the contemporary philosopher is likely to distinguish the types of meaning and make room for both.

Thus Gunnar Myrdal, the Swedish social scientist who directed the massive study of American society and the racial problem, argued influentially that inquiry in the social sciences is impossible without some value premises. These are not dogmatically held; they are subject to scrutiny and revision. But they are always present and are better acknowledged than hidden. Such premises do not permit the inquirer to skew his data; but they enable him to define a problem and determine what data are relevant.[14]

---

[13] Crane Brinton, *Ideas and Men* (New York: Prentice-Hall, Inc., 1950).

[14] Gunnar Myrdal, *An American Dilemma* (New York: Harper and Row, 1944), Appendix 2, "Note on Facts and Valuations."

Similarly Norbert Wiener, the specialist on cybernetics, argued in his last book that computers could not make moral decisions. Wiener reintroduced into philosophical discussion such words as "sinful" and "moral" —words that embarrass many philosophers. He insisted as a moral proposition that machines must be designed to pursue human goals, not machine-determined goals, and that in all moral and policy decisions the "feedback" must be routed through persons.[15]

In commenting on Myrdal and Wiener, I have chosen men who are not philosophers in the strictest sense of the term; but the strictest sense of the term is again broadening. An inspection of the professional journals of philosophy will show that philosophers, after something of an exile, are returning to the arena of the "Big Questions." We can expect them to be heard in the ethical discussions of the years ahead. They will rely on science, not their philosophical assertions, for the factual component in ethical decisions. They will themselves seek to sharpen thinking and talk about ethical matters.

RELIGION

Religion is the human activity in which man confronts the questions of his own nature, his destiny, his ultimate loyalties, his response to a world from which he was born, which sustains him, yet which in many ways is alien to him. Religion inquires into the mystery and meaning of the universe and of human existence. It combines this inquiry with acts of commitment and devotion. It rarely if ever restricts its concerns to morality and ethics, but it always has moral consequences and ethical significance.

In assessing the religious situation and prospect in the United States, I shall consider three aspects of religion: the social phenomenon, the intellectual discipline, and the religious element in public education.

The Social Phenomenon

Religious affiliation has been on the increase in the United States. The percentage of Americans holding membership in church and synagogue has risen from 50 percent at the end of World War II to 64.4 percent in 1965. The growth was rapid in the immediate post-war years, leveled off in the early 1960's, then resumed slightly at mid-decade.[16] However, church attendance did not match the rise in membership.[17]

---

[15] Norbert Wiener, *God and Golem, Inc.* (Cambridge, Mass.: M.I.T. Press, 1964), pp. 62-63.

[16] See data in *1966 Yearbook of American Churches,* published by the National Council of Churches, New York City. Data on church membership are notoriously inexact. Some churches report as members baptized infants; others report only youth and adults. The figures quoted are gathered from religious organizations reporting their membership. Polls of people generally indicate a higher percentage of church membership than the organizations report. The Harris Poll in 1965 reported that 73 percent of the population say that they attend church or synagogue at least monthly.

[17] The Gallup Poll reported that in 1964 49 percent of adults attended church during a typical week. During the following decade the percentage showed a fluctuating decline, reaching 44 percent in 1965. One finding of the Gallup Poll is that church attendance rises with educational attainment. See *Information Service* (National Council of Churches) XLV, No. 3 (Jan. 29, 1966), p. 7.

The growth has been largely a suburban phenomenon. A survey of the Washington (D.C.) Council of Churches showed that 60 percent of people living in single family homes and less than 5 percent of apartment dwellers are church members.[18] The churches, especially the Protestant ones, have confessed increasing perplexity about their confrontation with the city.

The same years have been marked by deep questioning and self-criticism within the churches. A host of churchmen have charged that the growth in church membership is largely a matter of cultural accommodation of the church to society, that the churches have been unfaithful in their mission, and that religious conviction actually has little influence within our society. Sociologist Gerhard Lenski produced a significant body of data to show that church membership is a major influence upon attitudes and behavior.[19] But the influences he found were not always those that might be expected from examination of the doctrines and ethical teachings of the churches.

In the midst of their self-criticism for lethargy and loss of a prophetic voice the churches have recovered something of their role of social protest. Catholicism and Calvinism (especially in the Puritan tradition) had always advocated social involvement of the churches. But this motif was often lost in the individualistic piety of the American churches. The Civil Rights movement put the churches back in the midst of public life. The organized churches mounted massive campaigns for the enactment of civil rights legislation, and many groups within the churches joined the numerous protest movements connected with the struggle for civil rights. Many church members, however, resisted such social involvement. At present it is impossible to foresee what future directions the churches will take on this issue; but their recent deep involvement in social struggle is almost sure to have some continuing influence.

Another movement of the times has been the awareness and acceptance of religious pluralism. Will Herberg's widely read book, *Protestant-Catholic-Jew*[20] showed that Americans were increasingly ready to claim their religious identity within a specific tradition, while recognizing the coexistence of other differing traditions. President John F. Kennedy demonstrated that a Roman Catholc could win election to the presidency and could occupy the office without meeting religious antagonism. Conjectures about presidential candidates for the elections of 1968 include prominent Jewish and Mormon figures. Religious prejudice has not vanished from American society, but an era of increased good will has arrived within the pluralistic culture.

---

[18] United Press International dispatch by Louis Cassels, Nov. 22, 1965.

[19] Gerhard Lenski, *The Religious Factor* (Garden City, N. Y.: Doubleday, 1961). Lenski's data show clearly a correlation between church membership of four groups in the Detroit area (Catholics, Jews, white Protestants, Negro Protestants) and measurable ethical judgments. But his correlation does not necessarily show a causal efficacy of the churches. In fact, the wide differences between white and Negro Protestants would indicate that Lenski's "religious factor" may actually be to a considerable extent an "ethnic factor."

[20] Will Herberg, *Protestant-Catholic-Jew* (Garden City, N. Y.: Doubleday, 1955).

The Intellectual Aspect

The intellectual life of religious groups evidences an intense desire to grapple with issues connected with social change. Because any specific religion grows out of a tradition, religion often clings to its traditions in a time of change. But the intellectual leadership of churches and synagogues is often seriously eager to meet the modern world in all its newness. The Second Vatican Council (1962-65) showed unexpected strength among the progressive forces in the Roman Catholic Church and led to dramatic changes in traditional teaching and practice. The World Council of Churches has called a conference for July, 1966—in the tradition of the famous Oxford Conference of 1937—on the theme, "Christians in the Technical and Social Revolutions of Our Time."

During the period marked by World War II, theology took the direction of recovering many of the long-neglected themes of the orthodox traditions. It sought to maintain the faith and to call men to responsible decisions in the face of temptations to compromise with the idolatrous ideologies of the time. This theological movement, sometimes called "neo-orthodoxy," is now giving way to new tendencies, not yet clearly named or defined. Sometimes the term, "Christian radicalism," is used. The new impulse is to welcome rather than distrust the contemporary world with all its revolutionary dynamism. Theologians frequently quote Dietrich Bonhoeffer's letters from a Nazi prison, in which he declared that the world has come of age and that the believer should immerse himself in the secular life of the world.[21]

Two best-sellers have introduced the theological debates to a wide body of readers. Bishop J. A. T. Robinson of England in *Honest to God* (Philadelphia: Westminster, 1963) popularized some of the ideas of such major theologians as Bonhoeffer, Rudolf Bultmann, and Paul Tillich. Harvey Cox in *The Secular City* (New York: Macmillan, 1965) hailed secularization of society as a fulfilment of biblical faith.

Most recently the new radicalism has won attention in the debates over "the death of God." This specific theme shows all the signs of a fad, nurtured by heavy publicity and dramatic slogans. When it blows over, atheism will remain a live option, as it has always been. The discussion between believers and atheists will continue, with possible benefits to both. And the profound rethinking, of which this specific theology is a surface symptom, will go on.

In an era of revolutionary social changes religious groups can expect to share the perplexities of the entire society. They will be quite mistaken if they assume that religion offers a haven from intellectual and ethical struggle. They will also be mistaken if they seek only to adapt their traditions to contemporary caprices.

Looking at their history the churches can see the perils both of stubborn resistance and of easy acquiescence to change. Too often the churches have resisted healthy changes; sizable blocs of Christians opposed the elimina-

---

[21] Dietrich Bonhoeffer, *Prisoner for God* (New York: Macmillan, 1953). Also published as *Letters and Papers from Prison* (New York: Macmillan paperback, 1962).

tion of human slavery and the progressive social movements of the nineteenth and twentieth centuries—movements now universally recognized as beneficial. On the other hand, in the time of Hitler many Christians learned that the cost of fidelity is resistance, even to death, of the new movement that asks their loyalty.

In the years immediately ahead we can expect both the vitality and confusion that mark a time of major social and intellectual change. The shape of the next major dominant theological movment is not yet discernible. We may assume, however, that religious thinkers will seek to escape the ghetto mentality, to avoid provincialism (although not necessarily particularity), and to reckon seriously with the emerging new forms of culture.

Religion in Education

The relation of religion to public education is currently in major change. The American traditions of public education (less in the West than elsewhere) have shown a curious anomaly with regard to religion. Public schools have frequently engaged in ritualistic devotional observances, while avoiding any serious educational treatment of religion. This pattern is the exact reverse of the one that might be expected in public schools, which are established for the purpose of education and not of worship.

The Supreme Court clarified the issue in 1963 when it outlawed the practice of prayer and Bible reading in the public schools. Defining the position of the government as that of a "wholesome neutrality," it insisted that children not be subjected to religious or irreligious pressures in the schools. But then it pointed to a legitimate educational concern with religion:

> In addition, it might well be said that one's education is not complete without a study of comparative religion or the history of religion and its relationship to the advancement of civilization. It certainly may be said that the Bible is worthy of study for its literary and historic qualities.

> Nothing we have said here indicates that such study of the Bible or of religion, when presented objectively as part of a secular program of education, may not be effected consistent with the First Amendment.[22]

A major increase in the study of religion in higher education is currently under way. Robert Michaelson, describing the "quiet revolution," writes of "a substantial increase in formal provision for the systematic study of religion, an increase that has been especially dramatic on the campuses of state universities."[23] Such studies obviously do not have the aim of serving purposes of sectarian indoctrination. They have the educational purpose of communicating information and opening the possibility for appreciative and critical understanding.

---

[22] Decision of June 17, 1963. Text from New York *Times,* June 18, 1963.

[23] Robert Michaelson, "The Study of Religion," *Journal of Higher Education,* XXXVII:181-86 (April, 1966).

Any comparable movements in elementary and secondary education are much slighter than in the universities. But teachers' colleges are giving attention to the issues involved and to the preparation of teachers. It may be expected that this style of education in religion will grow in the period ahead to the extent that local communities desire such education and administrators learn the methods of implementing it.

Similarly there are signs of increasingly cordial relations between public schools and the parochial schools maintained by some religious bodies. The public (and the Congress) have decided that society has a stake in the improvement of education for all children—whether in public or private schools. And religious parochial schools show many signs of desire for increased participation in the life of the culture. Administrators of parochial schools are frequently deciding that they need not provide *all* of a child's schooling, and public schools are often showing readiness to offer facilities and instruction to children enrolled in parochial schools. The emerging patterns of cooperation show great variety, depending upon local needs.

THE SIGNIFICANCE OF VALUES FOR EDUCATION

This paper has touched upon many issues involving ethics and moral values, philosophy, and religion. All of these areas are loaded with implications and problems for public education. They raise issues of the competing claims in public education of a value orientation and of neutrality.

I would argue that some forms of neutrality are, in our culture, possible, necessary, and desirable. At the same time I would maintain that some type of value-orientation is equally possible, inevitable, and desirable.

On some issues all of us want the schools to be neutral. In a pluralistic society we certainly do not want public educational institutions captured by any sectarian group that might aim to indoctrinate students for its sectarian purposes—whether these purposes be political, cultural, or religious. We are not a totalitarian society, and we do not want the schools to do everything. The family, the church, and other groups have their rights too.

But on some issues we want the schools to show a value-orientation. We do not want them to be neutral about crime and delinquency, about issues of ordinary honesty, about respect for the society and its traditions.

The educational process usually carries on both explicit and implicit education in values. The explicit values are the subjects of its verbalizations, its rituals, its exhortations. These are the common stock—unhappily often the common cliches—of educators, journalists, political leaders. The implicit values are those that are communicated, often unconsciously, by educational methods of organization. Such education is likely to be more effective than the explicit style, which is in danger of verging on propaganda. For example, an effective racially integrated school communicates certain values more powerfully than lectures about integration. Again, the patterns of authority and of appreciation for dissent that actually function in a school are more influential than study about authority and dissent. The prevailing behavior on honesty and cheating has more effect than an infinite quantity of platitudes on the subject.

Thus schools inevitably communicate values implicitly; usually they also communicate some explicitly. In a time of change and conflict, like our own, the issue becomes: which values shall education acknowledge? Shall it adopt the ethos of authority or of inquiry, of the establishment or of the revolutionaries? The issue arises in regard to sex, economic practices, politics, the use of drugs, national loyalty. American public education is always on the edge of, sometimes in the midst of, controversies on such issues. Society wants education to be a force for good, but society does not always agree on the good.

In the decades ahead the American society will have many opportunities to experiment with answers to the question of how a pluralistic society incorporates values in its public education. To the extent that Gunnar Myrdal is right in describing an "American creed," to which we all give assent even though we often violate it, the task will be made easier. To the extent that the public educational process itself generates certain values—respect for truth and co-operative inquiry, concern for opportunity for all persons, the appeal to evidence and rationality rather than prejudice—another asset is available.

But in the momentous social changes through which we are living, the task will not be easy. And nobody knows the outcome.

CONCLUSION

I shall resist the temptation to "wrap up" the reflections of this paper in any slogans or formulae. To do so would be to refute one of my major theses: that no findings, however well-based, can save us from the continuous effort of mind and struggle of spirit that are needed to face our future.

But perhaps I may return to emphasize two themes that have run through this analysis. First, the undermining of authority—which I have identified as a fact that may be both threat and opportunity—lays new responsibilities on the moral imagination. It requires the internalization of ethical sensitivity and values, without which ethics degenerates into rigid obedience to increasingly irrelevant authority or into capricious choices that can be disastrous in so complex a society as ours.

Second, an ethic for our time requires a scientific awareness of empirical evidence and an equally scientific readiness to project new possibilities and courses of action. Yet, since ethical decisions involve a valuational component that cannot be reduced to fit any of the standard models of scientific method, they require also the imagination of the artist and the prophet.

Decision-making in our world requires both fidelity and adventure. That makes this a good world in which to live.

CHAPTER 16

Major Problems Of Society In 1980

RICHARD L. SHETLER*

With the cooperation of Tom O. Paine** and Alex Groner***

In asking me to describe the world of 1980, your program chairman has given me an extremely difficult assignment, but one that I have accepted at my own peril.

The forecasting business gets more hazardous all the time. At no previous period in history have our lives, our institutions and our entire society been so completely enveloped in change. Moreover, the rate of change shows not the least promise or prospect of slowing down in the next decade or so. Given the premise of accelerating change, and given the fact that changes in any one aspect of our society interact with changes in all the others, it was probably less dangerous for Nostradamus to call his shots 1,000 years ahead of time than it is for us to gaze at our crystal balls for a look at the world 15 years hence.

Nevertheless, there are certain assumptions that we can make about the years to come that can help us detect the broad outlines of what is likely to happen. One is that man will continue to aspire to a fuller, better, richer and more comfortable life. Another is that his technology will advance at a rapid rate. I think we can be pretty sure that the environment of the 1980's will be shaped—as in the past—by man's *aspirations* interacting with his *technology*.

Does this mean that history is bound to repeat itself? Not always, I suppose. But our two assumptions can help us pinpont certain areas in which the past can be a pretty good guide for the future.

I have chosen to discuss three important trends in the world today, because their patterns in the past appear to indicate that they will continue to be dominant aspects of our environment, in 1980 and beyond. The three are: (1) world urbanization, (2) industrial automation, and (3) the information technology revolution.

Added together, the effects of these three might total something very close to what we call civilization, or at least modern technological civilization. What is more, their total is probably considerably more than the sum of the parts, since urbanization, automation and communications not only produce independent effects, but they also react on and intensify each other. We must therefore consider them not as separate and discrete forces, but as part of a larger unity in human society.

*President, General Learning Corporation, Washington, D.C.; formerly Vice President, General Electric Company.

**Manager, TEMPO Division of General Electric, Santa Barbara, Calif.

***Assistant to the Director, Corporate Development Department, TIME, Incorporated.

World Urbanization and Industrial Automation

Before trying to project ourselves ahead, let's take a brief look back over our shoulder to see where we've been for, say, the past 10,000 years. What about the aspirations of society and its technology back then? I would guess that one of those fellows might tell a visiting anthropologist that he aspired to some *food, shelter, fewer head and stomach pains, security from violent enemies,* and a *mate* to help raise a family.

And, of course, the available technology to realize these aspirations consisted largely of a *cave,* an *animal skin, fire* and *a club.* Even so, the demands for skill in hunting and defense were high, and a viable society had to pass these skills on to the young through some form of apprenticeship. This was a verbal and demonstration process, but it constituted effective communication, and thus education.

Communication was at first almost entirely vocal. But the magic of pictorial communications was dimly appreciated. The artist felt the power of graphic representation, and he created for others to see and feel some of this power. Thus, following spoken language, there was a second breakthrough in the refinement of communications.

Thousands of years later, symbols and pictographs evolved into *writing,* for an even more significant breakthrough in communications. This took place simultaneously with early developments in technology and *pre*-urbanization, when survival was a bit less demanding and men presumably could take a little time out to think. Writing first developed in the great river valley civilizations that were based on the *new* technology of agriculture. The hoe and the plow, used to raise grain, which was storable food, started man on his way toward city building. Fully 10 percent of the population could be supported in cities, where writing and an elite literary class arose, and where men could ponder the great seeming truths of the visible universe.

Geometry, arithmetic, codified laws, history, astronomy, architecture, the wheel and the sailing ship—technology and science interacted with rising aspirations as the age of the cities arrived.

Education in the new world of written communication took on new forms. Specialization increased. New coordination skills were called for. Literature emerged, empires arose, bards sang, and such innovations as democratic city government were tried. Along with soldiers and kings, philosophers and poets, *great teachers* were recognized for their contributions.

The technological innovation of *movable type,* together with inexpensive paper, moved the ability to transfer information another giant step. I need not describe its consequences. Progress, of course, is never without its price, and along with such salutary products as *Playboy,* movable type also ushered in such deplorable things as today's debate over "publish or perish."

In the 1800's *mechanical technology* transformed Europe and America. Railroads opened our continent, as power from combustible coal replaced wind, falling water and animal muscle as the chief source of energy for the world's work. The urban shop, then factory, helped bring about the Industrial Revolution, bringing with it great social changes. Agricultural productivity increased dramatically with the changes in technology and transportation—with chemical fertilizers and with petroleum-powered internal combustion engines.

The impact on our lives of mass production, plus the technology of the internal combustion engine, is immense and continuing. More and more of our once pastoral countryside is disappearing. Automobiles have changed the face of America, the way we live, and the way we teach our children. They help jam us more tightly into cities, even while providing a means of escape from the cities.

Today the problems associated with autos frequently replace the weather as a topic for lament. Smog, traffic jams, accidents, freeways slicing through our cities, hot rods—we decry them all, often while we drive smoothly along in our air-conditioned new models. All of these are the stresses and price of progress.

Even so, the mechanical revolution has lifted the burden from its ancient resting place, the backs of men. We have substituted technical skill and educational processes for human drudgery. Our urban industrial society has its problems, but a little perspective also shows its substantial rewards.

Figure 1: *World Urbanization*

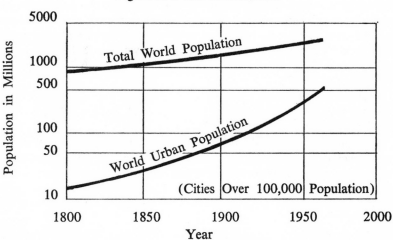

As more and more of the world learns to use less and less land to meet its food needs, there is a progression from an agricultural to an industrial society. It would appear to be quite safe to look ahead and project a continuation of the "population implosion," or drawing together of masses of people, that is urbanizing the world. The lower curve in Figure 1 clearly shows the trend for more rapid population growth in cities of over 100,000 than elsewhere.

Figure 2: *Income vs. Urbanization*

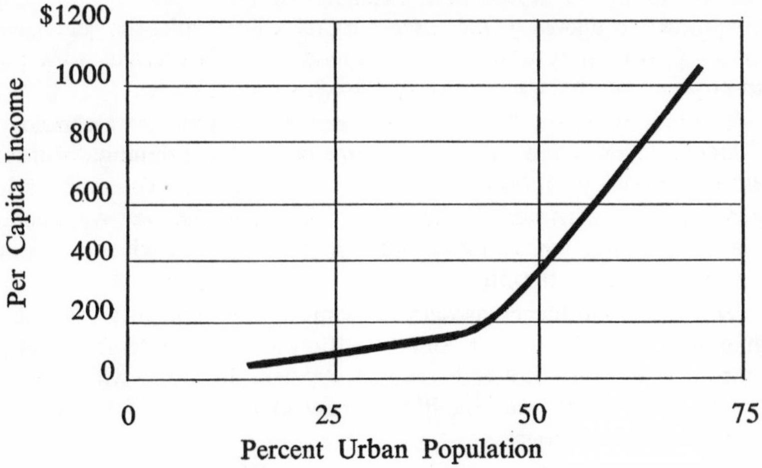

The rewards to the individual of successful urbanization and the development of a viable industrial society are indeed great. Figure 2 shows the relationship between percent of the population living in cities and per capita income. The lure of higher income is the great driving force behind the "population implosion." But once they have reached the cities, people find the demands for technical and institutional competence very high. As a result, effective educational systems become imperative in a large-scale society.

Fast as the cities in our own country and in Western Europe and Australia are growing, others will grow faster yet. Current projections of the rate of urbanization in the developing nations in Africa, Asia and South America show extremely large growth rates for the rest of this century. There is a veritable passion for education in these countries, where each successive step on the educational ladder can be immediate-

Developing Nation Urban Population in Millions

	1960	2000
Africa	58	294
Asia	559	3,444
South America	144	650

ly translated into higher income. Educational demands, already straining the budgets of some of the new nations, will continue to grow—and that will pose a major challenge to all of us. Teachers are in woefully short supply, and teachers with any semblance of proper qualifications are all but non-existent in some places. New approaches to education are urgently needed around the world.

SOME IMPLICATIONS FOR EDUCATION

More than 50 years ago, H. G. Wells concluded from his study of history that the whole world was engaged in a fateful race between education and catastrophe. This is perhaps even more true today. It is a race to which we are already deeply committed on the side of education, and to which we must continually re-dedicate ourselves. Sometimes education seems to be losing the race.

To keep a balanced picture, however, there is also much progress being made abroad. Schools *are* being built. Teachers *are* being trained. Girls are being educated for the modern world, and they will help educate others. This is a route America has already travelled, as we progressed slowly and laboriously toward universal education through high school. Now we can help show others the way, and we can offer them better new methods, reflecting the experience we have had.

Horace Mann's vision of an educated America took shape slowly, sometimes painfully, over the course of a century. Millions of disoriented, ill-trained immigrants flocked to our shores to go through the rural-urban transition even while they sought to absorb a new language and culture. Their life was hard, and the education process was often labored and inefficient. They learned the hard way.

But somehow the public school system responded. If the first generation had trouble establishing a meaningful place in our industrial society, there was always another generation coming right behind them. Somehow we need to help the vast and populous developing parts of the world do the same things now, and through 1980.

What's more, we still face the challenge of the disinherited in our own country, the 20 percent who lead substandard lives even in these times of widespread affluence. As rural farm workers from Puerto Rico and from our Southern states crowd into the slums of our northern cities, we must make provision for their education, the golden gateway toward equality of opportunity. For equal educational opportunity has now come to represent a consensus aspiration for Americans. We must provide the teachers, the new curricular approaches and the educational innovations that will help fulfill that aspiration.

Even while we are applying the lessons of the past, the future will pose *new* conditions that must be met—some of them unpredictable, others that will herald their own coming.

One of the major new environmental features of the U.S. in this century has been the steady downward trend in working hours. This is almost certain to continue. Industrial automation is still further reducing the man-hours worked per capita. During the past fifty years we have cut the average male work week almost in half, by the grace of mechanization. The worker is now better educated and older when he enters the labor force, he works shorter hours, gets more holidays and vacations, and he retires earlier. Needless to say, this has important implications for schools, as well as for the trend of our total environment.

People will have time to do more of the things that appeal to them. Since what appeals to them will reflect, to a considerable extent, their educational backgrounds, more leisure will thus impose new and larger responsibilities on our educational system. For the educational system will have an even greater impact than it does now on our culture.

Greater and more widespread cultural sophistication can be expected. The boom in the arts should asume even greater importance than it has. Just as education tends to beget more education, added emphasis on the arts should help nurture the arts to even greater heights.

Technology should help accent the enjoyment of our leisure hours. Advances in electronic communication are more likely to *stimulate* than they are to compete with the theater and other performing arts.

Uniformity and conformism need be no greater than we want them to be. In any event they will not be *imposed* on us by mass production, since technology and mass production have actually had the effect of *widening* our areas of choice, rather than narrowing them. And education, even while it stresses unity and equality, will be able to offer, through technical innovations, increasing opportunities for diversity.

THE COMPUTER AS A NEW TOOL

We have now tried to look ahead a bit at some aspects of our future environment: Greater world urbanization, some consequences of automation, and some of the implications for education. I would like to conclude with some reflections on the computer, a new tool we are just beginning to learn how to use, and the most recent breakthrough in man's continuing effort to achieve better communications.

The new technology of the computer and information system bids fair to be the dominant technological factor that will influence the environment of the 1980's. Project MAC at M.I.T., among others, is doing pioneering work in the college-level application of giant computers that share time among many users. The implications, as you can well imagine, are enormous. We seem to be discovering new dimensions of potential for the computer and information system almost daily.

The pencil and tablet, the data handbook, and that old engineer's companion, the slide rule—all of them are beginning to bear some small resemblance to the quill pen. For a great many important tasks, they are already obsolescent.

Much closer to the 1980 look are remote terminals with rapid communication access to a central computer, making for an electronic information network of enormous power and flexibility.

Some of my more enthusiastic associates even believe this new development is comparable in importance to the invention of movable type. And perhaps it *will* prove to be of equal significance. Just imagine the staggering possibilities of having all the world's great libraries, the accumulated knowledge of mankind, at your fingertips, of being able to select from them the information that is desired, and at the same time having a machine that can analyze, sift, integrate and calculate for us. These are machines that can, in a moment's time, go through successive calculations that would require hundreds of years in the slow motion calculating ability of our minds.

The imagination, ingenuity and inspirational qualities of the human being, in partnership with the vast memory and infallible calculation capabilty of the machine, together make up a strikingly *new* intellectual factor in our environment. We are only beginning to see where its possibilities can lead us.

New techniques for talking with the machine in our own language— that is, for communicating directly with computers in English—are under intensive development. By the 1980's they promise to be commonplace, removing one of the current barriers to more widespread use of the machine.

Advanced techniques of feeding out, or displaying, information will also facilitate electronic data handling. The military is using a type that will be commercially feasible in the 1980's. Less and less data will have to be put on paper and handled physically; instead there will be data banks to store information and communication networks to get it where it is needed.

Already much technical detail is recorded and stored on magnetic tapes, discs and drums. A librarian of General Electric's "Tempo" installation in Santa Barbara has more than 25,000 miles of magnetic tape in his library. Miles of tape may very well replace numbers of books as a standard of measuring stored information.

Much larger computer memories than we now have can easily be forseen by the 1980's. This will open new opportunities for education in our society.

Perhaps remote terminals in the home, connected to data banks and computer utilities of the 1980's, will change the whole picture of our normal daily movements. For a great many activities, the home may become the most efficient place to work, and the present pattern of morning workbound and evening homebound traffic jams will become memories of an annoying past, like the coal bins and shovels that some of us remember from our own childhood.

The same equipment that the family bread-winner would use for his work could also become effective self-teaching machines for all members of families that had them. In such an environment, the study habits and teaching methods for children could become quite different from what they are today. Some of the children whose parents now complain about the new math may be the equally nonplussed parents of the 1980's, should they be asked to explain the operation of a computer. Fortunately for them, nobody is likely to ask them, because the computer itself could explain its own operation much better.

SUMMARY

In summary, the environment of the 1980's may not match our private notions of a brave new world, but it cannot fail to be exciting and stimulating. It will be, of course, an extension of the world of today, just as today's world is an extension of the world of our own childhood.

There will be more years devoted to education, greater access to continued education throughout our lives, more time for leisure, more emphasis on cultural pursuits, and far greater technological advances in all areas, particularly in electronic information systems.

Our own country, of course, is far from being the whole world. One of the great problems of our recent rapid technological gains is that the breach is being widened between us and the nations that started out far behind us, technically and industrially. Urbanization and industrialization will be placing major new demands on the developing areas, many of which are still unable to feed themselves, even while there will be enormous strains on their educational systems. Just as we have accepted the social responsibility of solving our own problems of equal opportunity, so may it be imperative that we take on the responsibility of assisting other people into the Twentieth Century, into the last half of the Twentieth Century—yes, even into 1980.

Perhaps some of you have noticed how assiduously I have avoided mentioning another era in which there may well be some massive break-throughs by 1980—the field of molecular biology, of imposing changes in and around the living cell, thus possibly changing the character and quality of life itself. All the overtones of 1984, of Orwell and Huxley, are there, of course. But there are other and more hopeful overtones, too—of conquering disease and ignorance, and of opening boundless new horizons to human experience. I hope we have the good sense and humanity to use such a tool wisely, and not monstrously, if we are able to use it at all. But I have enough faith in our instincts to hope that we do not shrink from the adventure of using it.

By contrast with the cave man, we today are given the opportunity to live not just one, but many lives. We have compressed space in a manner that also compresses time. Just think, a mere 100 years ago, there were just a handful of people on earth who had been around the world—as many of you must already have been. And just 500 years ago, there was probably not one human being who had made the trip.

But more than compressing time and space, we have developed a remarkable capacity to compress human experience—through record-keeping, through communication, through education. Finding our lives so enriched, I can think of no more noble calling than that of helping to enrich the lives of others.